Marxism a

Ju

Judith Orr is the editor of *Socialist Worker* and the author of *Sexism and the System: A Rebel's Guide to Women's Liberation* (Bookmarks, 2007).

MARXISM
AND
WOMEN'S
LIBERATION

Judith Orr

*To Rachel
in solidarity
Judith Orr*

Bookmarks *b* Publications

Marxism and Women's Liberation
By Judith Orr
Published 2015 by Bookmarks Publications
c/o 1 Bloomsbury Street, London WC1B 3QE
© Bookmarks Publications
Cover design by Yuri Prasad
Typeset by Peter Robinson
Printed by Russell Press
ISBN print edition: 978 1 909026 97 1
ISBN kindle: 978 1 909026 98 8
ISBN ePub: 978 1 909026 99 5
ISBN PDF: 978 1 910885 00 0

Contents

Acknowledgements

The single author's name on a book cover never tells the whole story of collective effort that has gone into its production. I owe many people thanks for their role in making this book possible.

First I want to thank Sally Campbell as the publisher. She has seen it through from when it was no more than a few chapter titles and has been a source of constant encouragement and political feedback.

Thank you to Yuri Prasad for a great cover design, and to Lina Nicolli, Peter Robinson, Eileen Short and Carol Williams for all their work on production. I'm grateful to Sarah Bates, Alex Callinicos, Esme Choonara, Amy Leather and Sheila McGregor for taking time to read earlier drafts of the book and give comments. Of course any flaws are my own.

I very much appreciate that Charlie Kimber and Simon Basketter ensured I was able to take time away from *Socialist Worker* to write. Special thanks must go to Martin Smith for all his support, and my good friends Anna Gluckstein, Emma Bircham and Fiona Watson for always being there.

I was lucky enough to witness some of the 18 days in Cairo's Tahrir Square when the Egyptian Revolution erupted. Women were central to the struggle from the first day but are now victims of the counter-revolution.

So I want to dedicate this book to Revolutionary Socialist and human rights lawyer Mahienour el-Massry, who as I write is in an Egyptian prison for her role in the revolution. But Mahienour always insists that she with her high profile does not need solidarity as much as the countless women she shares cells with, who "will only be remembered with pride at their own family gatherings." In that spirit this book is for Mahienour and all Egypt's political prisoners.

Great expectations

Why are women, half the human race, still discriminated against? Women are overrepresented among the poorest on the planet, they face oppression in all societies and are treated as inferior beings in a million different ways. Why are women more often to be found on the sticky floor of low pay than above the glass ceiling where the rich and powerful reside? In Britain two thirds of those on the minimum wage are women and only six of Britain's top 100 companies are run or chaired by a woman. In fact more people called John run such companies than women.

Women on average earn around 18 percent less than men. Britain has fallen out of the top 20 countries for gender pay parity because the gap between men's and women's incomes is so wide. The latest economic crisis has hit working class people hard, but it has hit working class women the hardest. Women in Britain have suffered as much as 85 percent of the cost of the cuts and austerity launched by the Tory led coalition government of 2010-15. This is calculated on the basis of the impact of the cuts in tax credits and other welfare benefits on which working class women are more reliant. Women also disproportionately work in public sector jobs which have been cut or have seen their pay slashed or frozen.

The sexual freedom we thought had been won in the struggles of the 1960s appears to have just given us the opportunity to be even more crudely defined as sex objects than ever before. Old fashioned sexism hasn't gone—the *Sun* newspaper still insists on putting pictures of semi-naked women on its page three.

But today there is also a different sort of sexism—raunch culture. It has a twist; we are meant to revel in it as ironic. No longer is stripping demeaning, it's been rebranded as lap dancing and sold as empowering. In the 19th century Karl Marx wrote of the ability of capitalism to turn intrinsic parts of our humanity into alien objects to be bought, sold and possessed. This affects even the most intimate aspects of our lives, including our sexuality, which are transformed into things alien from us. New freedom of expression, which was hard fought for, is distorted by the system's drive to turn everything into a source of profit.

Women's sexuality has become trapped in a new cage of clichéd stereotypes in the name of liberation. Women's bodies are treated as sex objects whether they are an Olympic champion encouraged to pose in bikinis for magazine covers or a shop worker whose contract mandates the wearing of make up.

Women feel the pressure to conform to ever more exaggerated caricatures of what is deemed to be sexy, while men are encouraged to see themselves as helpless prisoners of their testosterone—sexually aggressive and insatiable. A fresher arriving at any university campus in Britain will find sexism has become a routine part of student life. They will be faced by posters, flyers, club nights and pole dancing societies using sexist stereotypes of women which are flaunted as fun and proof of liberated times. The more traditional sources of sexist behaviour have thrived in this atmosphere—they don't feign irony, they simply have more confidence to express pure misogyny. For example protests forced the students union of the London School of Economics to suspend the Rugby Club in 2014 for a year after it gave out a grossly offensive leaflet at freshers fair calling women "mingers" and "slags".

Sexual harassment is not just a problem for young people in college, as the Everyday Sexism project has shown. Thousands of women have posted their experiences online and it makes sobering reading. A YouGov poll found that two-thirds of people agree that sexism is still a problem in the workplace, three-quarters of women compared with 56 percent of men.[1]

It can sometimes feel like the clock has turned back and the struggles of the past were in vain. But women have made important material gains that would have seemed completely out of reach by previous generations. A hundred years ago women did not have the right to vote and had marched in their hundreds of thousands to demand suffrage. Fifty years ago abortion was illegal and a woman died every ten days after going to the back street. In Northern Ireland abortion is still illegal today. Only 25 years ago rape in marriage was not a crime—a wife was seen to have consented to be sexually available to her husband whenever he wanted.

Today in Britain women can divorce, access safe abortion and have a right to equality under the law. Women have grown up with the assumption that they will work for a living and have financial independence from men. They have access to jobs and a level of education denied to their grandmothers. The number of women going to university has outstripped men since 1992.[2] Women have never had more freedom in their personal lives. They have won the right to express their sexuality, they can choose never to marry, to have children outside marriage without being ostracised or not to have children at all.

Some women have done very well. In fact we are often told that women in the West are living in a golden age. The US trade advertising magazine *Ad Age* described our time as "a new era in American society and culture: The New Matriarchy" because "women have increased their economic power in society and taken on more and more leadership roles".[3] In Britain Prowess, an organisation devoted to women in business, wrote in 2015, "It may indeed be the best time there has been for ambitious women who want to get to the top".[4] Business woman Stephanie Shirley has compared her working life in the 1960s with today and railed against women complaining of sexism saying, "We've never had it so good. It's time we stopped whinging and got on with it".[5]

But pointing out that discrimination and oppression is still the lived experience of the majority of women is not whinging. Much has changed for women but too much has not and indeed in some aspects of our lives things are going backwards.

The higher you go in society the fewer women you see. Women are 51 percent of the population but you wouldn't know it by looking at the green benches in parliament. When the government headed up by Tory prime minister Margaret Thatcher was elected in 1979 women made up 3 percent of MPs. The 2015 general election saw more women MPs elected than ever before, up by 14 from 2010—women now make up 29 percent of the House of Commons. But this means men are more than two thirds of all MPs—no wonder Westminster is still a bastion of chauvinism. Some members of the ruling class can barely hide their distaste at the presence of women in institutions they still see to be the preserve of men.

Cameron tried to counter the view of the government as run by a bunch of public school boys when he appointed women to a third of posts in his cabinet after the May 2015 election. Previously his cabinet contained more millionaires than women. Yet Cameron's true attitude towards women was revealed when he cracked sexist "jokes" at women MPs on both sides to play to the reactionary gallery that is the Tory party. He described fellow Tory MP Nadine Dorries as "extremely frustrated" during one House of Commons debate. During another he told Labour MP Angela Eagle, then shadow chief secretary to the Treasury, to "calm down, dear" to guffaws from his back benchers.

Parliament and the top 100 companies are not the only institutions dominated by men. Only 5 percent of all newspaper editors are women and within the legal system just 13.6 percent of the senior judiciary are women, and when you get to the highest court in the land there is the sum total of one female supreme court judge.[6]

If you are in work and have the temerity to get pregnant get ready to fight for your job. Some bosses don't even hide their reluctance to uphold equality laws; four in ten admit being wary of employing women of childbearing age—that covers a lot of women.[7] The numbers of women taking out tribunals for unfair dismissal because of pregnancy went up by a fifth between 2008, the start of the recession, and 2013. Since 2013 funding cuts mean complainants now have to pay £1,200 to go to a tribunal and this has had a dramatic and immediate impact on the number of women getting justice—pregnancy and maternity claims have fallen by a quarter.[8]

Look beyond Britain and the impact of capitalism and crisis can be a matter of life and death for millions of women. A woman in Sierra Leone is 183 times more likely to die in childbirth than a woman in Switzerland. Across the globe 22 million women undergo an unsafe abortion every year, although denial of abortion rights is not only a problem in the global south. Savita Halappanavar died in an Irish hospital on 28 October 2012 after being denied an abortion when she was miscarrying.

Women own just 1 percent of the world's wealth; those lucky enough to be earning are paid up to 30 percent less than men. And they are sometimes in the worst conditions. In Bangladesh 85 percent of the country's 3.5 million garment workers are women. They earn £25 a month, well below the living wage set at £45. Women workers suffer sexual harassment and discrimination and face 14 to 16 hour shifts seven days a week. It's also dangerous: factory fires in buildings with locked doors and no escape routes are common and 1,130 workers, mainly women, died when the Rana Plaza garment factory outside Dhaka collapsed in 2013. Women also make up two thirds of all those in the world who cannot read and write—that's 493 million women.

But oppression is not simply economic. Sexual repression and objectification are a potent part of the way women are both trivialised but also in some cases brutalised simply because they are women. In Mexico women are being targeted in a wave of violence and murder that has reached epidemic proportions. It's estimated that seven women are murdered every day and the number is rising. A well of anger about the issue of sexual violence burst across the globe in 2012 when a 23 year old woman died of appalling injuries as a result of being gang raped on a Delhi bus on her way home from the cinema. Tens of thousands joined protests across India and worldwide to demand justice. The case brought home the shocking reality of women's oppression in the 21st century.

Sexual violence

In Britain the revelations that broke in 2012 of the scale of horrific sexual abuse carried out by celebrity and establishment figure Jimmy Savile have opened up the floodgates of reports of child sexual abuse. Hundreds of Savile's victims, children and teenagers, mainly young women, have come forward. But the scandal goes far beyond Savile. The cover-ups and corruption that allowed such abuse to carry on unimpeded exposed the rotten core of the British establishment, some of whom were abusers themselves. Child abuse cases have been brought against dozens of celebrities, politicians and other public figures. Many people, including middle aged women and men who suffered sexual abuse as children, have spoken out for the first time. They hope that finally they might be listened to and get some sort of justice, even if decades after their ordeals. Police, politicians and the media colluded in the cover up. Those who did complain were disbelieved, ignored or told to keep quiet.

The police declare that such a scandal would never happen today. They claim that their treatment of women who come forward is sensitive and supportive. Yet time and time again the police are found to be dismissing and failing to pursue allegations of rape—often without even informing the woman. The government admits that only 15 percent of all rapes are reported. Reports of rape have risen by 22 percent, yet at the same time the proportion of rape convictions has actually gone down. As many as 77 women in Britain were murdered by their partners or ex partners in the year 2012-13.[9] This is all at a time when rape crisis centres and refuges are seeing their funding cut back.

In 2014 Rashida Manjoo, a United Nations representative who came to Britain to investigate the position of women, described it as having a "boys' club sexist culture". She denounced the impact that cuts were having on services for women, in particular those who have suffered domestic violence. She cited figures showing that 7 percent of women in England and Wales reported having experienced domestic abuse during the previous year. Organisations dealing with domestic violence have seen their funding cut by a third between 2010 and 2012.[10]

To document the sheer extent of the suffering of women could take a book in itself. Instead this book is not simply about describing the problem, but about answering the question of why women face this sometimes brutal inequality and oppression and how we can fight it.

Today's debates

The rise in sexism and anger about sexual violence has led to an explosion of ideas and activity. For many new activists the ideas of feminism are the first and automatic political expression of being against sexism and for gender equality. Feminism stands for a basic rejection of discrimination and oppression of women and that is what all of us who oppose sexism have in common. Feminist ideas are not a single school of thought and never have been, so a single definition of "feminism" will by necessity not cover all the possibilities. Even when there was an organised women's movement it included people with myriad different political outlooks.

Many feminists also see themselves as socialists and there is much common ground between feminism and socialism. But there are also some important theoretical differences about the cause and sometimes the way to fight oppression, which will be explored in this book. The influence of the left and the organised labour movement on the Women's Liberation Movement (WLM) of the 1970s and feminist ideas has always been stronger in Britain than in the US (see Chapter 7).

US Marxist feminist Martha Gimenez has pointed out that Marxism has been a constant touchstone for ideas on women's oppression. Even those feminists who reject Marx, such as Shulamith Firestone and Kate Millett, often shape their polemics in terms of that disagreement. Gimenez writes:

> If Marx's work (and the Marxist tradition by implication) were indeed substantively afflicted by all the shortcomings that social scientists and feminists attribute to it, it would have long been forgotten. But Marx's intellectual power and vitality remain undiminished, as demonstrated in the extent to which even scholars who reject it must grapple with his work's challenge, so much that their theories are shaped by the very process of negating it.[11]

The resurgence of interest in ideas and activity around the politics of women's liberation of the last decade takes place in a situation brimming with the contradictions of gains, retreats and new problems. While many politicians, academics and writers may see no alternative to looking for answers within the system, many newly politicised young activists see no solution within capitalism. They see that some women can reach the top and yet oppression is still endemic. This is a generation of women growing up with expectations that the system won't and can't meet.

So today's debates about class, sexuality and the nature of gender take place against a very different backdrop to the 1960s and 1970s. That means even when some of the debates today echo those of the past they cannot be addressed by simply repeating old arguments.

The new interest in women's liberation has spurred a raft of new books. From the late 1990s several titles appeared on what was then called the "new feminism".[12] From the mid-2000s feminist societies and women's groups sprouted up in numerous college campuses. The size of the audience for such ideas can be seen in a number of 1,000-strong feminist conferences organised in London since 2008 as well as by the numbers on the annual Reclaim the Night demonstrations, relaunched in 2004.[13]

Alongside the many new titles publishers have reissued numerous older theoretical and academic works from the 1970s and 1980s. Some of these revisit themes of privilege and intersectionality as well as materialism and Marxism. Silvia Federici, Lise Vogel, Mariarosa Dalla Costa, Michele Barrett and Sheila Rowbotham have all had books republished in recent years.

These have been widely discussed online in ways that were simply not possible nor imagined by activists looking for ideas to explain their experience only a couple of decades ago. Many of those very same activists, both in Britain and the US, have found a place in academia and so are playing a role in shaping the theoretical response of new activists. But none of this is simply an academic or theoretical debate. Struggles to challenge or end oppression will only have a chance of success if they are shaped by an understanding of where and how it has become so deeply rooted in human societies. As Marx wrote, "Philosophers have only interpreted the world in various ways; the point is to change it."

The theoretical development of different feminist strands that came out of the WLM will be explored in Chapter 8. But what is worth noting is that today the dominance of forms of what has been called "cultural feminism", which concentrates on the politics of discourse, symbols and language, is being challenged. There is a welcome renewal of interest in materialist explanations of women's oppression.[14] The impact of the Occupy and anti-capitalist movements is cited as lending "new relevance to the Marxist feminist project" by Kathi Weeks in her introduction to the new edition of Michele Barrett's *Women's Oppression Today*.[15]

Other recent books which explore materialism, Marxism and feminism include Canadian academic Shahrzad Mojab's collection of writings under the title *Marxism and Feminism* and Heather Brown's *Marx on Gender and the Family*. Mojab wants to "remove the hyphen in Marxism-feminism". She echoes a common theme which asserts that although Marxism is a useful tool for understanding society, it alone is insufficient to fully explain or address women's oppression. Marxism is accused of reducing women's oppression to economics and class, because Marxists see exploitation as the core social relationship that drives and shapes society. As the experience of oppression reaches across the class divide then some conclude that a class analysis can't explain it. In short, there is an argument that Marxism isn't enough; it needs feminism.

Yet far from reducing oppression to economics, Marxism argues that the full impact of oppression cannot be fully appreciated without understanding the economic system in which it functions. When Marx was writing at the end of the 19th century he didn't see economics as a narrow discipline solely concerned with wages and profits. Instead he wanted his ideas and political method to help understand all aspects of society.[16] He wrote that "the economical subjection of the man of labour...lies at the bottom of servitude in all its forms, of all social misery, mental degradation, and political dependence".[17]

Oppression transcends class; nevertheless this book will argue that it is not independent of class. We have to go below what appears to be the common sense and discover the real forces that shape the lives of women and men within the system. As Marx wrote, "all science would be superfluous if the outward appearance and the essence of things directly coincided".[18]

So it's absolutely true that oppression is clearly not restricted to the working class. Rich and powerful women also face society's sexism. High-flying women in the city of London face sexual harassment in male dominated workplaces where the gender pay gap is actually higher than the average. The media's obsession with the clothes, grey hairs and pregnancy bumps of the future queen of England Kate Middleton is plainly sexist. But does that mean you can compare that treatment with the suffering of someone who cannot leave a violent partner because the refuge has been closed or with a shift worker on the minimum wage trying to sort affordable childcare? If we ignore class differences we are doing a disservice to the experiences of the majority of women.

We also have to be able to explain why the success of those few women who have reached positions in big business, the civil service or the city of London is predicated on the exploitation of other women who service their lives. These powerful women can "have it all"—a family and a career—but the price paid by the working class women who facilitate their achievement is often that they have to give up their own family. The last 30 years has seen an army of the world's poorest women forced to rip up their own family ties and leave their children with grandparents while they travel perhaps thousands of miles across the globe to care for the offspring of their richer "sisters". The mass emigration of women from the Philippines, where two thirds of all migrants are women, is one symptom of this development. The income migrants send home supports up to 54 percent of the total Filipino population.[19]

The world's nine richest women have a combined wealth of $230 billion. The wealthiest women have been getting even richer in comparison to the majority. Since the mid-1960s the percentage of total female earnings going to women in the top earnings group has doubled.[20] In 1980 women in the top 1 percent of female earners were paid just over 4 percent of total female earnings. By 2008 they were earning 8 percent of the total income of all women.[21] Such women have options way beyond the majority of women. When Sheryl Sandberg, ex Google executive and now with Facebook, found it awkward getting across the Google car park when she was pregnant she ordered parking spaces for pregnant women nearer the building. This was promptly taken care of.

Sandberg has written a book arguing that women who want to make it to the top have to "lean in" and fight for promotion before and right up to having children. She writes that, "More female leadership

Marxism and Women's Liberation

will lead to fairer treatment for all women." Yet the evidence shows that such a link is not automatic. Yahoo! chief Marissa Mayer started her job while pregnant but didn't think about her employees' problems with juggling childcare with work when she swiftly abolished the flexible working arrangements of her employees. She may be a working mother but those issues were not her concern. She had the resources to have a nursery built for her baby, right next her office.

Polish-German revolutionary Rosa Luxemburg did not mince her words when she wrote of such women in 1914, "The women of the possessing classes will always be rabid supporters of the exploitation and oppression of working people, from which they receive at second hand the wherewithal for their socially useless existence".[22] The fight for equality at every level of society is an important one but as Eleanor Marx, daughter of Karl, pointed out, such struggles, for example for the vote, could not be divorced from class. When she refers to suffragette campaigner Millicent Fawcett, who had opposed legislation to shorten working hours, she said:

> We see no more in common between a Mrs Fawcett and a laundress than we see between Rothschild and one of his employees. As women we certainly have a lively concern about winning for women the same rights as men, including working men, already possess today. But we believe that this "women's question" is an essential component in the general question of the emancipation of labour.[23]

The importance of class in a Marxist approach to women's oppression is not just to acknowledge that working class or poor women suffer more. Class as a measure of economic inequality is recognised by many who don't share a Marxist perspective. Class is seen as having a detrimental impact in the same way as other forms of disadvantage such as race, gender or sexuality.

Marxists argue that class cannot only be understood as suffering disadvantage; it is also a source of collective strength. Women are now part of the working class in bigger numbers than ever before. Although this development represents another burden on already tough lives it actually places women at the centre of potentially the most powerful social force in the system. This is the force that Marx described as the "gravedigger" of capitalism because he believed workers had the potential to bury the system once and for all. Such a view of class does not fit the mainstream narrative. This either sees class as a matter of lifestyle, or as something that is only relevant when referring to male manual workers (see Chapter 11).

So why look at the ideas of Karl Marx and his collaborator Friedrich Engels, two men of the Victorian era? What can they possibly have to say about women's oppression in the 21st century? Marx and Engels were first and foremost revolutionaries. They had been active in the 1848 revolutionary upsurge across Europe—Engels fought on the barricades and Marx was eventually exiled from Germany because of his revolutionary activity. Although this book will be looking in particular at Marx and Engels's ideas and political method, other writers including August Nimtz and most recently Heather Brown have explored their lives and political activity.[24] They show how both men saw women as an essential part of the socialist and working class organisations they fought to build.

Central to Marx and Engels's analysis was showing how women's oppression was not just structured into society but originated with the rise of class society and was specifically shaped by the role of the family in that society (see Chapter 4). Seeing women's oppression as being shaped by the family is different to believing that it is rooted in women's biological ability to procreate. Some in the past even speculated that freedom was only possible if women no longer had to give birth.[25]

A Marxist approach does not see biology as a defining factor holding back women's liberation, but it points to a critical moment in the development of human society, the division of society into classes, when women's ability to procreate did have a decisive impact on their position, separating them from production (see Chapter 3). So rather than the biology of reproduction being the problem, it is the way society is organised around reproduction within the privatised family that is the significant factor for women's oppression today. This book will look at how the family, despite its many transformations, serves a social and ideological function, which flows from the vital material economic function the family has in wider capitalist society. This analysis then points to the possibility of ending oppression with the end of class society.

This book seeks to offer an analysis of the position of women in modern capitalism building on the tradition of Marx and Engels and the many revolutionaries who followed them. So the insights of 20th century revolutionaries such as Clara Zetkin, Alexandra Kollontai and Rosa Luxemburg will be joined by those of the new generation of writers trying to get to grips with the contradictions of women's oppression in society today.

The socialist tradition has a rich history of theory and struggle over the issue of women's oppression, one that is often overlooked. It was socialist women led by German revolutionary Clara Zetkin who first declared that there should be an International Working Women's Day.[26] This was envisaged as a day to advance the campaign for the vote "in conjunction with the entire women question" and the date was chosen in tribute to textile workers in New York's Lower East Side who were fighting for the vote and decent wages and living conditions.[27]

Around the world women have been fighting back whether it is fast food workers in the US demanding a living wage, Greek public sector workers struggling against austerity or the women who took to the streets in the Arab revolutions of 2011. In Britain women workers have been at the forefront of resistance to Tory austerity. The biggest strike of women workers in British history took place when 2.6 million public sector workers walked out over pension rights in November 2011. It has been working class women most affected by the bedroom tax who have led the campaign against it. For these working class women gender equality would be a material improvement in their lives. But if society's greatest divide of class is left unchallenged then equality is nothing more than a mirage and there can be no hope of liberation.

This book is not about identifying another "wave" of feminism, it is about looking at how we fight to combat women's oppression at a time when we are being told that the major battles have been won. It will also address why struggles against oppression today risk the sort of fragmentation that marked the demise of the Women's Liberation Movement in Britain. Then the divisions represented a political rejection of the possibility of a "grand narrative", a unitary theory of capitalist society that could explain oppression.

Now the time is ripe to raise the argument that Marxism can indeed offer such an explanation. But not only that, it can point to a way forward. History has shown the power of women workers standing alongside men as part of the collective power of the working class. The experience of such working class fighters is often not the subject of academic or theoretical study. Ordinary women and men who have taken part in struggles against exploitation and oppression are rarely named in history books or commemorated in statues or art galleries. But their resistance offers hope of a different future—a socialist society where women's liberation can become a reality for the first time. This book seeks to pay tribute to much that we owe those who have fought in the past, but with one aim in mind—to convince you the reader to carry on the fight they started.

2

Oppression explained

Oppression is discrimination against individuals or a group of people on the basis of perceived or assumed difference. This can be on the basis of, for example, actual or perceived gender, skin colour, racial group, sexuality or religious belief. Oppression can sometimes appear to be simply a product of individual prejudice. But while bigoted ideas are often part of the expression of oppression, the experience of oppression is more than just facing bigotry or intolerance.

Oppression has both specific material roots and very real material consequences. It can result in low pay, domestic violence or the mass murder of ethnic or religious minorities. It can mean that whole sections of society are demonised, in order to legitimise their mistreatment. Oppression can affect people in all walks of life: racism, homophobia and sexism, for example, are experienced across class divisions.

Chapter 1 pointed to how women MPs, business leaders and academics are judged by their appearance and face sexual harassment and unequal pay. Their family arrangements—children, or lack of them—are scrutinised in a way those of men in the same position are not.

Critics of Marxism claim the evidence that oppression appears to function independently of class means Marxism lacks the tools to understand it. But this book seeks to show that on the contrary a Marxist understanding of oppression allows a deeper appreciation of the burden it imposes. It is impossible to adequately express the suffering oppression produces without reference to class, while at the same time recognising that oppression and class exploitation are different phenomena.

A glance at the predominantly white and male members of the ruling class who fill most positions of power shows that class and oppression are not working independently of each other. The class divide remains the greatest divide within society and shapes every aspect of our lives (see Chapter 11).

Exploitation at the heart of the system

The class divide is based on exploitation, the fundamental basis of the whole system of capitalism. In essence exploitation is the process through which workers "sell" their capacity to labour—Marx calls this their "labour power"—to an employer in order to live. If you live under capitalism you need money to buy food and pay the bills so you are forced to work for a wage. This means workers must turn a human attribute into a commodity to be bought and sold in the marketplace of capitalism, or face the even greater impoverishment of unemployment and reliance on benefits.

Marx argued that labour power "possesses the peculiar property of being the source of value". What he meant was that, unlike every other commodity, when bosses buy a worker's labour power they have the potential to accrue more from it than the price they paid. Employers keep all the new value created by workers over and above the fraction that is paid as a wage. This "surplus" value is the source of their profits. Today the term exploitation is often only used in the mainstream when referring to extremely low pay or bad working conditions. But it is the surplus value workers create not the level of pay that is critical to whether a person is being exploited in a Marxist sense. Even well paid workers do not receive the full return of their labour—indeed they may be more exploited than low-paid workers if their higher productivity means they create more surplus value compared to their wages.

The rate of exploitation can be concretely calculated from how many hours worked, wages paid, cost of equipment and investment in machinery and technology and so on. This exploitative relationship between boss and worker is what defines class divisions in capitalism. Class divisions are based on whether you have to sell your labour power in order to live. They are based on a social relationship, not categories to which you're allocated or on your accent, what food you eat or music you listen to.

The role of oppression

Oppression is not part of this core process that drives capitalist accumulation. But in today's capitalist system, it is generated by this process and can help facilitate it in the interests of the ruling class.

Different forms of oppression have developed in different circumstances and at different points in history (see Chapter 3). The oppression of women is the oldest oppression and grew out of the birth of class society over 10,000 years ago. No wonder it is often seen as something that is just a natural part of human life. So today women are seen as mainly responsible for rearing the next generation in the family and looking after the sick and elderly, even though their role in society is much more than this. But this hasn't always been so. Different forms of the family may reproduce the oldest oppression but it is still a relatively modern development when looking at the whole of human history.

For 90 percent of human history there were no hierarchies and no systematic oppression. Such an understanding of our history shows us something that should inspire and inform our actions. Whatever forms future struggles take, oppression is not an inevitable product of human nature. If we have a past without oppression, a future without oppression is also possible.

To fully understand the roots of oppression and how it functions the first step is to look at society as a totality. This means avoiding the dangers of seeing the roots of oppression as located within interpersonal relationships. Instead we have to look at oppressive relationships as taking place in the context of an oppressive society. They are evidence of oppression not its cause. Marxism seeks to go beyond simply examining the empirical evidence of discrimination and inequality. Part of a common feminist analysis is that women's oppression is rooted in the behaviour and sexist ideas of men, who have a collective interest in keeping women down. This view of what is seen as "male power" is often termed "patriarchy" and, as Martha Gimenez points out, there is a danger that this can lead to a "fall into tautology" where we end up simply "explaining male domination on the basis of phenomena used to infer its existence".[28]

It can also lead to an analysis that sees oppression as being caused by forces unconnected to the capitalist social relations in which it manifests itself. So for example, some socialist feminists agree that capitalism is to blame for exploitation but see patriarchy as existing as a process of oppression that developed independently of class and so needing separate and different struggles to combat it. This approach has been coined a "dual systems" analysis.

Such responses can even accommodate those that maintain that oppression is a product of natural roles that flow from our biological differences. This is the view that claims women are oppressed because men are naturally competitive and domineering and women more gentle and caring.

Patriarchy is a broad and flexible set of ideas and has led some activists to conclude that unity with men in struggle is either not possible or not desirable. Marxists have developed a critique of patriarchy theories and their consequences over a number of decades.[29] The issue will be discussed in more detail in later chapters but at this stage it is important to point to the weakness of a theory that sees all men as in some way having anything in common, apart from their body parts. When you look at society the experience of men or of women is not a common one across their entire sex.

The minority of men at the top of society has no more in common with a male refuse collector than with a working class woman. This is equally true for the few women that are part of the elites of the ruling class. Ordinary people's lives are alien to them. The economic crisis has only exacerbated these differences. Gill Riley, a managing director, boasted to the *Guardian* about how close she is to the staff of her company, saying of the impact of the financial crisis: "Before my office junior would go, or anybody, my Porsche would go".[30] For her office junior and the vast majority of women workers the choices they have had to make because of the crisis have been rather more prosaic. As German revolutionary Clara Zetkin pointed out over a century ago, whatever the outward appearances, when struggles break out the idea of unity of interests between all women against all men melts away like "scintillating bubbles".[31]

Women's oppression in particular has been, and sometimes still is, dismissed or regarded as a problem of individual psychology. So when women suffer depression or other mental health problems, including

Marxism and Women's Liberation

eating disorders such as anorexia nervosa and bulimia, these are dealt with as individual problems rather than conditions connected to anxiety produced by society's expectations. The Health and Social Care Information Centre reported a "national rise of 8 percent in the number of admissions to hospital for an eating disorder" in 2013. Nine times as many women were admitted and 15 years olds were the largest group.[32]

Sometimes the solutions proposed themselves reflect the oppressive and sexist values of society. So from a younger and younger age women and girls are faced with images of women's body shape that bear no relation to reality. Women suffering from issues of low self-esteem or confidence are encouraged to go to ever more extreme lengths to fit society's mould for the perfect female, even if inability or disinclination to fit that mould was the problem in the first place. For example, one British cosmetic surgery clinic whose website is called "Transforming lives" declares "it's all about feeling good about yourself". One woman who has had her breasts enlarged is pictured saying she now has "loads more confidence. I'm so much happier".[33] (See Chapter 9.)

All this is based on an acceptance of the notion that women's feelings of self-worth are based on fulfilling a desire to be both stick thin and busty—a physical combination that rarely comes naturally. Cosmetic surgery is now simply another consumer choice. But the surgeon's knife is not the answer to women's problems about body image. These are generated by a society that holds up an unattainable and stereotyped ideal of women. It is just another example of how women's oppression, which is bred and structured by the world in which we live, becomes an issue of individual psychology that can be medicalised away.

Medical intervention as a solution to the problems caused by women's oppression is not confined to the modern form of elective cosmetic surgery. There is a history of women who have trouble conforming to sexist templates of womanhood being treated as mentally ill. In the 1950s women who got pregnant before marriage could find themselves in a psychiatric hospital and their baby taken from them. Some became institutionalised and languished in such places for decades.

The term "hysterical" has sneering dismissive connotations associated with supposed female instability; the term comes from hysteria—the ancient Greek word for the uterus. This female "condition" has in the past been treated with everything from electric-shock treatment and long-term debilitating medication to lobotomies. After 1941 the majority of the 15,000 lobotomies performed in England were on women. "A well recommended psychiatric book in the 1970s, suggests a lobotomy to help a women stay within a marriage to an unsuitable husband when medication has failed to work, and when separation is impossible due to religious beliefs or financial or emotional dependence upon the husband".[34]

The brutality of a lobotomy and its devastating effect on a person were seen as of lesser importance to women patients and were said at the time by psychosurgeons to be "potentially more effective with women because it is easier for them to assume or resume the role of a housewife".[35] With added racism these attitudes were mirrored in the US. Walter Freeman, dean of American lobotomists until 1970, said of lobotomies that "women respond better than men, Negroes better than whites".[36]

Such medicalisation of oppression must be opposed. Oppression is not all in your head. But at the same time it is important to acknowledge that oppression can cause deep personal pain and so can have a real impact on mental health. Many people face very real mental health problems, some of which are caused or exacerbated by how they are treated and diagnosed in a sexist society. The question is how many women's bodies and brains are going to be cut before we decide society needs to be transformed to fit women rather than the other way around?

Part of the problem of understanding oppression is the extent to which it is not simply imposed from outside forces, or from "society" in an abstract way. Oppressive ideas about behaviour, appearance and roles can be internalised and even policed by other women. Mothers can tell their daughters to "make an effort" to look nice when going out, or assume sons will not take responsibility for housework and cooking or, if they do, will do it badly.

Ruling class women have played a vital role in policing the lives of working class women. They can be found heading up reactionary campaigns attacking women's personal freedoms in the name of "family values"; anti-abortion Tories like Ann Widdecombe and Nadine Dorries are recent examples. During the 1960s and 1970s religious campaigner Mary Whitehouse appealed to women to join her as she railed against the depiction of sex on television and in the 1980s Victoria Gillick fought a high-profile campaign and an ultimately unsuccessful legal case to ban teenagers from getting access to contraception without their parents' consent.

Even among peer groups there can be pressure among girls and women to conform to what are seen as the current norms of hair removal, make up and fashion. Celebrity magazines obsessed with the weight and appearance of a few celebrities are overwhelmingly bought by women.

The process of socialisation shapes expectations of what is "normal" behaviour for women and men, and its internalisation means sexist mores are absorbed into our day-to-day lives and become part of the society's "commonsense". A recognition of such a process contributed to one of the initiatives of the women's liberation movement of the 1960s—"consciousness raising" groups (see Chapter 6). It is also seen right up to the present day, for example in youth projects that try and involve young women in activities and discussion to build their self-confidence and assertiveness.

Building women's confidence and encouraging women to reject the limits of roles that society has socialised them to expect is a positive thing. And we should fight to do that wherever we can. But it has its limitations; women's oppression will not be solved by a change of mindset. Sexist ideas flow from the fact that women's oppression is a material problem structured into the system and rooted in the way society is organised.

Laurie Penny's writes in her book, *Meat Market*: "If all women on earth woke up tomorrow feeling truly positive and powerful in their own bodies, the economies of the globe would collapse overnight".[37] Obviously this is not meant to be a literal prediction as it would somewhat overstate the impact of women's positive thinking. It would also imply negativity about women's bodies was the responsibility of women themselves, something that Penny has argued against elsewhere. But the role of consciousness raising still has a resonance within much feminist thinking today.

If it really was the case that getting rid of oppression and exploitation was mainly an issue of consciousness then that would determine how we fought. Marx argued that "being determines consciousness". In other words, the world we are born into and grow up in shapes the ideas we have in our heads. So oppressive ideas don't create an unequal world, they reflect and are generated by the unequal world we live in. That does not mean we ignore sexist or oppressive ideas, we should challenge them as we challenge every manifestation or symptom of sexism. But ultimately to win real and lasting change we will have to challenge the system that produces the rotten ideas in the first place.

Personal accounts

Some accounts and debates about oppression describe and understand it simply as the subjective experience of an oppressed person or people. Personal accounts of the experience of oppression can be a powerful testament to the appalling reality of life in a brutal system. But alone they cannot be a replacement for theory that leads to an understanding of the roots of the systemic inequality. As Gimenez writes: "Experience in itself, however, is suspect because, dialectically, it is a unity of opposites; it is unique, personal, insightful and revealing and, at the same time, thoroughly social, partial, mystifying, itself the product of historical forces about which individuals may know little or nothing".[38]

Even in situations that seem to be rooted solely in interpersonal relationships, such as domestic violence, wider society is playing a role and not just an ideological one. So, for example, when a man is brought up in court for violent assault of a partner or ex-partner, he is able to plead mitigating circumstances that play to society's idea of gender norms. These can put the burden of blame on the victim of the assault and get him a lighter sentence. The state, through the legal system, both reflects and reinforces rules about women's behaviour and so condones the actions of violent men whom it regards as justified.

Marxism and Women's Liberation

So the family of Julia Pemberton, who was murdered along with her son William by her husband Alan in 2003, was told by the coroner at the inquest that although he did not condone the actions of Alan, he recognised there were "mitigating circumstances". He spelled out that these included Julia taking out an injunction—after Alan's death threats when she told him she was leaving him, "Julia's bombshell"—and that this was "excluding him from the house which he clearly loved." This was alongside the "awful and unpleasant allegations" she made against him. Julia and her family had reported her husband's threats to murder her to the police for over a year before her death. They did nothing.[39]

In another case in 1991 Joseph McGrail was tried in Birmingham for the murder of his wife who he repeatedly kicked in the stomach. He pleaded provocation on the basis that his wife was an alcoholic and swore at him. The judge commented that "this lady would have tried the patience of a saint" and let the man off with a two-year suspended sentence. In 1995 Brian Steadman was jailed for only three years after he hit his wife 13 times with a hammer, killing her. He pleaded diminished responsibility due his wife's constant nagging. In 2007 in Cwmbran in Wales a man killed his wife after a row by running her over. He had dragged her from their car in front of witnesses and deliberately aimed it at her. Although the judge "described it as a 'brutal killing' the court accepted his plea of guilty to manslaughter on the grounds of 'provocation'. He was jailed for seven years".[40]

Each of those men is individually responsible for their actions. But the legal judgments in such cases play a role in shoring up systemic oppression when they allow claims of "nagging" and the announcement of a separation as justification for violence and even murder.

Divide and rule

Women's oppression has a specific function in capitalist society, connected with pushing the burden of care of dependents onto the privatised family rather than being the responsibility of society. But all oppression is used by the ruling class to divide us in order to entrench their position. If politicians and bosses can convince people that immigrants are the cause of low pay or unemployment or the lack of affordable housing, for example, they can deflect the blame from themselves. The same goes for attempts to portray single mothers as a drain on welfare benefits or young unemployed people as lazy. The ruling class will make use of any possibility of fostering division in order to encourage us to blame each other for our problems. That is why those at the top of society so often scapegoat minority groups.

These actions are not driven by specific ideological prejudices, though members of the ruling class may well be racist and sexist. They are about making it easier to stay in control. In some cases bosses will even openly use migrant workers as scab labour to try and bring the rest of the workforce to heel. Women workers have also been used in the past to undercut male workers. In every case the greater and deeper the divisions in the working class are, the greater the ability is of the ruling class to impose its will.

Historically this has enabled bosses to pay all workers less or impose worse conditions on everyone. Economist Michael Reich in his book, *Racial Inequality*, researched the wages and conditions of black and white workers in the US and showed that during the 1970s "white workers' wages, the extent of unionism, and profit rates of manufacturing industries were each significantly influenced by racial inequality". In fact "wages and unionism were lower and profits were higher where racial inequality was greater." So black workers in the southern US states, where racism was most entrenched and open, were paid less than white workers. But southern white workers were paid less than black and white workers in the north because they allowed themselves to be played off against black workers. The beneficiaries were the southern ruling class.[41]

Similarly until the early 1970s working class Catholics in Northern Ireland had worse living conditions and wages compared to workers anywhere else in the UK. Protestant workers were told they were privileged by their allegiance to the British state and indeed they did live in better conditions than Northern Irish Catholics. But their living standards were still lower than those experienced by workers in the rest of the UK where the sectarian divide did not exist.

Marxism and Women's Liberation

The experience of oppression has generated powerful movements for liberation. The history of attempts to tackle the question of women's oppression will be examined in other chapters, but each time such movements have come up against the limits of the system. Important gains and reforms can be won. But if the system survives these gains may not reach across society and the ruling class will constantly attempt to undermine any reforms when the balance of forces shifts.

Struggles against specific experiences of oppression do not necessarily lead to unity across different oppressed groups. The suffering caused by the experience of oppression can lead to fragmentation and isolation. If you experience homophobia it does not automatically mean you will support migrant workers; women fighting for equal pay will not all believe that they have a common struggle with LGBT people or with the victims of Islamophobia.

However, in contrast, within the working class the experience of exploitation creates an intrinsic pressure to overcome division. Of course this does not mean workers do not have bigoted ideas or do not act in oppressive ways. They do. And in the past some trade unions have excluded or ignored the possibility of organising women and black workers, for example. But if workers are going to win, they are forced into collective organisation by the experience of being in a workplace and having to band together, sometimes despite their ideas, as the only way to extract concessions from their bosses. If one section of workers allows itself to be played off against another, then the result will be worse conditions for all.

Whatever the subjective ideas of workers, their objective interests are to oppose divisions on their side. This means the fight for the oppressed is not just an act of sympathy. Fighting for rights for all the oppressed makes the whole working class stronger. Overcoming divisions, challenging bigotry, fighting for equal pay and equal rights in the workplace is central to all working class struggle. Not only that, the working class is diverse, it is made up of the oppressed. They are not merely the victims of objective conditions, they are active participants in struggles and resistance to those conditions.

There has been a long history of debates about how to win equality and fight for liberation from oppression. Whether it has been the struggle for the vote, for birth control or the right to equal pay, arguments about whether oppressed groups are stronger if they fight alone or alongside others, whether the working class can play a role or whether we can win through gradual reforms have raged across the centuries. The debates of the late 19th century and early 20th century were shaped by struggles over suffrage, anti-imperialism and workers' rights. Then the experience of war, revolution and counter-revolution had a profound impact on the struggles that broke out against imperialism, racism and women's and LGBT oppression in the US in the 1960s.

Today we have new debates about the nature of oppression and how we can fight to eradicate it and win genuine liberation. The arguments of Vladimir Lenin, one of the leaders of the Russian Revolution, which in its early years of hope fought hard for the rights of the oppressed, still ring true today. He declared that a socialist should be a "tribune of the people" and such a tribune should be able to "react to every manifestation of tyranny and oppression, no matter where it appears, no matter what stratum or class of the people it affects".[42]

3

The origins of women's oppression

It can sometimes feel like the world has always been the way it is. Whether it is the world of work, home or the family we are told that the way we live is natural and inevitable. We are fed the illusion that there are static, unchanging features of human society, and those include inequality and social divisions. We are told women are naturally passive, home-centred and maternal, while men are more aggressive and competitive. Men are still seen as the dominant breadwinners, despite the modern reality in the US and Britain that half of the workforce is female.

The image of an average family most reflected in popular culture is a heterosexual couple and two children. It is assumed that such a set up is rooted in our nature and reflects biologically shaped gender roles that are as old as humanity itself. Anthropologist and Marxist Eleanor Burke Leacock led the way from the late 1960s onwards in challenging such superficial views of human history, women's role in society and the family. She wrote that in hunter-gatherer societies for example "the band, not the family, is the collective, whether several families share a tipi, or whether the camp is a series of small lean-tos... Care and responsibility for the young, the old, and the infirm is not an individual matter, but social, the concern of the whole group".[43]

The view of women as naturally caring and peaceful is shared even by some who support women's equality. But this is an ahistorical approach. Biology does play a role in human history and the development of women's oppression. Our human biological characteristics—our height range, our need for regular food and water and our offspring's lengthy period of dependence, among other things, all shape how we interact with the rest of the natural world.

This chapter will look at how at a certain point in human history the fact that women and not men bore children began to have a major impact on women's role in society. Marxist feminist Nancy Holstrom wrote in 1984, "As new needs and capacities are continually being created, biology remains an important determining factor, but human life progressively becomes less directly tied to its biological base".[44] So today the fact that women give birth is not critical to the role women play in society—physical strength, size and fertility are not relevant to whether you can pilot an airliner jet or drive a bus.

Marx and Engels and what makes us human

Friedrich Engels, Marx's great friend and collaborator, wrote a book in 1884 that revolutionised previous assumptions about the development of human history. Today, although in parts outdated, *The Origin of the Family, Private Property and the State* is still a brilliant account of the process by which class society arose and with it the development of women's oppression. In it he argued that for over 90 percent of their history humans lived in societies without classes and women did not face systematic oppression. He described human history as dominated by societies in which people lived in nomadic hunter-gatherer groups that were based on cooperation and egalitarianism, which he termed primitive communism.

Marxist anthropologist Karen Sacks argues that "Engels is almost alone in providing a materialist theory—one that sees women's position as varying from society to society, or epoch to epoch, according to the prevailing economic and political relationships of the society".[45] She acknowledges he made some errors due to the limited evidence available at the time, but says his framework is still the best way to understand results of research carried out with modern methods long after he was writing.

Marx and Engels argued that humans were products of the natural world, as living, breathing, biological beings. But they went on to say that we are unique among creatures because we *consciously* interact with the natural world. It is worth noting that throughout Marx and Engels's writing they use "man" and "mankind" to denote humans, as was common in their time. Marx describes the process: "By thus acting on the external world and changing it, he at the same time changes his own nature".[46]

Humans' conscious intervention means that they can plan, make choices and learn from mistakes. Marx stressed, "Free conscious activity is man's species character".[47] The fact that human labour is conscious marks us out from other animals. For while the actions of many other species change the world around them—birds make complex nests, beavers make dams, some even use twigs and other tools to access food—this is unchanging instinctual behaviour. Today starlings build the same nests they have for millennia; they don't construct thatched cottages, tower blocks or space stations.

Marx put it like this:

> A spider conducts operations that resemble those of a weaver, and a bee puts to shame many an architect in the construction of her cells. But what distinguishes the worst architect from the best of bees is this, that the architect raises his structure in imagination before he erects it in reality. At the end of every labour-process, we get a result that already existed in the imagination of the labourer at its commencement.[48]

This understanding of humans' conscious actions on their environment shows that at every stage there is constant interaction and change—a dialectical relationship between humans and the environment they are part of.

The environment is not a static backdrop to our lives. It undergoes perpetual change and is also itself in part human-made, even tens of thousands of years ago. In his study of ecology and human history Martin Empson points to a river mouth in South Africa where "archeological evidence from 75,000 to 55,000 years ago shows that early human beings were manipulating the landscape to improve their food sources".[49]

The tools, processes and materials we utilise to meet human needs are not somehow separate from human society—indeed, they form the basis of it. Those economic capacities, whether basic irrigation streams, the earliest smelting ovens or modern car factories, are all themselves both products of human labour and factors that shape human societies.

Marx and Engels's historical materialist method recognises this economic basis for human relations as well as constant interaction between the tools and materials we have, the ways we organise ourselves to use them and the ideologies, myths, art and politics that arise from them.

Historical materialism

Engels pointed out that the fundamental basis of any society is the need for humans to find the means to live. In his speech at Marx's grave he said Marx "had discovered the law of development of human history: the simple fact, hitherto concealed by an overgrowth of ideology, that mankind must first of all eat, drink, have shelter and clothing, before it can pursue politics, science, art, religion, etc".[50]

Humans have managed to, "eat, drink, have shelter and clothing" in vastly different climates and habitats, from the Sahara desert to the frozen Antarctic. As Marxist Chris Harman wrote:

> This is a fundamental difference between us and the existing apes. So gorillas are not to be found outside tropical rain forests, chimps outside wooded regions in sub-Saharan Africa, gibbons outside the tree tops of south east Asia, orangutans outside a few islands in Indonesia; by contrast, humans have been able to live across a vast swathe of Africa, Europe and Asia for at least half a million years. Our genetic "speciality" is precisely that we are not specialised, not constrained by any limited range of instinctive behaviour.[51]

Engels described how the method of producing and creating the means to live shapes all aspects of human society. This approach is reflected in what used to be called the iron, stone or bronze ages, for example. As Gordon Childe explains in his study *Man Makes Himself*, the names acknowledge that the development of productive ability was the defining feature of the society and its social relationships. Humans "must be in a position to live in order to be able to 'make history'" and finding the means to live is a "fundamental condition of all history, which today, as thousands of years ago, must daily and hourly be fulfilled merely in order to sustain human life".[52]

Engels argued that this "production and reproduction of the immediate essentials of life" had a twofold character. There is production to satisfy human physical needs and there is:

> the production of human beings themselves, the propagation of the species. The social organisation under which the people of a particular historical epoch and a particular country live is determined by both kinds of production: by the stage of development of labour on the one hand and of the family on the other.[53]

The way that the "production of human beings themselves", reproduction, takes place cannot be understood in isolation from the economic production in any society. It is not timeless and unchanging—"the production of life, both of one's own in work and of fresh life in procreation, now appears as a double relationship—on the one hand as a natural, on the other a social relationship".[54]

Humans as social beings

Basic human needs have only ever been met by acting cooperatively. This fact contradicts the popular image of humans as naturally competitive and striving to control one another. Such ideas are promoted to convince us that capitalism is merely an expression of natural human behaviour. But a careful look at the earliest human history shows us a very different picture. It also sheds light on how class society developed and with it the oppression of women.

Engels and Marx always stressed that humans were social beings. Marx dismissed those "Robinsonades" (after Robinson Crusoe, the character marooned on an island in the Daniel Defoe novel) who saw humanity as a collection of self-sufficient individuals. He saw production of the means of living as a social process, with the implicit necessity to communicate being part of that development, writing in the *German Ideology* that, "Language is as old as consciousness...language like consciousness, only arises from the need, the necessity, of intercourse with other men".[55]

In his pamphlet *The Part Played by Labour in the Transition from Ape to Man* Engels argued that the transition to walking on two feet and making tools with the newly freed and increasingly adept hands was a critical one: "The decisive step had been taken, the hand had become free and could henceforth attain ever greater dexterity; the greater flexibility thus acquired was inherited and increased from generation to generation".[56]

The idea that tool use—human labour—decisively shaped the nature of early humanity was a revolutionary challenge to the dominant thinking of the time, including that of Charles Darwin. This saw big brains as developing first, allowing the development of human communication and tool use. Engels's insight was remarkable and stands today as a significant contribution to our understanding of how we became human. As Harman wrote, humans:

> began to use sounds and gestures not merely to indicate what was immediately in front of them or what they immediately desired (which is what some animals do) but to indicate how they wanted to change something and how they wanted others to help them... The development of labour and the development of communication thus, necessarily, go hand in hand. And as they both develop, they both encourage the selection of those new genes which made people more adept at both: the more agile hand, the larger brain, the larynx that made a wider range of sounds.[57]

Our biology gives us the ability to imagine, fight for and create new ways of living that transcend the limitations of our physical make-up. We have no wings yet we can fly, our voice box enables us to shout only so loud yet we can communicate with people thousands of miles away. But all this would be impossible without collective and collaborative labour. For example, air travel requires aircraft designers, builders, technicians, pilots, air traffic control and crew—the list goes on.[58]

Anthropologist Chris Stringer has compiled evidence from the earliest human societies that shows social interaction both for acquiring food and in the development of culture. He has written that "the degree of coordination that a sophisticated social brain can help to deliver means that the group acts more like a food-gathering machine than the host of individual and 'selfish' foragers typical of a monkey or ape group".[59]

His most recent research shows that humans lived in Britain 400,000 years earlier than previously thought.[60] Scientists carried out new excavations and re-examined old finds with new methods of investigation and dating. The world's magnetic field occasionally switches direction. The direction of the magnetic field can be seen in sediment from the time. The last time it switched was 780,000 years ago. So when the researchers found stone tools in sediment laid down in Norfolk when the direction of the magnetic field was the opposite of today, they knew this meant humans had lived here long before anyone had previously thought possible. This is important because Stringer shows that evidence of cooperation and the inherent social nature of humans can be seen in even the very earliest human societies.

At one site in Britain researchers found tools and flint flakes from sharpening them alongside bones of large animals with butchery marks on them. A huge range of different animals have roamed Britain because of the extremes of climate Britain experienced over hundreds of thousands of years. This included woolly mammoths, sabre toothed cats, bison and lions. Hippos swam in the rivers of the Yorkshire Dales and the Thames.

The researchers concluded that the bones of the animals they found would be too big for an individual to kill on their own and so would have to have been brought down or scavenged by a group working together. At one site a total of 300 flint axes were found. This might indicate people working together not just to hunt but also to butcher what would be a large amount of meat. Such a kill would then need to be shared among those who took part. All of which takes a level of social organisation and some communication. Many other tools used over hundreds of thousands of years will have been destroyed. It's likely early humans used twine, nets for fishing, wooden tools and traps, for example.

Stringer has also exhibited evidence of social interaction's impact on culture and rituals in an exhibition in the Natural History Museum in 2014. These include decoration for burial and seasonal gatherings. One glass case contained the remains of a man whose ceremonial burial included periwinkle shells and ivory rings carefully sewn into his clothing 34,000 years ago. All this is evidence of an increasingly complex social life. The use of symbols and communication and sharing of culture is what marks out the modern human.

Human needs change and develop and part of the material world that shapes us is also other humans. Humans are born completely dependent, they need to be fed and clothed and looked after by others for many years. But they are not just dependent on others for their physical needs. Even our basic abilities to talk, use our vision and hearing are dependent on social interaction and experience and not simply biology. Children who grow up without human interaction do not learn to talk.[61] Marx wrote that not understanding humans as social beings was "as much of an absurdity as is the development of language without individuals living together and talking to each other".[62]

In his 2009 book *Karl Marx, Anthropologist* Thomas C Patterson describes how even attributes assumed to be individual are in fact a product of social interaction: "human individuals—their consciousness, their personalities, their ambivalences, their subjectivities, their individualities, their identities and their cultures—have a profoundly social character...sociality permeates all aspects of the individual's life, even when he or she is seemingly alone".[63]

Engels's revolutionary breakthrough

Since Engels was writing in the late 19th century there have been numerous advances in knowledge about early humans and prehistory. Then much of his analysis was based on the reports and studies of indigenous populations in North America and elsewhere. These were seen as remnants of much older societies whose customs and living arrangements could shed light on how our ancestors lived and how and why change occurred. Yet despite all the scientific advances the basic premise of Engels's argument stands the test of time today. He based much of his writing on that of Lewis Henry Morgan. Morgan was an American lawyer in the 1870s who became interested in the customs of the Iroquois Native Americans in New York State.[64]

His publications became seen as groundbreaking studies of kin relations and group organisation. His research and his conclusions were controversial and explosive, blowing apart the assumptions of the day. His best known book, *Ancient Society* published in 1877, was much admired by Marx, who made detailed notes on its findings. These *Ethnological Notebooks* were not published in Marx's lifetime, but they became part of the basis for Engels's great work. Engels wrote in the preface to the first edition of *The Origin*, "Morgan in his own way had discovered afresh in America the materialistic conception of history discovered by Marx forty years ago."

Morgan's studies were based on previous studies and first hand research among the Iroquois, and other Native Americans, usually referred to as American Indians at that time and into the first half of the 20th century. He was drawn by their system of kinship, which at first he believed was unique to the group. His research into Native Americans and later other indigenous groups, and studies of earlier travellers and missionaries led him to conclude that in fact some form of generalised social evolution had taken place in human societies that began with common features. These included egalitarianism and lineage through mothers, termed matrilineal. These societies were also often matrilocal, that is they organised their kin relationships and families according to the relatives of the women in the group. For example, a couple would live with the woman's mother and family.

Morgan divided human development into three stages using terms that reflect the language and assumptions of the period—savage, barbarian and civilised. His insight was that his observations of the Seneca tribe of the Iroquois Native Americans revealed features common to other groups across North America but also elsewhere on the globe. This proved something that much of the ruling class did not want to hear—that the laws and traditions and family arrangements the Victorian establishment saw as sacrosanct were in fact a relatively recent development.

Morgan's work was flawed—there was limited access to archaeological evidence. Genuine scientific anthropology was very new and much previous information about indigenous groups had come from the missionaries intent on swiftly changing those societies. But in her introduction to an edition of *Ancient Society* published in the late 1970s acclaimed Marxist anthropologist Eleanor Burke Leacock wrote, "There are inconsistencies in Morgan's work, as well as confusions and even glaring mistakes. Yet they seem insignificant in the face of his staggering accomplishment".[65]

Engels acknowledged that he inherited some of Morgan's inaccuracies. He wrote in the preface to the 1884 edition of *The Origin*, "Some of Morgan's minor hypotheses have been shaken or even disproved. But not one of the great leading ideas of his work has been ousted by this new material. The order which he introduced into primitive history still holds in its main lines today".[66] Hal Draper notes that in the preface to the 1891 edition of *The Origin* "Engels distinguishes between holding to 'Morgan's hypotheses pertaining to particular points' and maintaining 'his principal conceptions.'"[67] So Engels understood the limitations of the material he was working with but held fast to the broader view that hierarchies and oppression were not a feature of the earliest human societies.

Since Marx and Engels's day there has been a revolution in new research techniques such as carbon dating and DNA mapping, which have provided a mass of new evidence about human history. Yet far from undermining their basic theses this has provided reinforcement for their insights and analysis. New research published in 2015 based on studying the kin arrangements of hunter-gatherer populations in the Congo and the Philippines provides fresh evidence to confirm the view that sexual equality and egalitarianism were features of pre-class societies. The anthropologists involved concluded that such features acted as an evolutionary advantage. One of the researchers, Mark Dyble, argued, "There is still this wider perception that hunter-gatherers are more macho or male-dominated. We'd argue it was only with the emergence of agriculture, when people could start to accumulate resources, that inequality emerged".[68]

No wonder Patterson writes:

With more than 130 years of hindsight, it appears that "Engels got it right!" The broad outlines of his argument have stood the test of time. Nonetheless, the accumulation of diverse sorts of empirical evidence during that period has added unimaginable detail and enriched our understanding of the process.[69]

It is important to exercise caution when assessing anthropological studies from the past. The studies were mostly carried out by white middle class men, often from religious backgrounds and often in the context of expanding colonialism. No one else could afford to travel to remote areas of the world. The early missionaries of the 17th and 18th century did not travel simply to observe. They wanted to make new converts to the church thus "civilising" those they saw as backward peoples—and this included imposing new roles for women.

Those few groups still living in horticultural or hunter-gather societies in the 17th century let alone later, already had seen their lives disrupted and changed even by brief or minimal links with class societies. This could be through trade, repression, or even misguided benevolence. But nevertheless they can still shed light on the process Engels was describing.

Le Jeune's account of the Montagnais

One of the best known such missionaries was 17th century French Jesuit priest Paul Le Jeune. He travelled to the French colonies in Canada and carefully documented his experiences. His trip to work among the Montagnais Native Americans from 1633-34 to convert the group to Christianity led to over 70 volumes of notes, which were published in Paris. They have now been translated into English and can be read online.[70] They are full of preconceptions about people he refers to as "savages" and his horror at their way of life. He was out to destroy a society that welcomed him in. Despite all this they make fascinating reading, both for what they reveal about the Montagnais and what they show about the attitudes of the missionaries confronted with societies that defied all their assumptions about human nature, gender and inequality.

What comes across most vividly in Le Jeune's account is just how hard Christian missionaries had to work to break traditions that had been part of the Montagnais life for hundreds, and perhaps thousands, of years. They were shocked when they found an egalitarian society with no leaders, where women played a decisive role and where human relationships were fluid and children watched over collectively.

They introduced punishment, imposed European family structures, and encouraged male authority and female chastity.

Le Jeune complains that the Montagnais had no sense of hierarchy or respect for "authority" reporting that they "imagine that they ought by right of birth, to enjoy the liberty of wild ass colts, rendering no homage to anyone whomsoever, except when they like. They have reproached me a hundred times because we fear our Captains, while they laugh at and make sport of theirs."

The missionaries also bemoaned the fact that it was hard to impose the Christian institution of marriage on people who saw their relationships as being free: "The bond, so strong, which holds man and wife under the same yoke, will be very hard to fasten upon the Savages".[71] Elsewhere he praises the chastity of a newly converted woman: "she has never lived in the libertinage to which the girls and women here abandon themselves".[72] He observed that women were not deemed inferior, commenting that female "shaman" were often seen as more effective.

The transformation and effective colonisation of these societies was no gradual evolution, nor was it done with any pretence at morality. One missionary reports with pride that he had baptised a child against his father's wishes by pretending to give the baby sugar and "accidently" spilling some water on his head while hurriedly uttering the incantation of baptism. Another describes the brutal torture and murder of someone the group had been taught to believe was an evil "sorceress".

Women's role

Women played an important role in Montagnais society. There was a division of labour, but women were part of decision making and their work was not seen as inferior to men's. The importance of their role in providing food for the group was shown by the comments of one Montagnais to the missionaries, "If we take a wife, at the first whim that seizes her, she will at once leave us; and then we are reduced to a wretched life, seeing that it is the women in our country who sow, plant, and cultivate the land, and prepare food for their husbands."

David Livingston, the 19th century Scottish explorer and missionary, recounts that when travelling in Loanda in Angola, West Africa in

1854, he tried to evade the instructions of woman leader Maneko not to travel up river alone. He describes what happened when he tried to leave without her permission:

> Maneko was not to be circumvented in this way; she came forward with her people and seized the luggage, declaring that she would carry it in spite of me. My men succumbed sooner to this petticoat government than I felt inclined to do, and left me no power; and, being unwilling to encounter her tongue, I was moving off to the canoes when she gave me a kind explanation and, with her hand on my shoulder, put on a motherly look, saying, "Now my little man, just do as the rest have done".[73]

He had to acquiesce and he and his men watched in astonishment as she led the party at full tilt all the way while they floundered behind in the mud.

The intervention of missionaries and other outsiders quickly affected kin structures. This was particularly true of the role of women. Morgan wrote about women's autonomy and ability to choose husbands. Yet only 100 years earlier French Jesuit missionary Joseph-François Lafitau described a world in which women lived in dormitories under their control where they could receive lovers as they chose. Morgan described women's "patient drudgery", whereas a century earlier women's role was even more substantial, as Lafitau observed: "All real authority is vested in them. The land, the fields and their harvest all belong to them. They are the souls of the Councils, the arbiters of peace and war. They have charge of the public treasury".[74]

The Montagnais-Naskapi in Canada had been observed by 17th and 18th century missionaries as living in matrilocal societies. When Leacock studied their kin organisation in the 20th century she found that some attitudes and practices "affirm the existence of earlier matrilocality". But now the dominant way the groups organised was according to the men's relations, "the direct influence of traders, missionaries and government personnel, plus the indirect influence of the fur trade, have all favoured patrilocality."

In fact such a shift was widespread. "It is conceded that the weight of Western cultural contact consistently favours patrilineality, the cases of a recent transition from matrilineality to patrilineality occur again and again and no clear case of the reverse can be cited".[75] But the many studies of "primitive" societies proved irrevocably that humans have lived in a variety of ways, that women were not always oppressed and that there is nothing natural about the way we live today.

From egalitarianism to class and oppression

Homo sapiens, the modern human, evolved in Africa around 130,000 years ago. They are assumed to be, along with other human species including Neanderthals, descendants of Homo erectus, a split that took place 780,000 years ago.[76] Of the several other species of humans that came to Britain for example, the Neanderthals were the most recent, up to 400,000 years ago. Homo sapiens, to which all modern humans belong, arrived in Britain about 40,000 years ago.

Today the term Neanderthal is used to denote particularly macho chauvinistic behaviour. Yet this species were far from the brutal and primitive species of popular portrayal. Neanderthals were innovative and intelligent and there is no evidence that their societies, alongside other human species, oppressed women. In fact there is evidence that male and female Neanderthals were similar in physical size, something that might not be expected if their roles were very different.[77]

Neanderthals invented new methods of making sometimes beautifully crafted tools. They organised as social groups and there is evidence they looked after their sick and buried their dead. So they shared many attributes with Homo sapiens, the species that they co-existed with and which was to outlast them. It is sometimes suggested that Homo sapiens emerged victorious after waging war on Neanderthals. This plays to beliefs about humans being naturally violent and competitive, but there is no evidence to back up this speculation.[78] In fact there appear to be many different reasons for the eventual extinction of the Neanderthals, including climate changes.[79]

Their social and tool making attributes are not all we share. Now modern DNA mapping can break down our genetic make-up. It shows that all modern humans outside of the African continent have roughly 2 percent Neanderthal DNA. This suggests the earliest Homo

Marxism and Women's Liberation

sapiens who migrated from East Africa around 60,000 years ago co-existed and interbred with the Neanderthals in the Eurasian land mass. Researchers argue that it is from this group that everyone in the world outside of the continent of Africa is descended—"whoever we are, wherever we live, whatever language we speak, whatever our customs and beliefs, whatever the colour of our skin, at some point in the last 2 million years our ancestors lived in Africa".[80]

Homo sapiens developed more intricate tools and were more adaptable than Neanderthals. Their social networks were larger and they routinely moved further distances than previous human species making them more efficient at finding food. They also developed culturally—they used tools not just for survival but to create representations of themselves and other animals in the form of art and decoration.

They lived in nomadic hunter-gatherer groups of 30 to 40, though there is evidence that they would come together in larger numbers at certain times of the year. "Their mode of production was based on sharing the foods they foraged, trapped, hunted or fished".[81] All members of the group played a part in production but most food came from gathering nuts and berries and hunting of small game, work done by women—productive labour which could be combined with childbearing.

Big game hunting was less reliable, more sporadic, and was mainly done by men. So there was a division of labour within groups but critically women's labour was equally valuable as men's—and in some cases more so. Engels called such societies primitive communism. Some writers and anthropologists, including feminists such as Evelyn Reed, who based a whole book on the premise, have claimed that all the earliest human societies were matriarchal, ruled by women: "the maternal clan system is as old as humanity itself".[82] Reed also acknowledges that the earliest societies were "communalist and egalitarian". But the absence of women's oppression does not mean that the first human societies were controlled by women. There is no evidence that there was systematic domination of any part of humanity over another in the hundreds of thousands of years before the first beginnings of a rise of class society.

It is impossible to know exactly what the day to day lives of humans living tens or hundreds of thousands of years ago were like. But what evidence there is suggests that groups moved when food ran out, possessions were few, there was no private property to speak of, and the whole group starved or feasted together. They kept to small bands as they had to sustain themselves—the number of children was limited to the number adults could carry.

These were highly successful societies that sustained human life for tens of thousands of years. Remains show that many early humans lived a long life into their 60s and 70s.[83]

In their masterful study of how inequality developed in human societies archaeologists Kent Flannery and Joyce Marcus break from empirical evidence briefly to play a game of "what if the foragers were in charge today?" They cite many differences in how such a society would be run:

> Our society's tolerance of variation would extend to marriage. A man with two or more wives, a wife with two or more husbands...would be accepted. We would permit same-sex weddings, such as those involving Native American "two-spirit" people... Since many foragers practiced infanticide, our new leaders would not outlaw abortion.[84]

In terms of economic inequality they point to the foragers' ethic of sharing that would "alter business as we know it. They would never allow CEOs to earn thousands of times what assembly-workers earn".[85] In fact the pressure would be to compete on how altruistic and generous those with more could be. None of this is to argue that a return to foraging is either desirable or an option for the world's population today, but the exercise in imagination illuminates the very different way humans lived for most of their history.

Yet change came and was to have acute and long lasting effects—especially on the role of women. In some cases climate change forced humans to adapt; the impact of growing populations also created more pressure on resources. Over thousands of years some societies began to practise slash and burn horticulture, leading to a significant increase in their productive capacity, which in turn over time led to changes in how society was organised. Sometime "between 20,000 and 10,000 years ago new modes of existence—pastoralism and plant cultivation—were grafted onto existing communities in various parts of the old and new worlds".[86] The point about new ways of producing foods being "grafted on" is important because it shows that in Patterson's words "human history is messy", it is not a linear ascent leading to today. There was sometimes an overlap of thousands of years between different modes of production. People would have continued to forage and use other subsistence methods while they cultivated crops that wouldn't be ready for a season or more.

The process of change to cultivation and early horticulture has been called the Neolithic Revolution, or new Stone Age. Following Morgan, Engels referred to it as the transition from "savagery" to "barbarism". It necessitated and enabled more settled communities, the first permanent villages, new tools to dig and hoe the soil, to cut and to skin animals. Settled living led to groups building more permanent shelters, making small pots to store seeds and a surplus of food when there was one. And this was a first—never before had methods been productive enough to produce a surplus, or communities settled enough to contemplate storage.

As methods of cultivation began to produce a greater proportion of the group's food even more human and other resources would be invested in that work. Patterson describes the process of change "as steadily more time was devoted to the preparation of fields, the construction and repair of walls and canals, to tending the crops, or to moving herds from one seasonal pasture to another".[87]

The use of ploughs, irrigation, dams, and so on—in different ways in different parts of the world—made a vast difference to productivity, but also began to have a significant impact on women's role in society. Such developments involved heavy labour; child rearing could not so easily be combined with being at the centre of production. Increasingly there was a premium on having more children who would go on to tend the fields. Women who were breastfeeding and more frequently pregnant were not able to travel as much or as often. Their work, which had in the past been the main source of nutrition, became more marginal to providing for the group's needs. So there developed a division between reproduction, now taking up more of women's time, and production of the surplus, increasingly controlled by men.

Those that produced the surplus controlled its use and this in turn gave them power in the group. The creation of a surplus frees some members of the group up from having to work every day. It also encourages contact outside the group—for there is now something to trade, something to steal and something to fight over. The existence of a surplus generates the need to allocate people to protect it and, over time, ideologies to justify the minority's control of it. This was the beginning of what would eventually become elaborate state structures to maintain the minority's privileged position. People did not always passively accept these new divisions. Flannery and Marcus write of how "each escalation of inequality required the overcoming of resistance. There seems to have been an ongoing struggle between those who desired to be superior and those who objected".[88]

Circumstances will have favoured some men and excluded others from control of the surplus, so the divisions arising also divided men from men. The section of men who had access to wealth, whether it was cultivated land, animals or grain, now became interested in their own line of inheritance for the first time. Monogamy became valued—and then enforced—as the only way for a man to ensure any offspring he passed his wealth onto were "his own".

As Karen Sacks writes:

> Thus changes took place in the definition of children. From new members of a societal group, they became either private heirs or subordinate, dependent workers. This meant that women's reproductive labour, like their productive work, also underwent a transformation from social to private. That is women bore men's heirs—to both property and social position—whereas before they had borne new members of a social group that included men and women.[89]

With the increasing numbers of offspring women had, in contrast to the limits on offspring that nomadic life imposed, there developed "an interaction between biological imperatives and social needs" and this underlay changes in the division of labour.[90] So the fact that women and not men gave birth became a factor at that point in history. In the very specific circumstances of the rise of the first hierarchies and classes, settled agriculture and the creation of a surplus for the first time, biology briefly mattered. Humans were driven to survive in new and changing circumstances. Over time the significance of women's work in wider society and in the household transformed and these material changes led to the eventual entrenched marginalisation of women shaped by their role within a new family structure.

Critiques of Engels's approach

Engels's analysis of the roots of women's oppression and the role of the family has faced criticism from some Marxist feminists in the past and more recently. He has been portrayed as "mechanical" in comparison to what is argued to be the more dialectical and nuanced analysis of Marx. Heather Brown has accused Engels of "economic determinism" when he writes of the conflicts occurring in early human societies being based on "the development of technology and larger surpluses of goods". She writes that Marx, in contrast, "was often careful to note the reciprocal, dialectical relation between economic and social factors" and claims that Marx contradicted Engels, because he saw contradictions in early human societies, including gender conflict.[91]

Others have argued that Engels's references to the twofold nature of production and reproduction in *The Origin of the Family* allowed some socialist feminists to wrongly argue that he was accepting a "dual systems" theory of women's oppression.[92] But these criticisms fail to convincingly refute Engels's central thesis. Brown's references to conflict in human societies arising independent of the material and economic roots that Engels wrote of imply alternative explanations for women's oppression without expanding on what these might be.

Brown gives an example she claims shows that Marx, unlike Engels, saw oppression as more than "economically based". She refers to Marx's references to how women suffer in the confines of the bourgeois family.[93] Yet both Engels and Marx looked at how women's oppression, although rooted in class society, affected all women, including bourgeois women. In the *Communist Manifesto* they are damning about the hypocrisy within the institution of the bourgeois family, for example writing, "The bourgeois in his wife sees a mere instrument of production".[94]

These attempts to drive a wedge between the two revolutionaries at the expense of Engels have to be challenged. Engels freely admitted his work was based on Marx's notes and research. Far from being mechanical it reflects a dialectical understanding that humans are not mere products of a particular method of production or particular technological developments, but nor can their lives be understood without reference to them.

Ideas

The rise of private property, the state and family structures laid the basis for the privatised family we know today. It was only with the rise of class society that "The man took command in the home also; the woman was degraded and reduced to servitude, she became the slave of his lust and a mere instrument for the production of children".[95] This shift resulted in women becoming subservient at every level, and this was reflected in the dominant ideology. Sexist ideas about women's behaviour, dress or natural roles are expressions of—and justifications for—the material structures of oppression, which the family is central to.

We are not born with ideas of gender roles any more than we are born with knowledge of the internet. Ideas about what is natural for a woman, whether in men's or women's heads, don't come from their mother's milk or, as Italian Marxist Antonio Labriola put it more poetically, "Ideas don't fall from heaven, nothing comes to us in a dream".[96]

Marx saw that ideas flow from the material reality of the structures and hierarchies of society, and that the ruling class has the power to generate ideologies which maintain the status quo, and their privileged position in it. But he did not view humans as empty vessels into which the ruling class can simply pour their rotten ideology. If that were the case there would never have been any resistance to the system, workers would never have formed trade unions, women would never have marched to win the vote and revolution would be impossible.

We absorb, reproduce and resist the ruling ideas from the day we are born into the world. Humans constantly test ideas against their experience, and at certain times when they find themselves at odds with the ruling class, the real forces in society are often revealed at their starkest.

Today the reality of women's lives and ideas about what we are capable of, what jobs we do, what we are paid and what we should wear are very different to those of women just a generation or two ago. The institution of the family has itself undergone many changes in the thousands of years since the rise of class society and the few hundred years since the development of capitalism. But despite these changes the family is still central to shaping women's oppression in the 21st century.

4

It's a family affair

The so-called "family hearth"—that archaic, stuffy and stagnant institution in which the woman of the toiling classes performs galley labour from childhood to death.
—Leon Trotsky[97]

The term family comes from famulus, the Latin word for servant or house slave—familia was the word for the group of slaves owned by one master. Its meaning grew to encompass a whole household, including servants, wives and children under the control of one man. Today the notion of family means many different things. The family is the most eulogised institution in western society and expectations of family life are built up to convince people that all their fulfilment and happiness will be found there.

The model nuclear family of modern capitalism is only the latest incarnation of an institution which has shaped women's and men's lives over thousands of years. Women's role within the family has always been shaped by their class position. Women in the ruling class have historically been used as "trophy" wives to be flaunted as another expression of someone's wealth, alongside the castle or more recently the private jet. The upper class wife is also expected to produce the traditional "heir and a spare" to ensure wealth is passed on within the family.[98] Marriage among the aristocracy has more commonly been a suitable match arranged between two families than a love match between individuals.

The family has proved to be a remarkably adaptable and resilient institution. The extended peasant household under feudalism was a centre of production, with all generations of the family taking part. Those with a piece of land worked for the lord who extracted his tithes in the form of hours of labour or crops, but they also grew their own food and made their own clothes and household goods. "Many a shepherd and cottar too, with his wife and children, appeared at Church in clothes which had been touched by no hands but their own".[99]

Those without land of their own relied on working for others for minimal wages. There was a sexual division of labour; women were responsible for care and supervision of children, who also worked, and domestic chores. But women also played an important role in much production both for home use and for trade. One study looking at the sexual division of labour in peasant families in England between the 12th and 15th centuries described the sort of work that was done:

> In agriculture and in animal husbandry, each sex tended to specialise in a particular range of occupations. Predominantly male tasks included ploughing, hedging, ditching, reaping, mowing, spaying and gelding.
>
> Planting, winnowing, gathering straw, stubble and chaff, and weeding were done by women, who also undertook the care of poultry and the dairy. But arrangements were generally flexible and sexually nonexclusive, and there is evidence of women being engaged in most male tasks—such as reaping, binding, mowing, carrying corn, shearing sheep, thatching and breaking stones for road-maintenance. Heavy ploughing was the only task from which they were almost totally excluded, and even here there is evidence that women were accustomed to drive the plough oxen on some estates.[100]

The transition from feudalism to capitalism saw production taken out of the home and into larger scale manufacturing, with further consequences for women's role in production. This wasn't a smooth linear process, and working class women continued to work in large numbers. Women's work outside the home on the land or in the new factories was still combined with taking responsibility for unpaid labour in the home. All members of the family worked if they could, and "women's work" was certainly not seen as such because it was in any way lighter.

Advice given to a servant maid in 1743 shows that working class women were expected to support themselves: "You cannot expect to marry in such a manner as neither of you shall have occasion to work, and none but a fool will take a wife whose bread must be earned solely by his labour and who will contribute nothing towards it herself".[101]

Industrial revolution

As the industrial revolution advanced millions of people were dragged into factory production to sell their ability to labour in mills and mines. The work was hard, dirty and dangerous.

Marx and Engels thought at one stage that the impact of the industrial revolution would destroy the basis of the working class family as men, women and children were forced to work long hours outside the home to survive.

There were different patterns of employment in different areas of Britain, and in some industries children were seen as ideal workers. Silk weaving, for example, involved all family members. In the 18th century there was even a "children's market" in Bethnal Green in east London: "In an open space, from 6am to 8am every Monday and Tuesday from 50 to 300 children from seven years of age presented themselves to be hired by the weavers".[102]

Ivy Pinchbeck's classic account *Women Workers and the Industrial Revolution 1750-1850* exposes the sheer brutality of life during this period. In the mining industry one foreman commented that women and children "work in places where no man, or even lad, could be got to labour in". Women would be responsible for dragging cut coal to the surface; originally this would have been a family working together with the man cutting the coal that his wife and children collected. Pinchbeck describes the conditions for such workers:

buckled round the waist [was] a broad leather belt, to which was attached a ring and about four feet of chain which passed between the legs and hooked onto a sledge shod with iron. Then with candles stuck in their caps, and crawling on hands and knees, girls and women dragged their heavy loads over soft slushy floors which added to their difficulty, as did the inclination of the roads which was frequently one in three to one in six.[103]

Marxism and Women's Liberation

One woman commented to mining industry inspectors, "the belt and chain is worse when we are in the family way".[104] Another reported that she had given birth in the pit and carried the baby up to the surface in her skirt.[105] In even less accessible shafts women carried coal on their backs climbing ladders out of the pit with the candles between their teeth—so much for the much lauded sanctity of Victorian womanhood. Elsewhere upper class Victorian women were seen to be such delicate flowers they had to rely on smelling salts to revive them from fainting on the sofa after some shocking event such as not getting an invite to the local ball. This was a time when even table legs in bourgeois homes were covered by cloths so as not to offend women's decency.

It is in the face of such brutal experiences that Marx and Engels thought the working class family might not survive as an institution. But it turned out to be more resilient than they predicted. It was recreated both because it served the needs of capitalism and because workers themselves fought for it. Workers, women and men, wanted to reassert control over their lives, which had been ravaged by the impact of the industrial revolution. They wanted an end to seeing their children stillborn, and for there to be more in their lives than the hard grind of the factory floor. Many saw the family as a means to achieve this.

Sections of the ruling class helped rescue the working class family because they needed fit workers. Working and living conditions were leading to stunted growth and early death among the working class. These concerns led to legislation in the mid-19th century which began to control the employment of children and then women, both by limiting their hours and by banning them from certain occupations, most importantly mining.[106]

The exclusion of women and children undoubtedly led to increased poverty and suffering for those working class families affected. Men had been promised a "family wage", that is an income sufficient to make up for the loss of wages of women and children no longer working outside the home. But of course a true "family wage" was not forthcoming for most male workers. This meant that many households' income went down as a result of new restrictions.

However, some men and some trade unions did support the restrictions on women's work because they argued women's lower wages had undermined male wages.

For many women who had endured long hours of gruelling work, even when pregnant and nursing, the move was welcome. The changes meant a reprieve from the double burden of wage and domestic labour. It also meant that larger numbers of women, men and children in the working class were able to have at least the possibility of better living conditions and some "home life" away from the factory floor.

Some feminist theorists have cited the exclusion by law of women from certain sectors of production during this period as evidence of a patriarchal pact between male bosses and workers. They say that men found common purpose in marginalising women from waged work and forcing them into unpaid and isolating labour in the home. Heidi Hartmann argued that this laid the material basis for patriarchy. She wrote, "Patriarchy is hierarchical and men of different classes, races, or ethnic groups have different places in the patriarchy" but "they are also united in their shared relationship of dominance over their women; they are dependent on each other to maintain that domination".[107]

Yet this denies the agency of the many women workers who wanted to leave the drudgery and dangers of the mines and factories. Male bosses did not see any unity of interest with their male workers and many ensured that men did not get paid the equivalent of what their wives and children had previously earned. Some men had to work longer hours to make up the difference in income lost from women's and children's labour.

One colliery women described how she welcomed stopping working in the pit, where she had earned seven shillings a week:

> We had to pay 2s and sixpence to a woman for looking after the younger bairns. I used to take them to her house at 4 o'clock in the morning, out of their own beds, to put them in hers. Then there was 1s for washing, besides there was mending to pay for and other things...then when I came home in the evening, everything was to do after the day's labour, and I was so tired I had not heart for it, no fire lit, nothing cooked, no water fetched, the house dirty, and nothing

Marxism and Women's Liberation

comfortable for my husband. It is all far better now and I wouldna' gang down again.[108]

It isn't hard to see why such women might support a move they see as enabling them to raise the quality of their own and their whole family's life. One historian pointed out that the image of a married woman at home came to reflect "the health, stability, and prosperity of a household". And that this was not a sign of families becoming wealthier or more middle class, but simply "a statement about the realities of working class experience".[109]

Of course the reality was also that many women remained in work throughout this period and into the 20th century. In one study on "Married Women's Work" originally published in 1915 the editor, Clementina Black, wrote, "I have become convinced that the moral and mental effect upon the women themselves of being wage earners is good".[110] So there have always been women who have worked outside the home. But the mid-19th century marked a point when the bourgeois family became the ideologically dominant model. Here women stayed at home in the "private sphere" and were assumed to be the "weaker sex". They were deferential to the male head of household who they and their children relied on for financial support. The lives of bourgeois women and working women were and still are a world apart, yet this model became the basis for the ideal family that is still regurgitated and has a powerful resonance today.

The role of the family in capitalism

The family is not simply a product of class society; it also plays an important part in helping maintain that society. The ruling class uses every opportunity to promote and enforce the role of the family in every way it can. Chris Harman has pointed out that it is important to get the relationship between the family and the system the right way round, writing:

> Capitalism is not driven forward by a desire to maintain the family (and with it women's oppression) any more than it is driven forward by a desire to propagate religion, maintain monarchies, advance

obscurantist beliefs etc. It has only one driving force—the exploitation of workers in order to accumulate. The family, like religion, the monarchy, etc, is only of use to capitalism in so far as it helps this goal.[III]

The way the family helps this goal is through both its economic and ideological roles, and these are inseparable from each other.

The family is not an abstract construction; it is made up of real women and men who struggle each day to provide for each other and their dependents. But because of the historic division of labour in society even if a woman is in waged work outside the home, it is still she who carries the greatest burden of work inside the home. Part of the ideological common sense in society is that women are better suited to caring for people, that the home is naturally the woman's sphere and that they are the most efficient at every aspect of home making.

The family has been remade once again since the vast expansion of the system in the post-war boom. This created the need to bring huge numbers of women into the workforce. Chapter 7 will look at how this helped create conditions for the Women's Liberation Movement. But the surge of women into the workforce and further education left an ever greater gap between the ideology of the nuclear family with a woman at its centre supported by a working husband and the reality.

Yet even as this gap widened the need for the family as a model to aspire to has become all the more important for the system. In fact it is even more important precisely because it doesn't fit reality. So the majority of adult women work outside the home, yet they still feel and are responsible for the bulk of the work of privatised reproduction inside the home. Even the difference in the availability of maternity and paternity leave is structured around the expectation that fathers will play a lesser role in childcare.

Rather than being a place of production the modern nuclear family today is an important place of consumption. Products are marketed at working mothers—more and more pre or partly prepared meals are offered as a solution to the problems of a busy life. Cooking from scratch has become something that is seen as a special occasion, yet the phrase would have been unknown to women a few generations ago who had few alternatives to getting out the vegetable peeler. The main aim of advertising campaigns targeting working mothers is to tell them they can still be the nurturing mother and caring wife even though they are not in the home full time—just buy this product!

Working class women and men try to square the circle themselves of low pay, lack of childcare, shrinking social provision, and inadequate and expensive housing. Women feel they have failed if they can't be a wonderful mother, wife and hold down a job, and men feel they are letting their family down if they cannot bring home a wage that is good enough for them all to have a decent life.

The value of the unpaid work done by women and men in the home in bringing up the next generation of workers at minimal cost to the ruling class is immense. Still the ruling class constantly wants to relieve itself of any residual burden of care. The Tory and Lib Dem coalition government of 2010 took advantage of the worldwide economic crisis to justify an unprecedented assault on state social provision of services and support for the vulnerable built up since the Second Word War. The outright Tory victory in 2015 opened the way for even greater attacks.

Such cuts have laid bare the economic role the family plays. Tory prime minister David Cameron was unusually frank when he said in 2010 that the family "is the best welfare state we ever had, the family is what looks after the children and cares for the elderly." Just the informal care of sick and disabled family members alone is estimated to save the government at least £119 billion every year.[112]

One US website annually calculates on Mother's Day "what is a mom worth?" In 2014 they calculated that if you paid someone to do all the work a mother who stayed at home full time does it would cost $118,905 a year. Even for a working mother it calculated that her unpaid work was worth $70,107.[113] For the first time in December 2014 the Office for National Statistics in Britain began to include the value of "unpaid work" into their calculations of economic activity. In 2013 they calculated that annual unpaid childcare was worth £343 billion based on 2010 figures, this is equivalent to 23 percent of GDP.[114] In November 2014 they also produced a report that concluded that simply "producing, repairing, washing, drying and pressing clothes" in the home was worth £97 billion, equivalent to 5.9 percent of GDP.[115]

But the burden carried in the family is not simply the unpaid work and the financial cost of bills. It is the 24 hour responsibility for others that is hard for money to buy—it is done by most out of love and compassion but those very human sentiments are ruthlessly exploited by successive governments. The Tories, following the previous Labour government, were intent on driving more and more responsibility for those that are not working off the state and onto individual working class families. Young people increasingly face low pay, exclusion from benefits, extortionate tuition fees for higher education, all of which means their reliance on the emotional and material safety net of the family has become even greater.

Lack of affordable housing is yet another factor deepening dependence on the family following the economic crisis and imposition of austerity. Government figures show that in 2013 in Britain over 3.3 million adults aged between 20 and 34 were living with a parent or parents—up from 2.7 million in 1996, the first recorded year, despite there being no increase in numbers of people in that age group.

The politicians rely on the fact that they know people will pick up the slack as they cannot leave their children, parents or other family members without the care they need. Women and men juggle shifts and complicated childcare arrangements as if caring responsibilities are their own personal problem to solve. Yet social provision of care should be the duty of any modern welfare state, let alone one of the richest countries in the world. It benefits the whole of society for children to be well fed, nurtured and educated and for old people to feel secure that they will have a decent retirement after a long working life.

Politicians have found they can't always assume working class people will accept every new demand to absorb the cost of cuts. These are sometimes contested and defeated. During 2013 and 2014 a groundswell of protests, mainly led by working class women, erupted against what activists coined the "bedroom tax". This was a cut in housing benefit imposed by the Tory government on claimants who it deemed had an "extra" bedroom. This had a particular impact on families looking after someone with special medical needs such as hospital type beds or other equipment.

Ideology plays an important part in the battle to drive working class people to conform to the needs of the ruling class. The family ensures people believe it is their own responsibility to feed and clothe their offspring and that if they are poor, undereducated or living in poor accommodation then it is their personal weaknesses rather than society's failings that are to blame. This was most plainly put when Tory prime minister Margaret Thatcher said in an interview with *Woman's Own* magazine in 1987, "There's no such thing as society. There are individual men and women and there are families. And no government can do anything except through people, and people must look after themselves first."

Living in nuclear families atomises people, it pushes people away from collective solutions to their problems. In Studs Terkel's oral history of the Great Depression of the 1930s one woman talked of how she went to meetings and heard great speakers talk of revolution and how "life isn't what it should be" but she said of her life as a working woman, "the trouble with my life is that I have been confined to housework, and I haven't been able to observe the world. My world has been closed. So my observation—even if I were capable—there was a fence around".[116]

Some older generations had the ideology of self-reliance so firmly instilled in them that they believed it was wrong to accept assistance even when it was available. Some had to be persuaded that they were not accepting charity when the welfare state and National Health Service were established after the Second World War and offered services for free. This is far from the popular caricature of working class people being greedy and "taking advantage" of the system that is constantly pumped out by politicians and the media.

Alongside self-reliance the family is meant to teach us our place in society—we absorb what can appear to be natural hierarchies, deference to those we are told are our "betters". Family law, fines for school children truanting, anti-social behaviour orders for young people are all predominantly used against poor and working class families, reinforcing the notion of the "feckless poor" as a threat to society.

Not only are families policed by the ruling class, those that don't fit the mould of the nuclear family laid out for them also suffer by being excluded from the family by law and prejudice. Relationships between LGBT people, perceived as a threat to the role and stability of the family, were until recently not legally recognised by the state. This had a huge impact not just in terms of stigmatising LGBT people but it affected child custody, pension rights and even the ability of someone to visit a loved one in hospital.

The overwhelming yes vote in the 2015 equal marriage referendum in Ireland showed how much attitudes are changing as LGBT people increasingly come out and demand the right to be treated equally. The arguments used by the no side revealed just how enduring the "traditional" model of the family is. No campaigners argued that marriage could only be between heterosexuals as it was about procreation and raising children. They fear the breakdown of traditional family structures as a threat to the stability of the system and their power.

After long campaigning against such discrimination and for the recognition that a legal union gives, civil partnerships between same sex couples were legally recognised in Britain in 2004. But this was still not full equality and therefore many LGBT campaigners continued to fight for the right to marry, which was finally granted by the Tory government in 2013. Equal marriage is a welcome shift towards equality for LGBT people—the joy expressed by thousands on the streets of Dublin in May 2015 after the referendum result was announced should leave no one in any doubt as to just how much the result means to those facing homophobia. But some activists have also pointed to contradictions in the demand for the right to have the state legitimise your relationship. Some LGBT people argue that marriage is associated with ownership of another person and women's oppression—they argue against being assimilated into a reactionary institution.

Certainly some in the ruling class do see the move as an attempt to incorporate LGBT people inside an institution in which it puts so much store as a method of maintaining stability in society. It is in direct contrast to the Tories' strategy in the 1980s under Margaret Thatcher. This included inserting a clause in the Tory Local Government bill in 1988 that effectively banned teachers from what the Tories termed "promoting homosexuality" to their students. The clause included the phrase, "a local authority shall not promote the teaching in any maintained school of the acceptability of homosexuality as a pretended family relationship."

Cameron has claimed that his support for equal marriage was a sign of just how important he believed the family to be: "I'm a massive supporter of marriage and I don't want gay people to be excluded from a great institution." But the ruling class was and remains split on the issue of equal marriage. The right of the Tory party still see marriage as an exclusively heterosexual union, which is the only sort of relationship they want to be legally recognised. Most importantly for the bigots of the right, it is the only relationship within which they think it is suitable to bring up children. Now they are shocked to find that LGBT people might want to and indeed are able to have children.

The reality is that the Tory right who yearn for a mainly mythical past of the ideal nuclear family are being outflanked by the lived experience of millions of ordinary people. People do not want to go back to the stifling times when "family values" meant an unmarried woman who got pregnant would find herself ostracised and be forced to give up her baby, or when a woman could be raped by her husband but it not be recognised as such by the law.

The families people live in or around are constantly changing. Extended families of second or third marriages with step children and siblings, co-habiting couples who never marry, some who are straight and others who are LGBT—this is what family life is to many people today. Others will simply avoid living in any traditional family unit at all.

The contradictions of the family

The family can be a place where we find unconditional love and support. But it can also be a very dangerous place to be a woman or a child, a site of violence, abuse and neglect. Figures show that nearly 5 million women, 30 percent of the adult female population of Britain, have experienced some form of domestic abuse since the age of 16. On average seven women are killed by their current or former partner every month in England and Wales.[117] As many as one in five children have experienced severe maltreatment; over 90 percent of sexually abused children were abused by someone they know and "children abused by parents or carers are almost three times more likely to also witness family violence" and a third did not tell anyone at the time.[118]

During Britain's biggest public holiday at Christmas, when television programmes, magazines and advertisements are crammed with images of happy families laughing together around a roaring fire, the Samaritans' helpline sees its highest number of calls. If you don't have a family, or you do and it is not a happy one, the holiday only accentuates the pain of crushed expectations. The very time people are meant to be at their happiest can instead be just the opposite. The peak time for married couples to consult lawyers to split up is 8 January, now coined Divorce Day.

Yet even as divorce rates continue to rise, remarriage rates also rise. Marriage is a very big business, with countrywide wedding shows, exhibitions and fairs where companies compete for business on everything from venues to favours—going home presents for guests. *Brides* magazine suggests a breakdown of costs to budget for your wedding that comes to £24,716; the average wedding in Britain costs around £21,000.[119] Stag and hen dos are no longer a night out before the wedding. Instead they can be several days away in a European city costing thousands in themselves. The industry is estimated to be worth up to £500 million a year in the UK.[120]

Weddings are still all about the bride. Dozens of different bridal magazines are devoted entirely to weddings all targeting brides. A long running reality television series, *Don't Tell the Bride*, is based on the idea that every woman has her dream wedding planned since she was a girl. The challenge for the usually hapless groom is whether he can deliver it.

Even for those who do not get married the modern nuclear family is still the model to aspire to. The ideology of the perfect self-sufficient nurturing family is projected onto the working class but is rarely adhered to in the ruling class. Servants take care of the domestic labour while children are looked after by nannies and as quickly as possible shipped off to boarding school.

The central role of the working class family, however, is still the place where the next generation of workers is born, nurtured, fed,

Marxism and Women's Liberation

watered and socialised. But people don't get together or marry in order to "reproduce the next generation of labour power". In the main they create families out of a desire for love, security and a sense of being connected to each other in the face of a sometimes hostile world.

Capitalism treats humans as cogs in a system whose ups and downs we are told we must simply accept. The health of the system dictates whether one family is driven into poverty or another can afford a holiday. Yet politicians' constant references to "hard working families" imply that some people can make their own prosperity, whereas others facing hard times have only themselves to blame. The family is for many the ship they hold onto to ride the storms of a chaotic system that appears to be out of their control. A host of sayings show the enduring importance of family ties—"Blood is thicker than water", "keep it in the family" or the compliment to someone not related that she is "just like family".

Marx wrote about the role of religion as a "haven in a heartless world"—and this is also what the family can represent under capitalism. A Marxist analysis therefore should not lead to placards demanding "Abolish the family!" In fact Alexandra Kollontai, a leading Bolshevik in the Russian Revolution of 1917, wrote that she had to reassure working women that the Bolsheviks were not out to take their children away; they simply wanted to organise society to collectively carry the burden that was at the time the sole responsibility of women in the family.[121]

Of course many people throughout history have attempted to escape the narrow restrictions of family life. But alternative lifestyles have often only been an option for a privileged few. Even if you live outside the family the oppressive structures of the system in which the family is rooted do not disappear.

For some the family can also represent defiance of the system rather than conformity. Michele Barrett, in her introduction to the new edition of her 1980 book *Women's Oppression Today*, points out that black feminists active in the 1960s and 1970s often had a different view of the family to white feminists like herself. They saw the state breaking up black families through immigration controls, for example. She quotes one of her critics, Hazel Carby, who wrote that in contrast to Barrett's analysis the family "for black people of both sexes—it is an island of solidarity in a hostile and racist society".[122]

In the US in the 1960s when debates about the family's role in women's oppression were taking place many black women argued that they saw the right to a family life as something their ancestors had won after generations of black slaves were denied the right or ability to live as families. Slaveholders bought and sold slaves as commodities regardless of any family networks. One judge in the US state of North Carolina in 1853 described the state's view of the legal status of marriage between slaves, writing that the law requires "no solemnity or form in regard to the marriage of slaves, and whether they 'take up' with each other by express permission of their owners, or from a mere impulse of nature, in obedience to the command 'multiply and replenish the earth' cannot, in the contemplation of the law, make any sort of difference..." Though the law recognised slave families to the extent that they served "the slave masters' economic interests. Thus, the legal principle was developed that the status of a slave child followed that of the mother".[123]

Many black women were not about to abandon an institution that had been so hard fought for against the domination of their oppressors.

But the changes that were ignited by the post-war boom and the subsequent expansion of educational and job opportunities for millions of women has had a big impact on the family across society.

What does the family look like in Britain today?

The Office for National Statistics reveals that family life is constantly being transformed. The majority of marriages are civil ceremonies and this has been the case since 1970. In 2012 they accounted for 70 percent of all marriages. The most recent census, in 2011, shows that an increasing proportion of the population are getting married later or not all. In 2011 over 15.7 million adults—35 percent of those aged 16 and over—in England and Wales had never been married, a rise from 12.5 million, 30 percent, in 2001.[124] Although the underlying trend is going down, there was a 5.3 percent increase in marriages in 2012 compared to 2011, 262,240 compared to 249,133.

Marxism and Women's Liberation

Marriage is no longer automatically shunned as a misogynist institution by the new generation of feminists. Numerous articles and websites are devoted to tips on organising a "feminist wedding". A new publication, described as a feminist wedding magazine, was launched in the US in 2015. It caters for those who want to get married but also want to subvert the traditional features of weddings.[125]

But cohabiting is still on the increase, and not just for the younger generation; couples aged 40 and over made up a larger proportion of the cohabiting population in 2011—41 percent—than in 2001 when they made up 31 percent. The majority of marriages are first time for both partners, 67 percent, but they don't all live happily ever after. Statistics show that up to 42 percent of marriages will end in divorce and most divorces, 65 percent, are granted to women.[126] The fact that more women work and have some degree of financial independence means that more are able to see a future outside an unhappy marriage. Now 15 percent of all marriages are remarriages for both parties and 19 percent couples where one partner had been married previously. The largest percentage increase in the number of marriages was for men and women aged 65 to 69.

As part of a long term rise in births outside marriage, almost half of all births, 47.4 percent, now happen outside marriage or civil partnership. People are also having fewer children and later, or not at all. Average completed family size peaked at 2.42 children for women born in 1935, and has been falling since. Today the average completed family size for women reaching age 45 in 2013 is 1.92 children per woman.[127]

The average age of mothers has been increasing since 1975. In 2012 nearly half of babies—49 percent—were born to women over 30, with 20 percent of babies being born to women over 35.[128] Among women born in 1968 the percentage who have remained childless is 18 percent compared to the 11 percent of women bon in 1941 who remained childless. The fall in the fertility rate between 2012 and 2013 was the largest recorded since 1975.[129] One of the major hurdles working parents face is finding affordable childcare. Childcare is expensive—the average British family spends over a quarter of their income on childcare. The only other country worldwide whose childcare is more expensive than Britain's is Switzerland.

Figures show as many as 68 percent of women return to work within 11 months of giving birth and 80 percent within 17 months.[130] Before becoming parents men and women are equally likely to be employed but afterwards 57 percent of mothers of under-fives are in paid work compared with 90 percent of fathers.[131] However, this is not a reflection of women's desire to work. One survey conducted for the National Childbirth Trust showed that women wanted to be able to combine working and being a parent with their partners. It reported that 55 percent of women respondents said their ideal family "had both partners with equal jobs and equal share of house work and childcare". The majority, 61 percent, said they "would work even if they did not need to financially". Only 5 percent said their ideal family was one where the mother did not work.[132]

For single parents life is hardest and under the most scrutiny from the state and popular opinion. Politicians, both Labour and Tory, have scapegoated single parents, who represent just over a quarter of all parents in Britain supporting almost a quarter of all dependent children. Parents end up bringing up children alone for many different reasons—only 6.5 percent of all births are registered alone. But there is still a stigma which politicians use to portray single parents as feckless and undeserving.

One of the first acts of the landslide Labour government of 1997 under Prime Minister Tony Blair was to cut benefits for single parent families, 91 percent of whom are headed up by women. This was the government heralded as including the most women in British history. Over a hundred women Labour MPs were elected in 1997; only eight, none of them new MPs, voted against the bill.[133] Gingerbread, an organisation that supports single parents and dispels myths on the subject reports that the number of single parents, 2 million, has been consistent since the mid-1990s; of those 63.4 percent are in work, up by nearly 20 percent since 1996. In fact, "once their children are 12 or over, single parents' employment rate is similar to, or higher than, the employment rate for mothers in couples—71 per cent of single parents whose child is 11-15 are in work".[134]

Single parents have seen benefit changes since 2008 that have relentlessly shifted the goalposts over when they are eligible for income support. In 2008 if your youngest child was 12 years old you were shifted from income support to jobseeker's allowance. This meant that rather than being supported in bringing up a child or children alone, you had to prove you were actively seeking work. This threshold has been shifted again and again and now once your youngest child is five years old you are no longer entitled to income support. When childcare costs are out of reach of many low paid workers this policy is punishing the poorest single parents.

Yet whether in work or not single parents are more likely to live in poverty than parents living in couples. Department of Work and Pensions figures from 2014 show children in single parent families are nearly twice as likely as children in couple families to live in relative poverty.[135]

Many families are also taking care of a disabled or ill relative. Estimates are that one in eight adults in Britain is a carer, that's 6.5 million people. And 58 percent of them are women. Some 45 percent of carers have given up work to care.[136] The continuing imposition of cuts in the name of austerity will only increase the numbers of informal carers and the pressures working class families face.

We live in a society that purports to revere the family and yet the ruling class constantly pushes it to breaking point in order to increase the burden ordinary people carry. This is a contradiction Marx and Engels exposed in the *Communist Manifesto*: "The bourgeois claptrap about the family and education about the hallowed co-relation of parent and child, becomes all the more disgusting, the more, by the action of modern industry, all family ties among the proletarians are torn asunder".[137]

Whatever the changes both superficial and profound that the family has undergone it still serves the same economic and ideological role of privatised reproduction within the system. Any possibility for women's liberation will depend on the socialisation of the responsibilities that working class women are told to carry inside this "archaic, stuffy and stagnant institution".

5

Gender: boys will be boys and girls will be girls

When I was a little girl I wished I was a boy
I tagged along behind the gang and wore my corduroys.
Everybody said I only did it to annoy
But I was gonna be an engineer

Mamma said, "Why can't you be a lady?
Your duty is to make me the mother of a pearl
Wait until you're older, dear
And maybe you'll be glad that you're a girl."

—Peggy Seeger

A major part of the socialisation of children in the family is learn-ing conformity to strict gender roles. The first question most pregnant women get asked is "Do you know if it's a boy or a girl?" Everything from clothes, toys and books to blankets and cots are gendered, pink for girls and blue for boys. Some have tried to assign evolutionary importance to this. One psychology professor said, "The explanation might date back to humans' hunter-gatherer days, when women were the primary gatherers and would have benefited from the ability to home in on ripe, red fruits".[138] However entrenched these apparently gender specific colours have become they are themselves, like so many of the trappings of gender expectations, socially created.

At the end of the 19th century all babies wore white, and boys and girls both wore long dresses until they were six or seven when boys "had their first haircut". When babies did wear colours the idea of what was gender appropriate was the opposite of today. In June 1918 an article in the trade publication *Earnshaw's Infants' Department* included the advice, "The generally accepted rule is pink for the boys, and blue for the girls. The reason is that pink, being a more decided and stronger color, is more suitable for the boy, while blue, which is more delicate and dainty, is prettier for the girl".[139]

Today's convention only really became established at the time of the Second World War and was driven by companies who wanted to target new parents for a widening consumer market. The period of the late 1960s and 1970s saw a decline in gender specific children's clothes for a time as across society adults adopted more androgynous looks.[140] But by the 1980s they had returned with a vengeance. One author puts some of this down to the rise of prenatal scanning. The industry took advantage of the fact that more prospective parents knew the sex of their baby to market specific clothes, cots and nappies for girls and boys.[141]

Babygrows set the tone—a boy's will have "little rascal" emblazoned across it and a girl's "little princess". The idea that women and men have different roles in society permeates every area of our lives from the moment we are born. It can appear that the way society is structured is because of deep differences between men and women. Instead ideas about women and men are perpetuated because they reflect and act as a buttress for the material inequalities that class society produces.

Nature and nurture

The constant refrain that gender differences are innate can also masquerade as a materialist analysis—based on the genetic make up of humans and periodically backed up by studies that claim to be scientific.

An essentialist view, which assumes that biological differences determine what it means to be a man or a woman in a given society, is still the dominant one. It can be used to justify the status quo and portray the inequalities of society as natural. The logic of this view is, for example, that nature has made women want to concentrate on the home and the responsibility of bringing up children. But essentialism is also to be found in some feminist texts as part of a desire to challenge the status quo. For example, the idea that if there were more women at the top of society there would be fewer wars is one rooted in the belief that aggression and violence are intrinsically linked to masculinity. Such a view sees women as inherently peaceful and egalitarian.

Socialist and neuroscientist Steven Rose has pointed out the weakness in such a view of humans. He argues that all human behaviour has a social context. So for example when it comes to generalising about violence "aggression becomes the term used to describe processes as disparate as a man abusing his lover or child, fights between football fans, strikers resisting police, racist attacks on ethnic minorities, and civil and national wars".[142]

So any propensity for either sex for "violent" behaviour does not make sense in the abstract. Essentialism or biological determinism, whatever its political roots, does not take account of the enormous plasticity of human brains and behaviour and can lead to dangerous conclusions about how society should be organised. At its most crude it reduces the vast complexity of humans to merely a collection of cells. Even those theorists who have avoided such extreme reductionism see human potential as limited by competition for survival.

The ideas of biological determinism in the mid 1970s gained a wide audience in the form of sociobiology. Sociobiologists saw humans as merely products of their genes exhibiting physical, instinctual and behavioural patterns unchanged for thousands of years. Harvard scholar E O Wilson's 1975 book, *Sociobiology*, was hugely influential—it was incorporated into university courses and generated academic conferences—but it was also controversial. It drew widespread criticism for its crude determinism. Wilson regularly used phrases such as "genetic tendencies" or described certain genes as merely "predisposing" someone to particular actions to counter that view. But he was unashamed of where the logic of his views led when it came to gender inequality. In a *New York Times* interview he declared that "In hunter gatherer societies men hunt and women stay at home... Even with identical education and equal access to all professions, men are likely to continue to play a disproportionate role in political life, business and science".[143] As one academic wrote at the time, the ideas of

Marxism and Women's Liberation

sociobiology "end up simply as propaganda, or as mirrors reflecting the society in which they were developed".[144]

But the book that was to bring these ideas into the mainstream of popular culture came the following year in 1976—*The Selfish Gene* by Richard Dawkins.[145] This explained evolution as a process in which human bodies acted as no more than "survival machines" for genes. He understood behaviour as being driven by genes fighting to maximise their chances of replication. When it came to gender women were described as being "coy" because it had an evolutionary advantage.[146] Women must choose sexual partners carefully to maximise the chances of any offspring being from good stock as there is a limit on how many pregnancies they will have.

Men on the other hand would have evolved to be promiscuous so as to maximise the replication of their genes, as they had nothing to lose by having offspring by many different females. Dawkins always said human life was a bit more complicated than this model, but his portrayal had longevity in popular culture that embedded the notion that women and men were prisoners of their biology.

A decade later saw the growth of evolutionary psychology, which posed as being more sophisticated than sociobiology. This absorbed many of the assertions of sociobiology but tried to make itself more palatable and less mechanical. It stressed that humans' brains also enabled them to make certain decisions and choices about their behaviour. The science was effectively challenged but that didn't stop countless references in popular culture to innate gender differences. For example, London's *Evening Standard* ran a story claiming, "Men are genetically programmed to be better shoppers than women... Men's 'hunter-gatherer' inheritance means they are more effective at going in for the 'kill' on the high street—as they did on prehistoric plains millions of years ago. Even men's heart rates increase at the moment of purchase, an echo of the excitement at the climax of a successful Stone Age hunt".[147]

The claim for example that women choose to go for "high status" males is rooted in the desire to be with a good hunter thousands of years ago is deduced from experiments in which, for example, law students are shown different photos of the opposite sex. It concluded that women more often chose a man in a suit wearing a Rolex watch described as a doctor than one in a Burger King uniform described as a trainee, because they needed a man that would provide for them. Men on the other hand were said to be more influenced by attractiveness.[148] Many studies have looked at what males find "attractive", looking for what might be a product of evolutionary adaptation. In common with many such studies, one had 40 men look at digital silhouettes of different shaped women's bodies. It concluded that a "low hip to waist ratio" is most attractive because "a narrow waist is a visual cue of the absence of pregnancy and therefore current fecundity—a feature that ancestral men sought in women".[149]

One book that shot the specific subject of gender differences into the mainstream in a big way was the best seller *Men are from Mars, Women are from Venus*. Published in 1992 it sold 15 million copies worldwide.[150] John Gray, the author of this gender pop psychology, portrayed women and men as different species who have to learn each other's language in order to have meaningful relationships.

Some of the basic science at the root of sociobiology and evolutionary psychology may have lost credibility today but we are still regularly told that men and women have different brains and therefore different attributes.[151] Such crude determinism can't begin to explain the complexity of human behaviour, and some of it would be laughable if it wasn't for the experience of history showing us the terrible consequences of where the logic of such ideas can lead.

Biological determinism was the basis for the ideas of eugenics which grew during the 1930s based on the view of there being inherited characteristics that led to poverty, unemployment and what was seen as immorality. These claimed black people and women were deemed less intelligent, more childlike, more likely to be "feeble minded"—traits that were said to be inborn. This became a mainstream view and led to the forced sterilisation of mainly poor, vulnerable people and sometimes mentally ill people in the US and in other parts of the world in the early part of the 20th century. Black men and women were sterilised without their knowledge. These horrendous actions were a sign of how dominant eugenics became among some sections of the ruling class. However, it was the Nazis in Germany who pushed

Marxism and Women's Liberation

the logic of the ideology to its most horrifying conclusion with the Holocaust, an association that discredited eugenics for some time.

One reason the ideas began to creep back again during the 1960s and 1970s was as an ideological counter to the mass social movements that challenged values about race, gender, sexuality and class and terrified the ruling class. Even superficial and individual expressions of rebellion such as the first "unisex" clothes and men growing long hair, were seen as shocking snubs to the establishment.[152]

Modern determinism still comes dressed in the language of genes. But now technology has enabled scientists to map the human genetic code and much more is known about how genes work with each other. But it is still commonplace to talk of a "gene for" various attributes and behaviours including alcoholism, heart disease and even rioting. Yet the reality is that there is not even a single gene for something as simple as eye colour, let alone anything as sophisticated as nuances of social behaviour.[153] "Our environment, our behaviour, even our thinking, can all change what genes are expressed".[154] Genes interact with each other, and with other chemicals and proteins in the body and importantly with the environment. Women and men share roughly 99.8 percent of their genes.[155]

Yet it doesn't stop assertions such as the female brain has "outstanding verbal agility, the ability to connect deeply in friendship, a nearly psychic capacity to read faces and tone of voice for emotions and states of mind, and the ability to defuse conflict. All of this is hardwired into the brains of women".[156]

But it is difficult to break down the impact of "nature or nurture" even on a simple physical attribute like height. The height you grow to has a genetic element but the environment in which you grow up also has a role. Many immigrants to the US in the early part of the 20th century began to eat a different diet and saw increased height with each generation. But of course this height increase did not go on forever—it levelled off when any one person had reached the full height potential of their particular genetic inheritance. The most recent research shows that the average height of US citizens is now trailing the Netherlands and some other European countries. This has been put down to poor health care and diet—a sign that under capitalism even being the richest and most powerful country in the world does not guarantee its own poorest citizens meeting their full potential on the most basic measures.[157]

If we reject biology as our destiny are we nothing but blank slates? No, men and women are biologically different, we have different hormone levels and some body parts, different patterns of hair growth, there are average weight and height differences. Some of these are just different ends of a continuum—there are tall, strong women and small men just as there are hairy women and smooth skinned men. There are also intersex people, who are born with some genetic, hormonal, or physical attributes associated with both male and female sexes.

But biological differences don't automatically mean girls love pink or boys want to play with guns. All the past history of human societies has shown us that today's gender roles are not the only way women and men can be defined. For example it's estimated that more than 100 different Native American societies "included men who dressed and lived as women. Perhaps a third as many societies are estimated to have had women who dressed and lived as men. In Blackfoot language the word for two spirit men meant simply 'acts like a woman.'"[158] Among other societies there were up to seven kinds of marriage between different couples or multiple partners of both or either sex living as men or women.

But the determinists who argue we are prisoners of our biology are not all simply reactionaries who want to keep women in their place as second class citizens. The increasing activism of transgender people in recent years against the prejudice they face has also led to the reappearance of divisive arguments among some radical feminists about biology, gender and oppression. In her powerful account of transgender oppression and resistance Laura Miles writes of the experience of trans women being excluded from women only events in the 1970s being repeated 40 years later.[159] Trans activists have organised protests at non-inclusive events and women who have taken part have sometimes been boycotted.

This rejection of trans women because they are not "born as women" flows from the weakness of a theory of women's oppression rooted in patriarchy theory. So some radical feminists justify discriminating against trans women because they claim there is something intrinsically oppressive, either biologically or culturally, in maleness. Radical feminist Finn Mackay, who works both in organisations that include and exclude trans women, explicitly poses the issue of gender identification in the context of patriarchy. She writes that trans women were born into the "male sex class... It is the fact of sex class in the first place that is the problem, it is the fact of male supremacy in the first place that is the problem".[160]

Guardian columnist Julie Bindel goes as far as to accuse trans people of conforming to society's gender roles by having surgery that she describes as "mutilation" or wanting to identify as the "opposite" sex.[161] In fact many trans people define themselves as gender non-conforming and want to break from the binary straitjacket and look to more fluid notions of identity than society is willing to recognise.

One aspect of the greater discussion of trans oppression is the increasing use of the term "cisgender" or "cis" to describe non trans people. A cisgender person is one whose gender identity matches the sex they were assigned at birth. But the use of the term is often associated with the politics of privilege—assuming a cis person is privileged because they do not suffer transphobia (for a fuller exploration of privilege theory see Chapter 8). Finn Mackay rightly questions this view, arguing that being cisgendered does not necessarily mean you don't face oppression and bigotry. She describes her own experience as a cis woman whose "gender presentation is more masculine than most women". She writes that she is often read as a man and, because she looks younger than she is, often "read as a young man or teenage boy. In most of my daily interactions, I am not read as a woman".[162] She recounts how she has been questioned in women's toilets or even when accessing health care.

Is masculinity the problem?

Deterministic views of gender lead down various cul de sacs. A number of feminists argued after the financial crash of 2008 that testosterone was at the root of the risky banking behaviour of male bankers. The

Observer's business editor, Ruth Sunderland, referred to "the macho, tooth and claw brand of capitalism that caused the crunch in the first place".[163] In 2010 Christine Lagarde, then French finance minister now head of the International Monetary Fund, said, "If Lehman Brothers had been Lehman Sisters" then "today's economic crisis clearly would look quite different".[164] The implication is that there is an alternative, gentle, feminine capitalism that would bring harmony and wealth all round. After two banks collapsed in Iceland and a new government headed by women was formed it was heralded as "the end of the age of testosterone".[165]

Feminist academic Valentine M Moghadam in a paper on gender and the economic crisis writes of the "hyper-masculinity that lies beneath the capitalist relations of production and the behaviour of the (predominantly male) transnational capitalist class...hyper-masculinity is also a defining feature of the corporate domain—with its risk-takers, rogue traders, reckless speculators, and manipulative financiers".[166] Note that masculinity is assumed to be solely associated with negative attributes— men are reckless, manipulative rogues.

In contrast economist and banking expert Dr Ros Altmann agreed that an "excess of machismo" was a factor in the crisis but went on to say "There was not the cooperative thinking there would be in a female environment...there would have been a natural tendency for a woman to say, 'Let's take the longer-term view'." She asserted that women have a "caring mindset, a nurturing mindset, a mindset that says let's worry about the future".[167]

Of course it is true that the world of banking and the City of London is utterly male dominated. A survey in 2015 by the *Financial Times* shows that "Women occupy only a fifth of positions at the level of managing director in the City".[168] The minority of women who do work there face unequal pay, and a series of high profile sexual harassment complaints show that sexism is a major problem. But it is another thing to say that male hormones caused a global economic crisis and that women in the City would by nature act differently. The few women who do succeed in high powered jobs in the City will, like the men, only get to the top by deploying the methods of cutthroat competition valued in that environment.

Gender: you've got to be carefully taught

Neuroscientist Lise Eliot has written extensively on assertions of biological sex differences. She argues, "Obviously boys and girls come into the world with a smattering of different genes and hormones. But actually growing a boy from those XY cells or a girl from XX cells requires constant interaction with the environment, which begins in the prenatal soup and continues through all the choir recitals, football games, secondary school science classes and playground politics that ceaselessly reinforce our gender-divided society".[169]

Far from coming naturally gender differences are fought for, encouraged and rigorously reinforced from the day we are born. Anthropologist Gayle Rubin writes, "far from being an expression of natural differences, exclusive gender identity is the suppression of natural similarities. It requires repression: in men, of whatever is the local version of 'feminine' traits; in women, of the local definition of 'masculine' traits".[170]

In one experiment to test gender expectations participants were asked to hold a baby, and depending on whether the baby was introduced as a boy or a girl it was offered either a plastic hammer or a doll to play with. But "The participants also touched the baby differently. It was found that baby boys are often bounced, thus stimulating the whole body, whereas girls are touched more gently and less vigorously".[171] In another classic experiment students were shown video clips of a baby reacting to a jack in the box popping up. If they were told they were watching a girl baby they described the reaction as fear, if they understood the baby to be a boy they described the same reaction as surprise.[172]

Children quickly pick up disapproval when they choose some clothes rather than others—for example, how often have you heard the refrain "put on a nice dress, just this once"? Although society is now open to girls dabbling in different less gender specific clothes, boys are more restricted in what is seen as acceptable. The private Haberdashers' Aske's Boys' School includes in its school rules precisely what it deems appropriate for boys: "hair-styles are required to be moderate: hair should be its own natural colour, lie off the collar and be of an even cut; very short or long on top cuts are inappropriate; 'business-like' should be the guiding factor." The final phrase is telling as to the assumed destiny of its pupils.[173]

But it is not just private schools that impose strict gender conformity. A 15 year old boy was threatened with exclusion when he arrived at his Kent school wearing make up. He had been doing his own version of the girls' #nomakeupselfie photos on Facebook. He thought it would be good to do the opposite and raise money for cancer research as his cousin was ill with the disease. His mother pointed out, "Most girls in his class wear more make-up than that on a normal day".[174] In another case a group of school students in Wales collectively protested at their school's gender specific uniform codes that stated, "Trousers are compulsory for boys and optional for girls. These must be full length and plain black." When the head teacher insisted the boys could not wear shorts in the summer they all came in wearing skirts.[175]

The greater public discussion of the imposition of gender norms, particularly on young people, is welcome. It can mean some of those who defy or even just feel uncomfortable with the imposition of society's strict gender norms might be more likely to see examples of others in the same situation to relate to. Nevertheless these are only minor fissures in the hegemony of gender specific practice and ideology.

Conformity from an early age includes how you play and what toys you play with. The popular assumption is that boys are more physical, but research shows that there's a connection between the toys they are playing with and their level of activity: "The amount of physical activity each child engaged in (climbing, running, banging, chasing and so on) was more influenced by the type of toy being played with than by whether it was a boy or girl doing the playing".[176] Gender socialisation is not simply carried out in families, and some parents go out of their way to challenge gender stereotypes and encourage their children to play with all sorts of toys and to dress however they choose. But children don't just learn from what they are actively taught, they also learn from what they see. So your home may be a bastion of equality but there's always school, the high street, films, adverts and television shows.

Research shows that even children as young as three are already responding to pressure to act in gender appropriate ways, and not just

Marxism and Women's Liberation

from adults, but from other children of their age. One study showed that three and four year olds adapted their behaviour and the toys they chose when another same age child of either sex was in the room. This was even true when the other child was sitting at a table colouring in and not interacting with the subject child at all.[177]

That's not to say that it is worthless trying to bring up children outside of gender norms, just that there are limitations to the impact this has when everything else in wider society is stacked up to perpetuate them. Gender conditioning does not stop as children grow older. In some areas social expectations become all the more overt, particularly when it comes to sexual activity.

Dangerous double standards

The double standards that surround sexual activity of girls and boys are not a new phenomenon and will be explored in more detail in Chapter 8. To put it simply, girls are brought up to see themselves as the protectors of their chastity and told that if they wear skimpy clothes or flirt "they are asking for it" while boys are told that real men are having lots of sex and they must be inadequate if they aren't.[178]

Girls are seen as both dangerous and manipulative temptresses and virtuous innocents who need to be protected. The notorious eugenicist and psychologist Cyril Burt used the term, "habitual little courtesans" in the 1930s to refer to very young girls in a paper on "female delinquency".[179] This attitude was starkly shown in a case in early 2015 when a male teacher who was found guilty of having sex with a 16 year old pupil received a non-custodial sentence. The judge, a woman, claimed that the man had been "groomed" by the 16 year old. Her judgement openly expressed the long held belief, too regularly upheld in the legal system, that women are responsible for their "purity" because men are helpless to resist.[180]

Such judgements are common in cases of child sexual exploitation. Young and underage women and girls have been regarded as willingly taking part in prostitution rather than being victims of grooming. After the conviction of nine men in Rochdale in 2012 for child sexual exploitation it was revealed that:

One young woman alerted the police to the abuse she was suffering as far back as 2008... She even gave the police an item of her underwear that had traces of DNA evidence of a 59 year old man who was eventually one of the nine convicted. After almost a year's investigation the Crown Prosecution Service (CPS) did not take the case to court because they decided the young woman would be an "unreliable witness" and would not be believed by a jury. These assumptions about the credibility of the young woman condemned her to yet more abuse until the case was taken up again.[181]

Because the majority of the men in this case were of Pakistani origin the media claimed they were not pursued because of "political correctness". The reality is that the police's and the legal system's attitudes towards young women meant that the abuse was not taken seriously.

How we internalise gender roles

Views about gender differences are not just imposed from the outside, they are also internalised. Researchers gave maths students a test, first telling some of them that it usually showed a gender difference; the women who had been told this performed significantly worse than those who had not. The male students did better when they thought there was a gender difference and those who had been told nothing got virtually the same results.[182] Other studies have shown that "the more men there are taking a maths test in the same room as a solo woman, the lower her performance becomes".[183]

It is no wonder women might believe they should find maths hard. In 1906 the medical advisor to the Board of Education, Dr Janet Campbell, advised teachers not to push girls too hard on "lessons requiring much concentration and therefore using up a great deal of brain energy, mathematics for instance". She went to say that if girls show signs of "fatigue" they could be introduced to "such subjects as cookery, embroidery or the handicrafts...as they cause comparatively little mental strain".[184] When a talking Barbie doll was produced in 1992 among the phrases she was programmed to say were "I love shopping" and "Math class is tough". The manufacturers had to reprogramme the dolls after an outcry at what this was teaching young girls.[185]

When women stray from what is seen as their natural role as a gentle carer focused on family, they receive very different treatment from men. For example if a women carries out a violent crime it is seen as more shocking than if the same crime was carried out by a man. Myra Hindley and Ian Brady murdered four children in the 1960s. Hindley is the one who generated the most headlines of horror. The same happened to serial killer Rosemary West who with her husband Fred was convicted of ten murders. Most serial killers, murderers and violent offenders are men but violence is not treated as such a shocking aberration when the perpetrator is male.

Women who pursue male dominated jobs or activities, especially if they have children, face sometimes virulent criticism for turning their back on the true vocation of family. Mountaineer Alison Hargreaves was lauded as a hero, "Alison of Everest", when she conquered mountains and competed with the world's leading male mountaineers. But when she died in bad weather descending from the summit of K2 in Pakistan in 1995 the media turned on her. Comment pieces berated her for taking such risks when she was a mother; she was denounced as reckless. *Guardian* columnist Polly Toynbee wrote, "What is interesting about Alison Hargreaves is that she behaved like a man".[186] This was in contrast to the coverage of two men: "Paul Nunn and Geoff Tier, both skilled mountaineers and fathers, died on a mountain near K2 a few days before Hargreaves's death. These men, in contrast to Hargreaves, were not criticised in the international press for being selfish and taking risks that put their lives in danger and left their children fatherless".[187]

Men

So if we see the role the institution of the family has on shaping women's oppression what does it mean for the role of men in society? And what impact have the changes in women's roles over the last century had on men's lives?

Some commentators have always bristled at every upset in the "natural order of things". One wrote in 1833 in moral outrage at the sight of women workers going out and getting drunk, "I can see now troops of young women that work in manufactories go to spirit shops, that would have been ashamed of it some years ago".[188] Any apparent encroachment of women onto what is seen as men's territory is a cause for anguish, especially if it means venturing outside the home. It is also assumed that growing opportunities for women necessarily means less for men.

Sociologists in 1957 were already declaring that women were "invading the strongholds of masculinity in work, play, sex and the home. She seems to say...'everything you can do I can do better'."[189] Women were also seen as the cause of a crisis in masculinity in the late 1990s. A number of books asserted that women's increasing dominance, particularly in the workforce, was to blame. One such book, *Why Men Don't Iron*, was written by a husband and wife team and included classic assertions such as women are more suited to cleaning as they have better "peripheral vision" than men.[190]

In 2001 former women's rights activist Warren Farrell wrote *The Myth of Male Power: Why Men are the Disposable Sex*, which became the key text for those calling for "men's rights".[191] His was a more serious attempt to address the contradictions of the models of masculinity to which men were expected to aspire, but it was still based on the idea that there are fundamental differences between how men and women function.

The rise of "lads' mags" during this period was part of the backlash against women's perceived ascendancy. Lads' magazines such as *Loaded* and *Nuts* sold hundreds of thousands per issue at their peak, and they managed to take soft porn off the top shelf and put it in the mainstream. Theirs was a narrow and patronising stereotype of "real men" as only interested in soft porn, beer and consumerism—"here's what to buy after you've spent all the rest on drink". It was a rebellion against the "new man" who was supposedly being forced to change nappies and eat quiche by his high-achieving girlfriend.

More recently the narrative continues as writers claim that women have now achieved so much that it's men who are oppressed. The publicity blurb on the back of *The End of Men* by Hanna Rosin sums up the genre: "Men have been the dominant sex since, well, the dawn of mankind. But this is no longer true. Women are no longer catching up with men. By almost every measure, they are outperforming them." Rosin writes about "the new American matriarchy" that sees men left behind.[192]

In *Manning Up* Kay S Hymowitz from the right wing think tank Manhattan Institute writes of the emergence of "alpha girl" which has led to "child men". There is nothing such authors like more than trying to coin a new descriptor for a phenomenon they claim to have discovered. The "child men" Hymowitz looks at are in their 30s and 40s yet she says they act like they are still in "pre-adulthood" because women no longer need to rely on them for marriage, income or security.

The jobs men might have done 20 years ago are gone, she writes, and "The fact for young people coming of age today and for the foreseeable future is that women are more drawn to, and are often better at, many of the organisational skills prized in the knowledge economy".[193] She equates these skills with those needed in the family: "By all accounts, women are better at remembering those hand written thank you notes after interviews and lunches as well as clients' and contacts' birthdays".[194] The women trying to get a job in the notoriously male-dominated world of Silicon Valley, for example, may be surprised to learn that they are dominant in the knowledge economy. Half of all the publicly traded technology companies in the US, including Twitter, have no women on their boards.[195]

One thing that is often missing from these writers' accounts of gender differences is class. There are references to male manual jobs that are no longer part of "post-industrial" economy, but rarely any acknowledgment that while some women have reached the top in the job market, they are a minority. There is no recognition or understanding that the majority of men have never been in a position of power or wealth.

The reality for the majority of men is that they are also subject to gender expectations within the family in society, which distort their lives and are often impossible to fulfill. Masculinity is both something boys have to have instilled in them and simultaneously something they learn that society is critical of. As the old nursery rhyme went, girls are made of sugar and spice and all things nice but "what are little boys made of? Slugs and snails and puppy dogs' tails."

A major part of boys' socialisation is learning early to suppress their emotions—don't be a sissy/cry baby/mother's boy. Boys in school are more likely to be excluded, more likely to be diagnosed with Attention Deficit Hyperactivity Disorder (ADHD) or other behavioral problems, and leave school with lower educational results than girls. In 2014 65.7 percent of girls achieved five or more GCSEs at grade A* to C or equivalent including English and mathematics compared to 55.6 percent of boys.[196] When it comes to university education women outnumber men. In 2014 the gap was at a record level—"more women than men were recruited into two thirds of subject areas in 2014, with a record 57,800 more women than men accepted overall". This includes more women accepted to study medicine, law and biology degrees.[197]

Young men are portrayed in popular culture as being a problem to be solved. Working class boys are demonised and entrenched racism means that this is even more explicit and virulent when the young men in question are black. Any group of young working class men are to be portrayed as suspicious, the most common piece of clothing after jeans, the hoodie, has now become symbolic of a threat and viewed almost like a dangerous weapon. Young people are no longer people, they are "hoodies".[198]

Yet when it comes to education class is still a far greater predictor of achievement than gender and class differences are more marked in boys' results. One overview of recent research concluded, "Social class remains the strongest predictor of educational achievement in the UK, where the social class gap for educational achievement is one of the most significant in the developed world".[199]

There are still some who call for girls to be educated in single sex schools as a way of ensuring they don't get distracted by boys or pushed away from the sciences and other subjects that in a mixed school might be seen as boys' subjects. Girls' high levels of achievement in single sex schools have been used to support this approach, but the fact that most such schools are private and in some way selective skews this evidence. Research shows that "social backgrounds and ability levels of the intake...are more influential in terms of examination results than whether or not a school is single-sex".[200]

The period of the 1970s and 80s saw many attempts by teachers and local authorities to address the impact of society's sexist ideas in schools. The chairman of one education committee was so scandalised by council proposals to challenge gender stereotypes in primary schools in Devon in the late 1970s that he declared, "If parents wish to bring up boys as boys and girls as girls, this would seem to be highly desirable and fundamental to family life. If boys are to be turned into fairies and girls into butch young maids, it should be for the parents to decide and not the education authority or schools".[201]

Class shapes the ability of both girls and boys to reach their full potential, and working class men are told their main aspiration and role is being the provider and protector of their family. Men are defined by their ability to sell their labour power. Decades of married women and women with children working outside the home in bigger numbers than ever have not changed this dominant ideology about men. If men are unable to work, either because they are denied jobs in times of crisis and high unemployment, or because of illness or age, then they are on the rubbish heap. It is not just that society judges them disposable; men often internalise the sense of worthlessness.

Men are more likely to die of heart attacks or other serious diseases. Doctors report that the pressure not to express anxiety and talk about physical and mental health problems is one of the reasons men present late to doctors and are at a higher risk of suicide than women. Government statistics published in 2015 showed that male suicide rates are three times higher than women's, the highest in over a decade.[202]

One of the most powerful accounts of the impact of job loss and unemployment on working class men in the 1990s was *Stiffed* by feminist writer Susan Faludi.[203] She talked to men whose lives had been shattered by the closure of shipyards on the US west coast. The men talked about their sense of loss, not simply of income but also of selfesteem, of doing something valuable and meaningful in society. Their words echo those of former miners in pit villages in Britain where the smashing up of the coal industry led to the loss of hundreds of thousands of jobs. Without those jobs many such working class men felt they had nothing else to offer—they had been brought up to believe that work gave them a place in society.

But simply being in work is not the answer unless it is matched by the space for gender roles in the family to be transformed. In Britain, which has some of the longest working hours in Europe, men work the longest hours when their partner has just given birth. This not only denies the woman the support she needs but also sets in motion a gender division where the woman becomes comfortable with the newborn and the "expert" at childcare and the man is denied the chance to spend time with the baby.

Today the sight of a man pushing a buggy is not remarkable; many men now relish the opportunity to play a different role in their children's lives than their fathers and grandfathers might have been able to. There is a recognition that men have missed out on a fulfilling and joyful experience when they have remained on the edges of their children's lives, simply seeing their role as breadwinner. In the past such involvement was seen as a sign of weakness, both of the woman whose real role it was, and of the man who demeaned himself by doing what was a woman's job.

A BBC television series and book, *A Man's World* looked at the lives and experiences of men in the first half of the century in their own words. Leonard Small from Bathgate near Edinburgh talked of helping with his children during the 1930s.

> I loved helping with the babies... My wife never objected to me helping at home but she did to anyone seeing me doing anything with the babies. Once we were going up a steep hill and I was pushing the pram. That was fine until some women neighbours started walking towards us. She slapped my hand and said, "Take your hands off you big Jessie".

Men who "began to develop a liking for baby care were ridiculed as effeminate. In Lancashire men who pushed prams were known as Mary-Annes".[204]

When the introduction of family allowances was being discussed after the Second World War some in the ruling class were concerned about such state support undermining the "male breadwinner model".[205]

While views on fatherhood have shifted working class boys still grow up learning that society only values them for their ability to sell their labour power. Or in some cases it also values them for something else. A US army recruitment poster carries the slogan, "Army: be all you can be".[206] This epitomises the ruling class's attitude to young working class men, "all they can be" is killed or a killer in the name of the state. When army adverts on both sides of the Atlantic talk about how you can learn a trade, this isn't aimed at the sons of the wealthy— they don't need to join the army to get an education. It is the most extreme expression of working class lives being disposable.

The myth that men have a natural affinity for war and violence is exposed by what the army has to do to turn young men into soldiers. They brutalise them in boot camp training, teach them to obey orders without question to do the unthinkable—torture and murder and die in the name of their country. The scale of psychiatric problems veterans face shows that all of this is not enough to immunise them from the effects of war. Those who start the wars are politicians whose sons never serve in the front line. And these warmongers include women such as Margaret Thatcher and US secretaries of state Condoleezza Rice and Madeleine Albright—who famously said of the death of half a million Iraqi children from Western sanctions that "we think the price is worth it". Affinity to imperialist war is a class issue, not a gender one.

Changing gender roles

Capitalism consistently proves its capacity to absorb new developments and dilemmas and turn them into commodities. The fact that the majority of adult women work outside the home even when they have children requires different products and different advertising to that aimed at men. The 1955 advert showing a joyful woman in an apron admiring her newly installed washing machine as her children declare, "Hooray! It's mum's dream come true!" probably wouldn't be used today. Instead washing powder companies advertise their plastic sachets as being helpful for men who now have to help out, but who might not know how much detergent to use.

Similarly cleaning products are regularly directed at men, usually in some way branded as manly and "turbocharged" so that the man can do the job while watching the football without raising a sweat. Of course these still fuel the idea that the amount of detergent or ability to degrease an oven comes naturally to women. One advert for an oven cleaner attempting to play with changing gender roles fell flat when it used the catch line, "So simple even a man can do it". It generated hundreds of complaints from viewers who felt that it both demeaned men but also assumed that women are better at cleaning.[207]

New commodities and food products are produced to reflect the fact that women have less time for cooking and housework, yet still want to do the best for their family. Men are increasingly targeted as a growing market for skin care and other cosmetics—Lynx has created its whole brand on the basis of being the solution for men anxious about not being able to get a girlfriend. It plays to men's feelings of inadequacy in a world where they are told men are meant to be studs able to get plenty of sex, when negotiating and sustaining real life relationships is often very different.

Adverts and movies that reflect or try to capitalise on stereotypes new and old are no more than froth, but they reflect a deeper process. Gender roles are both static and unchanging in their ideological presentation but are also in practice becoming more diverse. The day to day lives of millions of ordinary women doing a multitude of different jobs, often working and living with men, do not fit shallow stereotypes. The complex interactions of the many factors involved in gender roles create tensions and contradictions which distort our relationships with each other and with ourselves—but also threaten to expose the damaging nature of gender stereotypes, for women and men.

Everything from people's sexuality and personal relationships to the clothes they wear is much more fluid than we are taught to believe in a society that crushes us into boxes labelled girl and boy.

6

The first wave of the women's movement

Historians have referred to past women's movements as the first and second waves—the first being the suffrage movement fighting for the right to vote, the second the Women's Liberation Movement (WLM) of the 1960s and 70s. This is a useful and important starting point—as the waves represent the high points of struggle from which we have much to learn. But it is an oversimplification if taken too literally. There was political agitation by women before the "first wave" at the start of the 20th century, and far from these movements uniting women from across society in fact the issue of class was present in every struggle.

Early stirrings

The idea that women should be treated as equal citizens was not invented by the suffragettes. Women rebelled against the poll tax during the Peasants' Revolt of 1381, as married women were to be taxed separately whatever their income or none. Court documents describe one rebel, Johanna Ferrour as, "chief perpetrator and leader of rebellious evildoers from Kent".

The poorest women were a part of the political turmoil of the mid-17th century, with the English Revolution at its centre. After the restoration of the monarchy one conservative writer exposed the disdain of his class for those who had been part of the struggle when denouncing the fact that during that time "the young women conversed without any circumspection or modesty".[208] The struggle to end a society based on the privileges of the landed aristocracy was being raised by those who wanted to establish a bourgeois democracy and capitalist relations of production. Yet the opening up of new possibilities could not be contained within the limits those leading the struggle tried to lay down. The talk of the right to freedom and equality meant that the questions of women's position, monogamy and the family all came to the fore.[209]

Gerald Winstanley of radical group the Diggers wrote that, "Every man and woman shall have the free liberty to marry whom they love". The Ranters opposed monogamy and celebrated sexual freedoms for women and men. One shocked Quaker described one female Ranter as "an impudent lass that said she was above the apostles".[210] The landless poor were portrayed as immoral vagabonds at the time and the assumed promiscuity of the Ranters was seen as an affront to those that wanted to impose discipline and respectability on society. Women Ranters came in for particular denunciation. One commentator wrote that they "speak highly in commendation of their husbands that give liberty to their wives, and will freely give consent that she should associate herself with any other of her fellow creatures which she shall make choice of".[211]

The French Revolution of 1789 saw the mobilisation of the masses and women are frequently portrayed in historical accounts. Much attention is given to the bourgeois women who were active in the demands for democracy and equality, such as Olympe de Gouge who wrote the *Declaration of the Rights of Woman and the Female Citizen* in 1791. But women from among the very poorest in society also rose up against the monarchy and took to the streets over a central issue for those at the bottom of society—bread prices. Revolutionary clubs and groups sprung up everywhere and working women led the march on the Palace of Versailles to capture the king and his family, chanting "Let's find the baker, his wife and apprentice."

The French Revolution led to wide political debates way beyond its shores. English writer Mary Wollstonecraft wrote a powerful pamphlet, *A Vindication of the Rights of Men*, defending the revolution. This was a response to an attack on the revolution in 1790 by Edmund Burke, who had become a defender of the establishment. She went on to write *A Vindication of the Rights of Woman* in 1792 and supported the call for women and all working class people to have the right to vote. She railed against the way women were treated in society—"all the power they obtain must be obtained by their charms and weaknesses. What were we created for?"—although her bourgeois class prejudices were revealed when she described the women marching on Versailles as the "lowest refuse of the streets".[212]

Workers and socialists in Britain were inspired by the struggle to defend the Paris Commune, set up in 1871 by workers organised against the government and its army. It opened up voting to all men but not to women, although women were a part of every section of its organisation. Women communards fought hard in the bloody battles, including, Louise Michel, who led a battalion of women to defend the commune. The struggle inspired revolutionaries in Britain and Karl Marx's daughters, Eleanor, Laura and Jenny helped organise solidarity with the commune. It also horrified the ruling classes, women and men alike. Communards were cruelly punished after the commune's defeat—some were executed and others deported to Australia. As prisoners were paraded through the streets, "fashionable women struck at the communards with their parasols, shouting for their execution".[213]

But working women had held up a banner that showed that women could fight alongside men in even the most brutal of class battles and deserved equality. Eleanor Marx went on to become one of the leaders of the workers' struggles of the 1880s and led the formation of the gas workers' union in 1889. It recruited 20,000 workers in three months. The organisation that Karl Marx himself was central to during this period, the International Working Men's Association, known as the First International, brought together socialists and revolutionaries from across the world and despite its name, included women.

Historian August Nimtz writes that "Marx was the most conscious of all the GC [General Council of the International] members in putting the issue of women on the agenda".[214] He reminded Engels, "Ladies are admitted" when suggesting that Irish nationalist Lizzie Burns should join. He was proud that the General Council voted to include its first woman, Harriet Law, against some objections, writing to a friend, "Everyone who knows anything about history knows that great social revolutions are impossible without the feminine ferment".[215]

Eleanor Marx and fellow revolutionary Clara Zetkin were delegates at the International Working Men's Congress in Paris in 1889. Zetkin was part of the mass revolutionary German Social Democratic Party and she spoke out on women's rights and the fight for socialism. She spoke as a delegate from working women of Berlin and argued that the question of women's liberation was not an isolated one but "rather constitutes a part of the great social question... The emancipation of women as well of all humankind will only occur within the framework of the emancipation of labour from capital." Her speech was met with huge applause, which was repeated when Edward Aveling, Eleanor Marx's husband and also a delegate, translated the speech into English and French.[216] Two decades later Zetkin was one of the revolutionary socialist women to propose the celebration of an International Working Women's Day.[217]

Women and the New Unionism

The upsurge in workers' struggles and explosion in trade union membership in the late 1880s saw the struggle of working class women in Britain reach a new level. Some women already had a tradition of union organisation: "By the 1890s women workers in the factory areas of Lancashire had acquired habits of organisation through activity in mixed trade unions".[218]

It was the famous strike of matchwomen in 1888 that both caught the popular imagination and unleashed a new era of workers' organisation known as the New Unionism. The young women, employed by Bryant and May in east London, worked long hours and in appallingly dangerous conditions. As one observer reported at the time, due to their close living conditions they "have always shown a remarkable power of combination...one girl's grievance being adopted as the grievance of every girl".[219]

The strike was provoked by the sacking of one of the workers, but it drew attention to conditions and low pay which shocked fellow workers and wider society. The women worked between ten and 11 and a half hours per day for a weekly wage of four to six shillings. Bosses extracted numerous fines and deductions from these, "if the feet

Marxism and Women's Liberation

are dirty, or the ground under the bench is left untidy a fine of 3d is inflicted". One woman who allowed the web to twist round a machine to stop her fingers from being cut was fined a shilling. She was told, "never mind your fingers". Another woman lost her finger when she followed this instruction and "was left unsupported while she was helpless".[220] Louise Raw sheds new light on the impressive self-organisation of the matchwomen in her recent book *Striking a Light*. This has often been overlooked in popular narratives that see the women as being led and rescued by outsiders, while the strikers themselves are "little more than a shadowy mass".[221]

The strike won huge solidarity from other workers. The strikers held firm in the face of the bosses' threats to move the factory and bring in scabs to break the strike. After three weeks out they won. Management conceded to all the workers' demands—they agreed to abolish the fines, allow workers to eat in a separate room away from where they worked with phosphorous, and all dismissed workers got their jobs back. It was a historic achievement.

Other workers who had previously been thought of as unorganisable were getting organised. Most significantly that same year London dockers, who were treated as casual labour, shut down the Port of London for ten weeks when they walked out in the great London Dock Strike in 1889. They demanded six pence an hour and won. The big strikes inspired many smaller strikes, not all successful, but all helping to build the new unions. For example, a strike by women tailors in Leeds saw 5,000 workers fill the town hall square for a rally called by Leeds trades council. The strike was unsuccessful but the Leeds Society of Workwomen saw its membership grow from "a mere handful to 2,000 members".[222]

By the end of 1889 union membership had doubled to around 2 million and the following year over 250,000 workers took part in the first May Day march to Hyde Park in London. Engels described the scene in a letter to Marx's second daughter Laura Lafargue, writing that the scale of the march was:

> nothing short of overwhelming, and even the entire bourgeoisie had to admit it...it was head upon head, as far as the eye could reach,

250,000 to 300,000 people. I can assure you I looked a couple of inches taller when I got down from that old lumbering wagon that served as a platform—after having heard again, for the first time since 40 years, the unmistakable voice of the English Proletariat.[223]

Between 1886 and 1906 a swathe of up to 90 new working women's societies and organisations were born—"little unions of dressmakers, upholdstresses, bookbinders, purse and pocket makers, artificial flower makers, feather dressers, shawl makers, lace makers, brick makers, paper makers, box makers, glass workers, tobacco workers, jam and pickle workers, munitions workers, shop assistants, typists, domestic servants..."[224]

Such a blossoming of organisations shows women workers' enthusiasm for trade unions; it also shows the huge range of jobs that women did during this period, though it was still the case that the majority of working women had no option but the gruelling drudgery of domestic service. But the birth of these small unions went alongside an even more significant development—the opening up of previously men-only unions to women. In the decade from 1886 the number of women in all trade unions rose from around 37,000 to nearly 118,000, by 1906 this had risen to 167,000, of these only 5,000 were members of women-only societies.[225]

The fight for the vote

Around 125,000 of these union members were cotton workers. These women had industrial experience and were also agitating around political demands. By the opening years of the 20th century reports revealed an extraordinary level of political debate in the cotton towns of Lancashire. Observers said they witnessed hundreds of workers gathering outside during the summer months "more after the fashion of Continental than English towns, and on certain nights of the week anyone going to the market-place can get an audience of interested and intelligent men and women, varying from 600 to 1,000 or even 1,500 who will stand for an hour or two to hear the question discussed."

Marxism and Women's Liberation

The campaign for the vote flowed from this wider labour movement in the north west of England and the Independent Labour Party (ILP) led by Keir Hardie, which had been formed in 1893. Thousands of women formed the working class base for the suffrage campaign. They went from "the mill and factory to the Women's Trade Union League and the cooperative Guild...from the cotton mill or sweatshop to the new Independent Labour Party".[226] Between 1872 and 1879 there were more than 1,400 meetings on the subject and 3 million people signed 9,500 petitions.

The struggles of the working class suffrage campaigners, suffragists, have often been overlooked as the Pankhursts and the Suffragettes became synonymous with the women's suffrage movement in popular memory. The Pankhursts, the mother Emmeline and her daughters Christabel, Sylvia and Adela, were part of the ILP when they set up the Women's Social and Political Union (WSPU) in their Manchester home in 1903. It was at first to be called the Women's Labour Representation Committee, reflecting the organisation's political roots. It was only changed when Christabel pointed out there was already a suffragist organisation with a similar name—the Lancashire and Cheshire Women's Textile and Other Workers' Representation Committee.[227]

Alongside the WSPU and the number of working women's suffrage organisations was also the National Union of Women's Suffrage Societies (NUWSS) formed by Millicent Garrett Fawcett in 1897. It sent petitions throughout the Lancashire cotton industry and called for the vote to be extended to women on the same basis as men—at a time when male suffrage covered only 58 percent of men. For working class women the campaign for the vote for women meant also granting the vote to the working class men denied it.

This argument was to rage through the whole period up to the First World War—whether to fight for women's suffrage on the same basis as men currently had it, or to call for universal adult suffrage for all women and men. Some in the labour movement were worried that to fight for the vote for women would only increase the vote of those with money and property. They feared it would weaken the impact of the working class vote and so adult suffrage was preferable. The

Labour Representation Committee and then the newly established Labour Party held this position until just before the war.

But for some Suffragettes the call for women's suffrage was achievable and the call for adult suffrage, although it sounded more democratic and radical, was beyond reach at that stage. They saw those that insisted on calling for adult suffrage as in reality blocking the chance of at least some extension of the vote to women in the immediate future. Many of the suffragists in their campaigns called and campaigned for the vote for women and at the same time openly declared their aim for full adult suffrage. Unlike the wealthier sections of the Suffragette movement they saw getting the vote for women as part of the wider industrial and social struggles they had been part of for years.

The different strands of the campaign exposed the class differences and priorities over the years of struggle, although there was overlap and collaboration. The Pankhursts moved their base to London in 1906 and this represented a shift in political direction and strategy. When the *Daily Mail* coined the term "Suffragettes" in the same year, the Pankhursts were happy with that as it differentiated them from working class radical suffragists.

Suffrage and the Great Unrest

The new unions were not just the first general unions open to women and unskilled workers, significantly they were also led by socialists such as Tom Mann, Eleanor Marx and John Burns, leader of the dockers. The militant struggles in Ireland were also led by socialists, Jim Larkin and James Connolly.

When a new wave of struggle broke out in 1910, known as the Great Unrest, workers' confidence soared. In 1911 alone there were ten million strike days. This unprecedented level of struggle among workers, the rise of agitation for women's right to vote and the battle in Ireland for independence from British imperialism came together in the years leading up to the First World War and threatened the very stability of the British state.

After a mass rally in Hyde Park in June 1908 the *Times* report of the day noted, "Its organisers counted on an audience of 250,000.

That expectation was certainly fulfilled and probably doubled, and it would be difficult to contradict anyone who asserted it was trebled." Similar monster demonstrations took place in Hyde Park in 1910 and 1911.[228] In the first six years of campaigning at least 100,000 meetings took place.

But the tactics of the Suffragettes became more about spectacle and gaining headlines. They attacked ministers in the Liberal government headed by Asquith, they broke windows, slashed art, set buildings on fire and blew up letter boxes. The logic was to make each action more and more daring and shocking. Many actions took an immense amount of coordination and showed great imagination. One day golfers around the country arrived to play and found the slogan "Votes for women" burned in acid across their greens.[229]

This focus on tactics involving individual acts of vandalism and violence alienated many working class supporters who saw them as elitist and no substitute for building a mass movement from below. They saw the fight for votes as part of a wider struggle in society. Emmeline Pankhurst rejected such a view and declared, "our members are absolutely single minded; they concentrate all their forces on one object, political equality with men. No member of the WSPU divides her attention between suffrage and other social reforms." As Paul Foot pointed out, "the [Chartist] violence of the 1830s represented the fury of the masses... The suffragette violence of 1912 and 1913 by contrast came on orders from above".[230]

In contrast leading suffragist Selina Cooper, who had worked in the cotton mills since the age of ten, said at an open public meeting in 1906 that women:

> do not want their political power to enable them to boast that they are on equal terms with men. They want to use it for the same purposes as men—to get better conditions... Every woman in England is longing for her political freedom in order to make the lot of the worker pleasanter and to bring about reforms. We do not want it as a mere plaything.[231]

Sylvia Pankhurst was part of a section of suffrage campaigners who had become politicised by issues beyond the right to vote. She was inspired by workers' struggles and the Irish fight against imperialism.

In 1912 she set up the East London Federation of Suffragettes (ELFS) as a branch of the national organisation. While still under the national umbrella its priorities became very different. The East London group targeted its work among the working class and poor and campaigned over pay, poverty and childcare. The group ran a maternity clinic, day nursery, school, two low cost restaurants for working women as well as a toy factory.

As the struggle intensified many suffragettes were imprisoned for their actions. They defied the prison authorities and organised hunger strikes to protest at their imprisonment. They faced force feeding, which amounted to torture. One Suffragette wrote an account of her own experience:

> In his right hand the man holds an instrument they call a gag, partly covered with India rubber, which part the prisoner never feels and the moment of battle has come. The prisoner refuses to unclose her teeth—the last defence against the food she out of principle refuses to take—the doctor has his "duty" to perform...he sets about his job in a butcherly fashion—there is no skill required for this job—only brutality.
>
> He puts his great fingers along her teeth—feels a gap at the back, rams the tool blindly and with evident intention to hurt her...he has to still hold it for 20 minutes or so while the food is being poured or pushed or choked down her throat...her feet are in a vice, her head is held...her jaw is forced to its widest. They pour the food down—it is a mince of meat and brown bread and milk—too dry, too stiff, they hold her nose so she cannot breathe...scraping their fingers clean on her teeth.[232]

The government was worried about the hunger strikes and eventually passed new legislation in 1913, which became known as the cat and mouse law. This meant hunger striking women would be released if they became so weak they might die, but then re-arrested as soon as they regained strength. The brutality the Suffragettes faced was not just in prison. In George Dangerfield's classic account of the period, *The Strange Death of Liberal England*, he gives an account of a demonstration in Parliament Square on what became known as

Marxism and Women's Liberation

"Black Friday", 18 November 1910. The then home secretary Winston Churchill had told the police that the women had to be kept away from the Houses of Parliament. After an initial gentle push to get the marchers out of the square the police found,

> the skirted warriors were not so easily repulsed; their method was simply to push, with gloved hands, against the constabulary chest; and push they did, returning to the fray over and over again...the police grew flushed and angry... Bannerettes were torn and trampled; women struck with fists and knees, knocked down, dragged up, hurled from hand to hand, and sent reeling back, bruised and bleeding into the arms of the crowd...they were pummeled and they were pinched, their thumbs forced back, their arms twisted, their breast gripped, their faces rubbed against the palings: and this went on for nearly six hours.[233]

The bringing together of the three issues threatening the ruling class—women's suffrage, Irish independence and mass workers' struggles—was symbolised in a rally at the Albert Hall in 1913. Sylvia spoke there in support of the striking workers of the Dublin Lockout and to call for the release of their leader Jim Larkin, imprisoned for his union activity. She spoke alongside socialist leader James Connolly, who would later be executed by the British state for his role in the Easter Rising of 1916. Sylvia's involvement in this radical political rally was too much for her mother and her sister. Christabel had by now escaped to the palace of the bohemian Princesse de Polignac in Paris to avoid arrest in Britain. She summoned Sylvia early in 1914 to reprimand her for associating with Connolly and Larkin.[234]

Sylvia travelled to Paris undercover to avoid rearrest as she was at the time a released "mouse". She was weak and in a state of exhaustion. In prison she had been on hunger and thirst strike and prison wardens had force fed her. When she arrived at the palace where Christabel had been running the campaign at a safe distance she found her "nursing a tiny Pomeranian dog". Without asking after Sylvia's health or any other preliminaries Christabel announced that the East London group was to be expelled from the national organisation and must take another name. Christabel said she was unhappy about the democratic nature of the East London group saying, "We want all women to take their instructions and walk in step like an army".

Most of all Sylvia's mother Emmeline and sister Christabel did not want to be associated with strikers and working class women. Christabel told Sylvia that a working women's movement was of no value, "working women were the weakest portion of the sex: how could it otherwise? Their lives were too hard, their education too meagre to equip them for contest. Surely it is a mistake to use the weakest in the struggle. We want picked women, the very strongest and most intelligent".[235] Dangerfield recognised the significance of this split in class terms, writing that it meant one portion of the suffrage movement was "tossing like a highly coloured cork, among the dark waves of proletarian anger".[236]

The expelled ELFS added red to its banner colours and continued to grow. In 1916 it changed its name to the Workers' Suffrage Federation. It had branches across east London and its paper, the *Women's Dreadnought*, had more than 10,000 readers. In 1917, inspired by the Russian Revolution, it became the Workers' Socialist Federation and changed the paper's name to *Workers' Dreadnought*. Sylvia was won to the cause of socialist revolution.

The split inside the Suffragettes was the logical conclusion of the Pankhurst leadership's long journey away from its labour movement roots. This included increasingly making their campaign about the evil of men. Christabel published a book in which she asserted that 85 percent of all men had venereal disease. Their slogan became "Votes for women and chastity for men". As soon as Britain went to war they dropped the suffrage campaign, renamed their paper *Britannia*, and collapsed completely into imperialist jingoism. They travelled round the country giving white feathers to young men they thought should be fighting at the front and called for foreigners to be locked up. In contrast many working class suffragists campaigned against the war. Socialist Hannah Mitchell argued, "War in the main is a struggle for power, territory, or trade, to be fought by the workers, who are always the losers".[237]

The war had seen tyrannies toppled by revolutions alongside soldiers' and sailors' mutinies. As soon as the war was over the

Marxism and Women's Liberation

government made accommodations to the movement for women's suffrage and granted the vote to women over 30. This affected 8.5 million women—householders, or wives of householders, occupiers of land and university graduates—but it still meant that 40 percent of adult women were excluded. The vote was also extended to all men over 21, and from 19 if they were serving in the armed forces. The number of eligible voters rose from 8 to 21 million. Finally in 1928 all women won equal voting rights to men.[238]

Going beyond equality

The struggles for the vote brought out in stark relief debates about how to fight for women's rights. There was no all-encompassing "women's perspective" that held a movement together. When it came to the big political questions of the period—workers' strikes, suffrage or the war—women and men split along class lines. Marxists challenged the bourgeois feminists who saw their goal as women's "equality" because this view overlooked the fact that the deepest inequality of class could remain intact. This did not mean that women should not fight for equality, but that working class and poor women could not be satisfied with that as their only aim.

Clara Zetkin led some of the sharpest debates with bourgeois feminists through the years before the war and revolutions. Her commitment to the struggle of women was unfaltering, and this has led some academics to describe her and other leading revolutionary socialist women as feminists, "because of the priority they gave to women's liberation".[239] But this is to negate Zetkin's and others' struggle to see the fight for rights for the mass of ordinary women as also representing a challenge to bourgeois feminists who professed to fight for all women. Zetkin saw that such women were repeatedly shown to be opposed to the expansion of workers' rights. In contrast Zetkin and other revolutionary women such as Alexandra Kollontai saw the fight for women's rights as being inseparable from wider social struggles against the system of capitalism.

As Russian revolutionary Nadezhda Krupskaya wrote in 1914 in the first issue of *Rabotnitsa* (Woman Worker):

Bourgeois women advocate their special "women's rights", they always oppose themselves to men and demand their rights from men. For them contemporary society is divided into two main categories, men and women. Men possess everything, hold all rights. The question is one of achieving equal rights.

For the working woman the woman question becomes quite different. The politically conscious women see that contemporary society is divided into classes. Each class has its special interests. The bourgeoisie is one, the working class the other. Their interests are counterposed.[240]

The revolutionary struggles at the end of the First World War in Russia and Germany had offered a glimpse of the greatest challenge to oppression and exploitation and made the debate about how to win liberation concrete (see Chapter 12). They would have a profound effect on the fight for women's rights and would transform the whole political landscape of the 20th century.

7

The second wave

After the Second World War capitalism experienced massive and rapid expansion and the US was confirmed as the dominant global power. The post-war boom created high levels of employment, rising income, the creation of welfare states and the expansion of further and higher education. This was the period during which British prime minister Harold Macmillan told people, "You've never had it so good".

The impact on women was immense. Greater and greater numbers of women were sucked into higher education and the growing job market. The government had lifted the ban on married women working in teaching in 1944 and then did the same in the civil service in 1947. In 1950 the law was changed to allow women to do evening work.[241]

In the home housework was changing as new labour saving commodities such as fridges, washing machines and vacuum cleaners were available to wider numbers of people. This would help free more women to work outside the home. At the start of the 1950s the ideal for middle class family life decreed that women would leave the family home only to marry and then very quickly have a family of their own. The dominant image was of the woman at home polishing the furniture and getting spruced up to serve her husband a meal on his return from work. Popular culture was full of "expert" advice for mothers and parents; Benjamin Spock's *Baby and Child Manual*, published in 1949 became a best seller.[242]

Moral panics were rife about "latch key" children—whose parents both worked—becoming juvenile delinquents. Psychologist John Bowlby was commissioned to write a paper for the World Health Association on the mental health of war orphans. The paper, *Maternal Care and Mental Health*, based on the limited and extreme examples of general deprivation that war babies and refugees experienced, concluded that a baby needed "a warm, intimate, and continuous relationship with his mother (or permanent mother substitute)".[243]

When he wrote "continuous" he meant it: "The provision of constant attention night and day, seven days a week and 365 days in the year". He also said the women must enjoy and take "profound satisfaction" from the care otherwise the child would sense it and turn out badly. As for the father, "little will be said of the father-child relation; his value as the economic and emotional support of the mother will be assumed."

Bowlby's argument was that without this attention the child would suffer from "maternal deprivation". This study became the scientific justification for a major ideological drive focused on women's role in society and the damage that could be caused if the mother worked outside the home. Bowlby's work went on to have an enormous impact on public policy and of course the anxiety of millions of mothers who worked.[244] At the same time as new myths were being generated some old ones were being undermined. Claims that the high infant mortality rates of the first part of the 20th century had been due to the numbers of married women in work were exposed as flawed when after the Second World War more married women worked and infant mortality went down.[245]

A number of reports published during this period reveal some of the tensions over women's role in society. John Newsom, the County Education Officer for Hertfordshire, was explicit about the need for the education system to help girls accept life as a housewife. He published *The Education of Girls* in 1948 and *Half our Future* about the education of "average and less than average ability" children, in 1963. He argued that those girls who didn't want to do domestic science because they already did enough housework needed "even more domestic training so they could learn just how fulfilling homemaking could be".[246]

Society's expectation that women would marry and then be dependent in every way on their husbands was backed up by severe legal and administrative constraints on women. A woman could not buy something on hire purchase (an early form of credit) without her husband's (or if unmarried her father's) signature. Hospitals would demand evidence of the husband's permission to carry out an operation on a woman; women couldn't take out a mortgage or sometimes even have their own bank account, and many jobs remained closed to married women.

But the seeds of change that would explode in the 1960s were already being sowed in the 1950s. The scale of female employment was higher than ever before—"In 1951 over 20 percent of all Britain's married women were employed as compared to some 10 percent in 1931".[247] In the US in 1956, 70 percent of families with a household income of between $7,000 and $15,000 had at least two workers in the family. In 1956 *Life* magazine ran a "typical" housewife photo feature with a headline that declared, "Women hold ⅓ of all US jobs".[248]

Birth control

One of the ingredients that helped accelerate the changing place of women in society was the transformation in women's ability to control their fertility. This included the development of the contraceptive pill and later the legalisation of abortion. The advent of the pill, which became publicly available on the NHS in 1961, revolutionised the ability of women to safely control when and if they became pregnant. The first pills, called Enovoid, were released in the US in 1957 for women with irregular periods. Their real purpose, to prevent ovulation, was already well known and written on packets as a side effect. They first went on sale in the US as contraceptive pills in 1960 and by 1962 around 1.2 million women were on the pill. By 1963 the figure was 6.5 million.[249]

It is difficult to overstate the impact of these changes on the lives of millions of women in Britain and the US. Up until then contraceptives, advertised in local papers as "Malthusian appliances", included the condom or cap and were often too expensive for most working class pockets. The alternatives were early withdrawal or sponges soaked in brandy or vinegar.[250]

The legalisation of abortion in Britain in 1967, and in the US after the Roe versus Wade court case in 1973, opened the possibility for the first time for women to terminate an unwanted pregnancy legally and safely.

Women risked their lives in back street abortions. One London pathologist reported that he saw a woman die post-abortion once every ten days.[251] Women who had the money would answer adverts that described, "Miraculous Female Tabules, positively unequalled for all female ailments. The most obstinate obstructions, Irregularities, etc of the female system are removed in a few doses.[252] Abortificants, including rat poison, lead plaster and gunpowder, were being used through to the early 20th century. One woman expressed the desperation that drove women to these lengths: "I'd rather swallow the druggist's shop and the man in't than have another kid".[253] Films from the 1950s and 1960s such as *Alfie* and *Up the Junction* are haunted by the chilling reality of a world where abortion was illegal.

Sometimes if abortificants didn't work midwives would say they could ensure a stillbirth, "a quiet 'un". Failing that some women even resorted to infanticide.[254] Women would beg doctors to sterilise them after they had given birth to ensure they would not have any future pregnancies. In 1948 there were 65 clinics offering birth control advice "with some 30,000 new users every year...by 1963 there were 400". Even so, around one in three working class married couples didn't practise formal birth control.[255]

The Home Office stated that in 1966 around 100,000 abortions were being carried out. By then a minority of well-off women might have been able to find a doctor willing to carry out an abortion under the Bourne judgment of 1938, which allowed an abortion if the woman would be made a "physical or mental wreck" by the pregnancy. Figures for deaths from back street abortions are difficult to estimate as women who attended a doctor would have had to lie about causes of haemorrhaging for fear of prosecution. But figures show that at least 40 women a year died as a result of illegal back street abortion until the law changed. A parliamentary committee calculated that in 1959 as many as 20 percent of all gynaecological admissions were due to attempted abortions.

The change in abortion law and access to contraception in the 1960s marked the beginning of a new era where for the first time women could effectively and safely separate an active sex life from procreation. The important issue was women themselves having control and choice—whether they wanted to prevent pregnancy or actively pursue it.

Many black women pointed to the racism in society and among some doctors which meant they were encouraged not to have children—for example black women were often advised to use the long term hormonal contraceptive Depo Provera. In the US many black women were subjected to enforced sterilisation. Leading civil rights figure Fannie Lou Hamer told of her own experience when doctors carried out a hysterectomy without her consent or knowledge when she was admitted for the removal of a uterine tumour in 1961. She only found out some time later. She reported that "60 percent of the black women who passed through the Sunflower City hospital in her hometown were sterilised, many of them without their knowledge".[256] The Student Nonviolent Coordinating Committee (SNCC), which worked with the civil rights movement, published a pamphlet exposing what they called *Genocide in Mississippi* in 1964.

But some feminists argued that sex without fear of an unwanted pregnancy acted only in men's interests, because they could have sex without responsibilities. This view, when it came from the right, was based on the assumption that women did not have sexual desires of their own (see Chapter 9). When it came from radical feminists it flowed from the idea women could not enjoy heterosexual sex as sexual intercourse with a man was inherently oppressive. US radical feminist Robin Morgan wrote, "The so called sexual revolution... has functioned toward women's freedom as did the Reconstruction toward former slaves—reinstituted oppression by another name".[257]

Independence

Between 1960 and 1965 there was a 57 percent increase in women gaining degrees in the US—the equivalent rise for men was 25 percent. The proportion of women living alone rose by 50 percent during the 1960s; for those between 20 and 34 years old the increase was 109 percent. These material changes transformed women's aspirations, which in turn shaped the struggles and demands they made. Each achievement of material improvements for women only served to open up even greater demands and expectations.

Waged work was seen as a way to find financial independence and some personal freedom: "For some women, working outside the home was now seen as an aspect of emancipation; whereas for earlier generations of women who had worked in the cotton mills, emancipation was seen to be an escape back into the home away from an insupportable double burden of hard physical work".[258]

Of course many women had always worked and continued to work throughout this period, out of necessity. This included many black women in the US who had had to work to support households for generations. Figures from 1900 show that 22.7 percent of black married women worked outside the home, compared to 3.2 percent of white married women.[259] These different experiences shaped the politics of feminist movements: "White feminists tended to see paid employment as a route to independence and self realisation; most black women regarded jobs as an unpleasant part of life, just something one had to do if one wanted to eat".[260]

The US: from civil rights to the new left

The Women's Liberation Movement grew out of the movements of the 1960s that saw a generation politicised by momentous anti-imperialist and national liberation struggles across the globe.

In the US the mass movement for black civil rights shook society to its core. Women were a part of every struggle. Movement leaders included Fannie Lou Hammer, who grew up on a cotton plantation, and activist Rosa Parks who led the year-long Montgomery bus boycott that began with her refusal to give up her seat at the front of a bus in 1955. The first "integrated sit-ins" were in 1960, when young women and men faced violence from the police and white racists when they broke the colour bar in shops and cafes. Leading activist Diane Nash defied racist violence by leading the Freedom Riders after brutal attacks nearly stopped them in Birmingham, Alabama in 1961. She said, "If we allowed the Freedom Ride to stop at that point, just after so much violence had been inflicted, the message would have been sent that all you have to do to stop a nonviolent campaign is inflict massive violence."

These courageous pioneer protests involving groups such as Students for a Democratic Society (SDS) and SNCC were just the start.

In the early 1960s thousands of mainly young people poured into the American South to get involved in the growing black civil rights movement. SNCC's activists in the South, women and men, travelled around the rural areas doing voter registration. They became recognisable by their denim clothes, including the bib and braces/dungarees usually worn by sharecroppers. (After the abolition of slavery landless freed slaves worked "shares" of land owned by others and had to hand over portions of their crop, usually cotton, in payment.)

The protesters' clothing was about both politics and practicality. From 1961 onwards, going into rural communities, being attacked by police and local racists, young black activists began to care less about the "respectability" their parents believed would bring them equality and more about identifying with the rural poor. Black women activists were encouraged by SNCC organisers to stop "frying" their hair and let it go natural. Some denounced all this as romanticising poverty and a uniform that the most oppressed blacks had been forced to wear. But for many young activists it became associated with rebellion.[261]

Taking on the racists and the state in the South took commitment and organisation. "In the summer of 1961 the Freedom Rides kept the prison cells filled...from those experiences there emerged a group of leaders bound by imprisonment, violence, and brutality endured, victories won".[262] In the spring of 1963 the police used dogs and high pressure water hoses on school children in Birmingham, Alabama; in August 200,000 protesters descended on Washington DC for a mass civil rights march for "Jobs and Freedom" where Martin Luther King made his "I have a dream" speech. This was followed only 18 days later by the bombing of a black church in Birmingham that killed four young girls attending Sunday school. The following year Freedom Summer saw the biggest numbers ever go from the north to register black voters in the South.

A generation of black and white northern activists who joined the Freedom Rides and Freedom Summer were deeply politicised by their time in the South. Sara Evans writes in her personal account of the period and the roots of the women's movement that:

> [activists'] experiences had an impact far beyond the borders of the South, moreover, for the white youth who joined the civil rights movement were crucial to the mobilisation of the "new left"… Students who had been to the South provided the leadership, tactics, and ideology for the developing movements against the Vietnam War, for "student power" and for women's liberation.[263]

By 1965 the ideas of Black Power were becoming popular in the civil rights movement. Black activists politicised by the open and violent racism in the South were becoming disillusioned with integration as their aim. Some became frustrated at the slow pace of the leadership and moved to organise separately from whites.

In 1966 after a close vote SNCC excluded white members in favour of black self-organisation. New social questions were raised as the focus for struggle moved from the South to the cities of the north. The rise of the Black Panther Party, which openly identified with Marxism and was influenced by Maoism, attracted a large female membership including prominent women activists in the leadership such as Elaine Brown and Kathleen Cleaver. Supporters included Angela Davis. The Black Power movement also had enormous cultural ramifications that still have influence today. The idea of black pride and "black is beautiful" had a particular impact on how black women saw themselves. Singer Aretha Franklin has talked about how this affected her: "I stopped shaving my eyebrows and using pencils and went back to a natural look…and wore my hair in an Afro. I began to appreciate myself as a beautiful black woman".[264] Such changes were profound in a deeply racist society that denigrated black people in every way.

The SDS became the main vehicle for many white activists who turned their attention to building the anti Vietnam War movement on student campuses across the US. Anti-war teach-ins turned into mass protests and at the height of the movement hundreds of thousands marched in Washington DC. Women were active in the anti-war campaign from the start. But only men were being drafted, and only they could burn their draft cards; women's role was sometimes seen as less critical. One sign of the belittling of women's role in the movement was the slogan of the time, "Girls say yes to boys who say no!" The "new left" which produced the Women's Liberation Movement (WLM), grew out of these struggles, rooted among students and graduates. At that time this meant its members were a predominantly white and relatively privileged section of US society. It had no organisational or political roots in the old Communist left in the US, as the name purposely signalled.[265]

The US Communist Party, which had built a mass base in the 1930s and 1940s, was a contradictory organisation. It had won some of the best class fighters to its membership, including black workers and women militants such as Elizabeth Gurley Flynn. But it had become distorted and discredited by bowing to the demands of the Stalinist regime in the Soviet Union. The new generation of activists looked at the Soviet Union and saw that oppression and inequality clearly still existed—leading to sharp debates about the possibility of winning liberation through socialist revolution.[266] The shadow cast by Stalinism in Russia shaped the political response of many new activists and led some to believe that socialism would not bring women's liberation.[267]

Radical feminist Anne Koedt summed up the anti-left view when she declared in a speech in 1968 in New York that the experience of a revolution from capitalism to socialism could be viewed "in terms of male interests". She rightly pointed out that despite gains women were still oppressed in the Soviet Union. She pointed to Soviet women who can be "teachers, doctors, assistants and food handlers" but "when they come home they are expected to continue in their submissive role to men and do the housework, cooking and take primary responsibility for child rearing".[268]

Anti-Stalinist revolutionary socialists were too few in number to have an impact and offer an alternative analysis—that the Soviet Union was not, whatever it claimed, a socialist society. Communist Party activists and supporters themselves had been driven underground by the vicious witch hunts of Senator McCarthy and the

House Un-American Activities Committee. The prospects of being blacklisted, demonised and losing your job and even home were very real. The fear of being found to have associated with Communist activity was so great that even as late as 1971, when Sara Evans was interviewing former Communist supporters, some refused to be named. "Many...are still terrified of being identified with the left, though their activism may have taken place 40 years ago".[269]

It was significant that many of the women who helped found the WLM in the US had grown up in old left families, with socialist, trade union organiser and Communist parents. Children of Communists were known as "red diaper babies". Evans found that many of the key instigators of the WLM were "red diaper" women: "They had a tradition out of which they could name oppression...daughters of the old left tended to grow up knowing, on some level, that women were oppressed." She wrote as a footnote, "It is important to note that in my research I did not seek out 'red diaper babies'. Rather, I pursued women and men who had participated in specific new left activities and in particular the women who provided the links between the new left and the early leadership of the women's liberation movement. Again and again I was surprised to discover a radical family background".[270]

Since Evans's book was published some of those former Communist Party members or supporters have become more open and spoken out about their political pasts. They have explained how the language of the WLM took on the terms the old left had used to describe women's situation—for example, oppression and male chauvinism. In the 1980s conferences were held for red diaper children to share their experiences.[271]

But such was the stigma at the time that these links were not acknowledged. For example Betty Friedan, seen as the first to express the sentiments of the alienation and oppression of the American woman, portrayed herself as an ordinary middle class housewife writing about her personal experience.[272] She made a great deal of effort to hide the fact that she had been a labour journalist for years, writing for trade union publications on class, racism and women workers.[273]

This meant that when the civil rights and anti Vietnam War struggles broke out in the US in the 1960s the traditions of the left that had existed, alongside an understanding of women's oppression as an issue to be addressed, had largely been buried. As one feminist historian noted, "the new left initially lacked critical consciousness of gender relations. Indeed this was one of the more unfortunate consequences of the yawning gap between old and new leftists." Activist Barbara Epstein, who had been involved in both the Communist Party and then inside the new left, said that within the SDS "'Male chauvinism' was a phrase that one did not utter unless one was ready to be laughed at".[274]

The record of the old left or Communist Party on the issue of women's oppression was far from flawless. Those that still looked to the Soviet Union as a model saw the family as central and regarded gender roles in a traditional way. "American Communists glorified women's maternal roles and prevented them from supporting birth control and abortion".[275] But the origin of the WLM shows that the work and struggles of previous generations of socialists, although often not openly acknowledged, played some role. The thread to early socialist ideas was not completely severed.

Many courageous women activists were involved in the struggles of the early 1960s. They broke from family backgrounds, travelled around the country, took part in protests and grassroots campaigning, sometimes in situations where their lives might be on the line. The scale of social resistance gave many a sense they could change the world. But the unity of the movement was short-lived, and its divisions were only just below the surface.

The dominant politics of the new left were shaped by an ideology that declared, "Let the people decide"—reflecting the influence of Maoist ideas. Activists focused on organising among the poorest sections of society and sometimes idealised even the most backward ideas and behaviour as "authentic".

This account of a large meeting at the University of Washington in Seattle tells how one SDS organiser recommended students could establish a rapport with the poor whites they were working with:

> Sometimes after analysing societal ills, the men shared leisure time by "balling a chick together". He pointed out that such activities did much to enhance the political consciousness of poor white youth. A

woman in the audience asked, "And what did it do for the consciousness of the chick?"

After the meeting, women formed Seattle's first WLM group.[276]

Some women began to feel that the mainly male leadership of the new left saw women not as equals in the struggle but as support staff. Two women, Casey Hayden and Mary King, wrote a paper to raise this issue at a staff retreat for SNCC workers in Mississippi in 1964. It came among 37 different papers on "goals and strategy" and was titled, "SNCC position paper (Women in the Movement), authors' names withheld on request". Their decision not to be named was a sign of their fear of the reaction.

Many activists later mistakenly recalled that a leading black activist, Ruby Doris Smith Robinson, presented this paper—she was outspoken and playing a leading role in the struggle. Evans argues this reflected the fact that in many cases "black women occupied positions of growing strength and power which challenged sexual discrimination".[277]

Hayden and King spelt out examples of women being relegated to clerical work or excluded from leadership positions and likened the position of women to black oppression. But afterwards women activists faced comments that would only confirm their need to stand up for themselves. Stokely Carmichael, one of the leading members of the Black Power movement, was chatting among a group of activists including one of the authors when the session finished and asked a rhetorical question, "What is the position of women in SNCC?" He answered his own question with the infamous statement, and to much laughter, "The only position of women in the SNCC is prone".[278]

This was not an isolated incident. Delegates at an SDS convention in 1965 laughed women speakers off the floor. One speaker was told she "just needs a good screw" and at the following year's meeting women had tomatoes thrown at them.[279] One early movement pamphlet described women's skills in the movement as "workers and wives"—they serviced organisers with both typing and clerical skills and with their homemaking and sexual skills. Even as late as 1969 one SDS chapter published a pamphlet for activists that included the advice, "the system is like a woman, you've got to fuck it to make it change".[280]

The US Women's Liberation Movement is born

Many women politicised by the struggle began to see their own situation in light of debates about oppression and inequality. They came to feel both dismayed and angry to find their experience of being discriminated against and trivialised in wider society mirrored in the movement. It came to a head when a motion from a caucus of SDS women at the new left's National Conference of New Politics in 1967 was brushed aside.

This growing disaffection then crystallised among some women activists in Chicago. They decided to get organised. It wasn't long before other women in other groups followed suit. At first this simply meant a few informal meetings to discuss the problem. Chicago activist Jo Freeman, who first coined the name Women's Liberation Movement for a national newsletter, explained, "Thanks to various national liberation movements, the phrase was in the air".[281]

The women who kicked off the WLM did not reflect broader American society. Alice Echols in her excellent history of the period writes that "most early women's liberationists were college educated women in their mid to late 20s who grew up in middle class families".[282] At the start the moves to highlight the position of women in society and in the movement were dominated by women who saw themselves as part of the left—they were often referred to as "politicos". By 1969 women were differentiating themselves as "politicos", defining as socialists and Marxists, or "feminists".[283]

Echols writes that one of the reasons the WLM was able to grow so fast was because the bulk of the early pioneers and leadership were of the left.[284] One early WLM activist said that the Chicago group "more than any other women's liberation group was responsible for the growth of the early women's liberation movement precisely because the women who were in it were so well versed in left-wing networks".[285]

From this handful of women grew a movement that reached across the US and inspired similar movements in Europe. There were WLM "consciousness raising" groups, protests and an explosion of books, pamphlets and discussion papers debating the nature of women's oppression and what sort of political ideas and action were needed to challenge it. Some tried to reach back to women from the "first wave", though one incident shows just how different the experiences of the first and second wave women were. One women's liberation group asked famous suffragist Alice Paul of the National Women's Party to join their rally at the new left's "Counter Inaugural" demo in 1969. There they declared they wanted to "give back the vote". For this new generation voting was a mockery of democracy and "a sop for women". Alice Paul, who had been imprisoned during the fight for women's right to vote, when asked to join them in publicly burning their voter registration cards, "hit the ceiling".[286]

One of the first major actions that drew public attention was the protest outside the Miss America pageant in Atlantic City in 1968. Women picketed and as part of hours of guerrilla theatre they crowned a live sheep. Contrary to popular myths the protesters did not burn their bras; instead they threw "girdles, bras, curlers, issues of *Ladies Home Journal*" and other items they saw as constrictive into a "Freedom Trash Can".[287] Some protesters had indeed planned to burn the contents but were stopped from doing so by the city in case it set the wooden boardwalk alight.[288]

There were fierce political debates from the very beginning—who was the real enemy? What was the most important arena of struggle— was it the war in Vietnam, racism, capitalism or sexism? How should women organise? The feminism that grew out of these debates and struggles was never defined as one specific ideology. Instead it always encompassed multiple and contested meanings. The first national action that involved tens of thousands of women across the US was called in 1970 to commemorate the 50th anniversary of women winning the vote. The demands raised were equal opportunity in employment and education; free abortion on demand and 24-hour childcare centres. They challenged gender roles in the family, fought for women's rights to control their fertility and demanded equality at work.

By the late 1960s and early 1970s different groups included "Seattle Radical Women, San Francisco's sisters of Lilith, SALT (Sisters All Learning Together), and Sudsofloppen (a nonsense term, to indicate the group's openness to new ideas), Boston's Cell 16, and Bread and

Roses... New York City's The Feminists, and several spin offs from New York's Radical Women including Redstocking and the first "coven" of WITCH [Women's International Conspiracy from Hell]".[289]

Activists looked to create a different culture for women; they looked for alternative ways to live, to dress and to behave to break from the old ways. Cell 16, who had a programme of "celibacy, separatism and karate" once ceremonially cut off the long hair of one its founder members at a feminist convention "as a protest against male defined standards of beauty. Their performance distressed many in the audience who felt the length of one's hair had very little to do with one's feminism".[290] The Chicago Westside group, dominated by politicos who wanted to expose consumerism, suggested a uniform for feminists, "to disassociate ourselves from the 'woman as consumer and clothes horse image'...(one such women's liberation uniform was produced by Californian feminists. However it is doubtful that many dresses were sold because the only thing which distinguished this dress from a Macdonald's uniform was its hand embroidered women's symbol)".[291]

The rise of radical feminism

Radical feminists, so named to differentiate themselves from "mainstream" or reformist feminists, over time became the dominant strand of the WLM. Beverly Jones and Judith Brown, two veterans of the civil rights movement, wrote in 1968 what became known as the "Florida Paper".[292] This laid out a radical feminist analysis with men firmly as the enemy. They tore into the women activists in the movement who they characterised as trying to "sweet talk" movement men into recognising the issue of women's oppression rather than fighting them.

They assert that the best thing would be if women were driven out of the wider movement, then "they will be forced to stop fighting for the 'movement' and start fighting primarily for the liberation and independence of women. Only when they seriously undertake this struggle will they begin to understand that they aren't just ignored or exploited—they are feared, despised and enslaved".[293]

This bleak assessment of the prospect of winning liberation in wider society saw men as the equivalent to slaveholders: "In the life of each woman, the most immediate oppressor, however unwilling he may be in theory to play that role, is 'the man'. Even if we prefer to view him as merely a pawn in the game, he's still the foreman on the big plantation of maleville".[294] Their solutions included women-only communes, where married women could come for respite.

This version of radical feminism posed women's assumed "natural" strengths, "attention to personal needs, caring for others, making decisions on the multitude of human data" as offering a solution to a system built on the principle of domination by men, "an entire sex bred for mastery".[295] This approach, coined patriarchy theory, gained hegemony. Patriarchy always meant different things to different people but essentially it was seen as a system of control and domination that pre-dated and acted alongside and separate to class society, by which all men oppressed all women.

Some of those moving to separatism and rejecting socialist ideas even argued that any sort of theory was unnecessary and relating each other's experiences of oppression was enough to understand it. This was challenged by other women, particularly the few working class women in the movement who saw the dumping of learning and theory as being a luxury only college educated middle class women could afford. The response of one working class woman who was determined to read and learn about Marxism is telling—she said she didn't believe it would destroy her "authenticity" and she "didn't want to be ignorant". Others wanted to reject any analysis which took account of class differences because, as the *Fourth World Manifesto* put it in 1971, they believed, "class is basically a distinction between males" whereas a "female is defined by her sexual caste status" and that women were a colonised "fourth world".[296]

Part of this increasing fragmentation of the movement was over sexual politics. In the early days lesbians had not been very visible, in fact some in the leadership of the biggest mainstream women's group, the National Organisation for Women (NOW) stayed in the closet. A section of the Florida Paper gives a flavour of the difficulties lesbians faced in their own movement. Judith Brown wrote,

"The radical woman is probably more uptight about homosexuality than other women. This is one of the curious paradoxes of the movement... Homosexuality, we imagine, would be too much to add to an already strained relationship with the society in which we dwell." She went on, "We have to stop throwing around terms like 'fag' and 'pimp', 'queer' and 'dyke'."[297]

A group of lesbians did a stunt that put sexuality right at the centre of the debate. At the second Congress to Unite Women on May Day in 1970 around 40 women rushed the stage wearing T-shirts stencilled with the words "Lavender Menace". This was a phrase Betty Friedan was reported to have used about lesbians in the movement. They called for supporters and women flooded to the stage. The conference was taken over for two hours by a discussion of "what it was like to be a lesbian in a heterosexist culture". The conference drew up resolutions on homophobia, and the Lavender Menace became the Radical Lesbians.[298] Sexuality was to become a recurring flashpoint as some lesbians argued that lesbianism was "feminism in action" and that "the only true feminists were those who renounced relations with the opposite sex entirely". This incurred angry responses from many feminists, lesbian and straight.[299]

The other gaping fissure in the movement was race. The WLM was dominated by white women from its beginning although the issue of race was central—the whole movement had grown out of struggles against racism in the South. But whatever the dangers, northern white women campaigning in the South could always go home—they had options that none of the black people they were organising among had. The rise of Black Power and the new left's shift back to the northern campuses were expressions of the divisions that existed inside the movement from its birth.

Some black women activists were alienated from the WLM because they saw their lives shaped by racism, which also affected black men, who were being brutalised and murdered. For them gender was not always the most important issue. But there was also hostility in some instances from white women who didn't want to be confronted with the challenges of the issue of racism, Echols writes of a debate that took place at a national WLM gathering about whether to contact women in the Black Panther Party to see if any radical black women would like to attend the 1968 WLM Lake Villa conference.

One woman complained it would be "counterproductive" to invite black women:

> Having experience with a black welfare group that had white women in it, I know that black militant women rule the day. They set the tone and they manage to completely cow white women in welfare organisations...they hold the cards on oppression...and they let white women know it. I don't want to go to a conference and hear a black woman tell me she is more oppressed and what am I going to do about it.[300]

Many other women argued against this position and said it was a mistake for the movement not to be inclusive, but in the end radical black women weren't specifically approached to attend.[301]

As women activists constantly grouped and regrouped around different and evolving political views weaknesses became all the more exposed. The movement, which had started from a mass movement to challenge the racist structures of the state and inspired many to an audacious vision of a world free from oppression, was becoming introverted and exclusive. It was often not able to reach out beyond the minority of activist women who started it even though the idea of women deserving equality was one that had a wide audience throughout society during this time.

In 1969 one group called The Feminists voted to make their actions compulsory for members to attend. They also said they would limit to one third the number of members who were married, or even living with a man because marriage was "inherently inequitable".[302] The Witches "betrayed their contempt for non-movement women" when they took their agit prop action to bridal fairs where they would picket wearing black veils and chanting at women entering, "here come the slaves off to their graves".[303] For some groups even women who got pregnant were seen as a problem, as this was simply fulfilling sexist expectations. Shulamith Firestone declared pregnancy "barbaric" in her book *The Dialectic of Sex*.[304]

In 1971 one activist from Washington DC admitted the problems of groups not being inclusive: "In trying to reach out to women different to ourselves, we still did not basically change the nature of our group. Instead we required that they become more like us to participate. Some did, but others found this impossible".[305] Radical feminist politics not only saw all men as the enemy but also patronised or openly excluded women who didn't accept that view and didn't or couldn't live accordingly. Instead of galvanising the mass of women and men against the system, women activists were being pitched against other activists. This fragmentation partly reflected the problems with organising a movement based on the notion that all women have a common interest.

The US radical movements of this period were in the main not centred on the organised working class. This lack of working class roots meant that when the struggles declined there was not the ballast of class organisation to hold sections of the movement together. This had implications for the WLM; it meant that the pull of looking to individual solutions to what were societal problems became strong when collective responses no longer seemed possible.

Britain's Women's Liberation Movement

In the US the movement reflected the class base of its mainly middle class founders who had been to college and did not want their newly acquired opportunities to be thwarted by discrimination and bigotry. In Britain the context for the WLM was different. Historian Sheila Rowbotham wrote in the first collection of WLM writing in 1972 that, "In the autumn of 1968 vague rumours of the women's movement in America and Germany reached Britain. We only had a hazy idea of what was going on." They didn't think of meeting; "the organisational initiative came from elsewhere".[306]

The most significant event that put the struggle for women's rights on the agenda was the 1968 strike by women workers in Ford's factory in Dagenham, east London. They were demanding to be upgraded in recognition of their skills as sewing machinists making car seat covers. The strike lasted three weeks and became the dispute that put the demand for equal pay on the map, and eventually on the statute books. They won 92 percent of men's wages but not the precious regrading to

C grade. They weren't to achieve that for another 16 years, when they walked out for seven weeks, and won.

The women workers were determined but at the same time astonished that they had the power to shut down the whole of Ford's. As striker Sheila Douglass said over 40 years later, "Because naturally you can't put a car on sale if it's not got a seat in. That's when we realised that we were more important than we thought. We hadn't really thought that far ahead, so when it happened it was a bit of a surprise... it had gone from C grade by then to equal pay—or equal rights".[307]

This struggle and others like it fundamentally shaped the birth of the WLM in Britain.

The early 1970s was a period of mass working class struggle. This included two national miners' strikes, a national dockers' strike and more than 200 factory occupations. So although the women's movement in Britain was inspired by the WLM in the US it was built in different circumstances, which included the presence of a stronger revolutionary left and a better rooted and organised labour and trade union movement. This backdrop shaped the dominant ideas and debates of the WLM in Britain. It also shaped the activity of newly politicised women. The campaigns they organised often reflected the demands and needs of working class women—equality at work, equal pay, maternity benefits for example. It was common for many feminists to take part in active solidarity with workers' struggles of the period.

An early campaign was to defend family allowances, the forerunner of child benefits, from being absorbed into the tax system—meaning it would cease to be a benefit that women could access directly. The Working Women's Charter, which involved sections of the trade union movement, listed and campaigned for demands in the workplace and over childcare and nursery funding which would force the state to lift some of the burden from individual women.

From a few disparate groups of women across Britain the beginnings of a movement grew. A newsletter appeared called *Harpies Bizarre* and later *Shrew*; different groups would edit different issues. In a single issue there would be denunciations of Maoists and Marxists as well as contributions from Maoists and Marxists.[308]

Marxism and Women's Liberation

Women organised actions, such as picketing Miss World in 1969, and they also leafleted workplaces. Rowbotham recalls:

> We made obvious beginners' mistakes. The Sheffield group for instance gave out leaflets on contraception at a factory gate at six in the morning. Not surprisingly the women teased them mercilessly. "Sex at this time in the morning? You must be joking." York organised a meeting on equal pay without contacting trade union women thoroughly first. No one came".[309]

Of course, the interesting thing is that women's groups were going to a factory gate at all—not something the founders of the US movement had done or seen as important.

Rowbotham recalled the excitement of the first national event of the WLM in Britain in early 1970,

> I can remember when we had the first Women's Liberation Conference in Ruskin [College]. About 500 people came and we weren't expecting them. That was quite amazing—you suddenly discovered that there weren't just these little groups of us but there were a few hundred of us. The following year we went on a march and there were thousands.[310]

The conference set up a loose national group to which local groups could send delegates, a Women's National Coordinating Committee to keep groups in touch with each other, and they organised around four demands: equal pay now, equal education and job opportunities, free contraception and abortion on demand, and free 24 hour nurseries.

The women joining the groups were "predominantly middle class, in their 20s and 30s, housewives and white collar workers".[311] But the influence of the left and class politics was still evident at the beginning.[312] The first anthology of writing from the WLM in 1974 included a section on "women and work" with pieces on trade unions, unemployment, equal pay and black women and work and an account of the night cleaners' strike.[313]

The second anthology, *Conditions of Illusion*, opened with a Marx quote—"The call to abandon their illusions about their conditions is a call to abandon a condition which requires illusions"—and a cartoon on its cover named capitalism as the problem. Its sections included

"Sexism, capitalism and the family" as well as chapters on equal pay, the working mothers' charter and the TUC's maternity leave recommendations. The final page was a cartoon that showed a boy and a girl each getting gradually boarded into coffin-shaped boxes of gender expectations. There was also a calendar of all strikes that involved women workers in the previous 12 months "compiled from *Socialist Worker* and *Morning Star*" alongside important milestones such as the date London buses recruited its first woman bus driver (May 1974) and first three women bus inspectors (August 1974).[314]

Above all the scale of strikes and escalation of unionisation of women workers in the early 1970s shaped the early movement. By 1975 women were 26.8 percent of trade union membership, up from around 10 percent in 1914.[315] Rising militancy against successive governments was especially significant in the expanding public sector, such as among teachers and in the NHS, where women workers became concentrated. Between 1968 and 1978 women members of the public sector union Nupe trebled, numbers doubled in local government union Nalgo and in the health sector union Cohse the number of women members quadrupled. All three unions are now part of Unison. The white collar union Astms, now part of Unite the union, saw its female membership increase sevenfold.[316]

A unionisation campaign around night cleaners in London became a symbol of the cooperation between socialists, feminists and women workers at the time. The cleaners faced poverty pay but as May Hobbs, one of the leading militants among the cleaners said, they needed to work "for little luxuries like food, rent and clothes for the kids".[317] Women's groups including feminists and socialists alike worked together leafleting the offices where the women worked and organising solidarity.

Tony Cliff recalls the scale of struggle among women workers, writing that in the same year as the office cleaners' dispute:

20,000 Leeds clothing workers (85 per cent of them women) went on strike. Flying pickets closed clothing factories further afield in Yorkshire. Tens of thousands of teachers, three-quarters of them women, were also on strike over pay for the first time in half a century.

1971 saw a London telephonists' pay dispute, while at Brannan's, a small thermometer factory in Cumberland, women struck to defend trade union organisation. In 1972 women joined the occupations of Fisher-Bendix on Merseyside and Briant Colour Printing in London. The same year women at Goodman's, part of Thorn Electrical Industries, successfully struck for equal pay. In 1973 hundreds of thousands of hospital workers (the majority women) went on their first ever national strike. In the same year 200 women in GEC, Coventry, struck for eight weeks over piece rates. Asian women at Mansfield Hosiery Mills struck over racial discrimination, and there was a national Nalgo strike—mainly of women.[318]

The influx of working class women into the trade union movement at the same time as the ideas of women's liberation were gaining ground had an immense impact. The unions were still predominantly led by men but many members identified with the demands of the WLM and fought for policies that supported the fight for equality. The influence of women's liberation activists was lasting, so that the principle, if not the reality, of women's equality became the common-sense of the union movement.

Yet WLM's methods of organising, just as in the US, often excluded working class women. The popular model for most groups was a small number of women who got to know each other well, although many such groups were unable to sustain themselves after the first year or so. They did not see it as necessary to reach out to recruit more and different women—some claimed their very strength was in keeping their group small. They limited the numbers they would allow to join because "relationships and solidarity have been built". The concentration was on changing women not society. The group in Tufnell Park in north London put it like this: "the safety and reflected power that makes it comfortable to identify with one's oppressor has to be given up and strength found to identify with one's own oppressed group and other oppressed groups".[319]

Rowbotham wrote as early as 1972 about this problem: "In Britain the student movement was collapsing as women's liberation started, and the Vietnam Solidarity Campaign was already dead. The real political initiative has come from the labour movement," which she acknowledged the left was "better equipped to intervene in than women's liberation." Women's liberation "serves an educational propagandist function but it is difficult to mobilise...it is almost impossible to act in any concerted way without any clear agreement of what your aims are".[320]

The mid-1970s saw a decline in class struggle and the women's movement had not become a mass social movement on a scale that could overcome the objective difficulties. Women in the movement increasingly split over issues of sexuality, class, politics and race. The women's groups that had sprouted up sometimes coordinated with others nationally, while others did their own thing locally over childcare or consciousness raising. But even these circumstances did not mean the end of the influence of class politics.

One example where the women's movement and the trade unions came together to great effect towards the end of the 1970s was in the fight to defend the 1967 Abortion Act. Socialists and other activists in the National Abortion Campaign (NAC) fought for trade unions to take up the issue, raising motions and debates at union conferences. Several private member's bills seeking to restrict access to abortion were beaten back. Eventually in 1978 the TUC passed a motion committing it to organise a demonstration in support of the right to abortion if any future attempts to change the law threatened it. They didn't have to wait long before they had to put this policy into practice—in 1979 Tory MP John Corrie tabled a new anti-abortion bill.

The TUC demonstration against Corrie in October 1979 was magnificent. Over 80,000 people marched; it took hours to make its way through central London. Workers, women and men, carried a seemingly endless stream of trade union banners from all sections of the working class, including many from unions with majority male members. Abortion was seen as a class issue and something that the trade union movement was rightly at the heart of defending. The power of that demonstration, and the fact that the organised working class took up the demand for a woman's right to choose, helped ensure lasting and solid popular support for abortion rights in British society.

Marxism and Women's Liberation

Working class women still predominantly organised where they were strong, in their collective trade union organisations. Women workers took part in high profile strikes such as in Trico for equal pay in 1976 and at Grunwicks, over union recognition in 1977.

Many feminists continued to look to the labour movement as a source of strength through the late 1970s and into the 1980s, but a layer of feminist activists argued against working within the trade union movement. For example Anna Coote and Beatrix Campbell denounced trade unions as only being capable of representing what they deemed narrow sectional interests. In their book on the women's movement in Britain, *Sweet Freedom* (1982), they argued "for men to champion the women's cause wholeheartedly required a degree of altruism that had no part in the tradition of trade unionism." They claimed that men had a "conflict of interest" with women and men acted on it "instinctively more than deliberately". Yet when faced with examples of trade unions throwing their weight behind a struggle beyond workers' sectional interests they dismissed them.

Referring to the 1979 TUC march against Corrie they claim that while "self-interest was not the only motive behind men's support of abortion rights", male trade unionists primarily mobilised because, "the defence of the 1967 act entailed no threat...to men's material circumstances. Indeed many men were spared financial hardship and social embarrassment by the 1967 act".[321]

Their anti union prejudice meant they showed a lamentable lack of understanding of the impact of illegal abortion on working class women and men. Male trade unionists marched alongside co-workers, sisters, daughters, wives and girlfriends because they recognised that having access to legal and safe abortion was their issue too. Rich women didn't die in the back streets; working class women did. That is why the march was so big. The characterisation of trade unions as simply representing male interests didn't address the question of male bosses. It also ignored the fact that women were joining unions in bigger numbers than ever before. And when women walked out on strike it was fellow workers, women and men, who they looked to for solidarity.

This view of working class organisation as being oppressive to women went alongside concerted attacks on socialist and revolutionary organisation by a section of the movement. This was the theme of a book originally published in 1979, and reprinted in a new edition in 2013, *Beyond the Fragments*.[322] The three authors, Sheila Rowbotham, Lynne Segal and Hilary Wainwright specifically target Leninist groups as being the problem in the movement. The book marked for many women a justification for a turn away from the working class as an agent for change in society. With the decline of the struggle both in the streets and within the trade unions many of those who believed they could change the world in the heady days of the 1960s began to think that maybe it was only going to be possible to reform it. For many in Britain this meant turning to the Labour Party.[323]

This was a contradictory development. This was the same Labour Party that had been viewed as firmly a part of the establishment during the first protests against the Vietnam War—it supported the US—and for equal rights in the 1960s. But it was also the party still seen as the major political expression of the working class movement. Activists joining the Labour Party may have lost their belief that militant struggle could bring equality and liberation but, in contrast to radical feminists who argued for separatism, they still saw themselves as being part of a class organisation committed to challenging inequality, albeit a mainstream reformist one.

It wasn't only former activists from the WLM who saw the Labour Party as their preferred political home during the 1980s; so did some of the wider left including former revolutionaries. Many became part of a move to set up women's committees and working parties in local councils across the country.[324] By 1986 these had been established in 33 local authorities. When the Greater London Authority was abolished in that year its women's committee, the first to have been established, employed 96 people and had a budget of £90 million.[325]

These committees helped put issues of equality on the political agenda. They pioneered issues of fair employment, for example opening up jobs in the fire service to women and ethnic minorities, that have a lasting legacy. However the committees often became an end in themselves for those involved and acted as a stepping stone for a layer of women to build careers within local and national Labour politics.

Arguments about class were not the only ones that divided the movement. The WLM arose alongside the gay liberation movement—the Gay Liberation Front was launched in late 1970. Within the WLM the argument that patriarchy was the cause of women's oppression led some to argue for a life free from men. The logic of this for some activists was that lesbianism became a political choice; among them were those who argued it was the only political choice for anyone who was serious about fighting oppression.

For example Leeds Revolutionary Feminists expressed the view that women should become "political" lesbians and spurn men on principle stating, "Every woman who lives with or fucks a man helps to maintain the oppression of her sisters and hinders our struggle." This followed the London workshop's reprinting of The Clit statement by radical lesbians in New York, an attack on heterosexual women: "Straight women think, talk, cross their legs, dress and come on like male transvestite femme drag queens." Of course also implicit in this attack is an insult to trans people. When this was published in New York other radical feminists vocally opposed the attack but reportedly, "British radical feminists remained silent".[326]

By 1978 there was so much division and acrimony in the movement that the National Women's Liberation Movement conference in Birmingham was the last held. "The split was so bitter and painful that no one was prepared to organise another such gathering".[327] Feminists and activists continued campaigning on single issue and local campaigns, though later in the 1980s many were to mobilise as part of working class resistance to the Thatcher government.

The campaign against nuclear weapons at the US base at Greenham Common became a focus for many radical feminists in the early 1980s. A women's camp was set up in 1981 and in the following years the campaign against cruise missiles mobilised tens of thousands. In April 1983 the Campaign for Nuclear Disarmament organised a human chain of 77,000 people along the 14 miles between Greenham Common and Aldermaston where the Atomic Weapons Establishment was based. In December of the same year, weeks after the cruise missiles were put in place, 50,000 turned out at Greenham to surround the base.

However the Greenham Common protests also showed many of the weaknesses of a set of politics that saw men as the enemy. Women were portrayed as naturally peace loving and the protest slogan was "Take the toys from the boys". They saw the missiles as an expression of manhood and counterposed women's inherent peace loving nature by hanging what they saw as symbols of "womanhood", including tampons and nappy pins, on the fences of the military base. "Women's strength that is growing here might be crushed when it's the only thing that can stop Cruise Missiles and the male domination of our earth... I know why I cannot walk at night without feeling threatened by attack. I know why there is militarism and imperialism and racism and sexism... It's because of patriarchy—male rule".[328] Yet slogans such as "Take the toys from the boys" didn't begin to address the fact the Tory prime minister in charge of the toybox was actually a woman.

The end of the second wave

Ultimately second wave feminism crashed on the rocks of the multiple identities of race, sexuality and political beliefs that tore the movement apart. The initial four demands of the movement, which focused on material gains that could be won through collective struggle, were added to over the years—in 1975 legal and financial independence for women and an end to discrimination against lesbians, and in 1978 at the last ever WLM conference a woman's right to define her sexuality and freedom from male violence. The focus on male violence signified a turn towards seeing interpersonal issues as the source of women's oppression.

This was a retreat from a view that saw oppression as rooted in the structures of society. The level of domestic violence suffered by women has often been hidden in a society that wants us to revere the family. Although it is experienced within interpersonal relationships, it has to be understood in the wider context of a society whose ideology and structures, particularly of the state in the form of the police and legal system, condone and justify this violence. The Reclaim the Night demonstrations which began in 1977 were a collective response to the issue but were limited by the dominant assumption that men caused the problem.

Marxism and Women's Liberation

Separatist feminists accused heterosexual women of "sleeping with the enemy"; feminists who supported Israel broke with those who sided with the struggle of the Palestinians; black and Asian women felt that their experience of racism was not appreciated by the white women who dominated the movement. The sometimes poisonous rows that broke out between individuals and groups led one US feminist activist, Ti-Grace Atkinson, to resign from the group she helped found in New York, declaring, "Sisterhood is powerful. It kills. Mostly sisters".[329] The editorial board of *Spare Rib* magazine had to bring in a therapist because it became so divided. An editorial in September 1980 admitted, "It has been difficult to produce work and get along in a sisterly spirit. The seriousness of it all made us decide to hold a series of special meetings, with a group counsellor, to help us sort out structural and personal problems".[330]

In the US the limitations of the small women-only groups centred on consciousness-raising became glaring. In a blistering critique written in 1970, *The Tyranny of Structurelessness*, Jo Freeman, the feminist who had coined the term Women's Liberation Movement, argued that the "movement will have to disabuse itself of its prejudice about organisation and structure" if it was going to effectively take any action more than talking. She said "consciousness-raising as the main function of the women's liberation movement is becoming obsolete". She pointed out that far from being more democratic, structureless groups in reality tended to elitism, even if this was informal. But her experience was that groups would have their own informal rules— they would only allow women who were young or old, who were lesbian or not, married or not, "hip" or not too "hip" and so on, and then "the mere act of staying together becomes the reason for their staying together." The editorial in *Notes from the Third Year* (1973) echoed this view saying that many women were seeing consciousness-raising as a stage in the struggle and that it was "limited as a tool". It called on groups to "move to analysis, small group actions and, most difficult, large collective actions and mobilisations".[331]

The process of fragmentation around issues of race, class, sexuality and politics did not happen in a vacuum. The movement grew at a time of mass struggles in the US and around the world. Its decline in the US and Britain cannot be separated from the more general decline of the 1960s insurgency and class struggle, during the second half of the 1970s and early 1980s.

Yet even through the 1980s there were examples of feminist activism that was inspired by class politics and workers' struggles. In Britain the historic year-long miners' strike of 1984-85 saw women in the pit villages play a leading role in the strike, from soup kitchens to picketing to doing speaking tours to raise money and support. Women Against Pit Closures saw women organising to win solidarity for the miners all over the country in what became a defining battle against the Tory government led by Margaret Thatcher. The bitter defeat of the strike led to a deep demoralisation in the working class about the possibility of beating Thatcher's all-out war on workers.

The achievements that women made during this period of struggle were considerable. They included equal pay legislation, abortion rights, greater rights to divorce, expansion of employment and education opportunities, and the right to political representation. The ideas of feminism, of women's right to equality, had permeated much of society. Other social reforms that reflected the progressive demands of the times included the decriminalisation of homosexuality in 1967 and the abolition of the death penalty in 1965.

The challenge to the stifling morality of the 1950s was exhilarating—sex was no longer assumed to be something most women simply endured, although many of the changes of the "swinging sixties" took years to filter through to the whole of society. One male interviewee in Elizabeth Roberts' oral history, a teenager in the late 1960s in the north west of England, probably reflected the frustrations of many at the slowness of change: "It was beginning to oscillate in Barrow".[332]

But the greatest winners were a layer of women, some from working class backgrounds, who benefitted from the increasing social mobility of the period of the 1960s and 1970s. They were able to secure positions as well educated women in the middle class. As the movement went down some were able to use their new found rights to break through the glass ceiling and become lawyers, surgeons, politicians and bankers.

Marxism and Women's Liberation

Some of these women have even gained benefits sufficient to glue them to the system, something the US feminist academic Hester Eisenstein examines in her book *Feminism Seduced*. She writes of how the system could absorb at least some of the ideas of feminism in order to function more efficiently: "Unhappily in recent years I have come to fear that...feminism in its organised forms has become all too compatible with an increasingly unjust and dangerous corporate capitalist system".[333] Feminist ideas have been marshalled in ways that completely contradict their roots.

Now bosses are encouraged to include more women as managers and commit to equal pay because "gender equality is good for business" as one Women and Work Commission study put it, rather than equality being a principled aim for which to strive.[334] Eisenstein quotes a US report which suggests the assertion that "equality is good for business" is valid. She quotes Catalyst, a research organisation that tracks women at work, reporting in 2004 that "the Fortune 500 corporations with the most women in top positions yielded, on average, a 35 percent higher return on equity than those with the fewest female corporate officers".[335]

These women were initially sneered at as "career women" by the tabloids, a sexist and derogatory term for women assumed to be shunning their responsibilities to their family in pursuit of selfish ambition. You never heard the term "career man". But this minority of women were able to seek out individual solutions to societal problems. They could afford to employ cleaners and nannies and farm out their ironing—a model that would be familiar to upper class women and the working class women they have employed across the centuries.

A great number of the most political activists who won a place within the system went into academia. This became a haven as well as a battleground for some of the women activists of the 1960s and 1970s. In the US there was an explosion of women's studies courses: "by the beginning of 1974 women's studies programs were functioning at 78 institutions and about 2,000 courses were being offered at another 50 campuses".[336] The next chapter will look at what this shift to the academy meant for the development of ideas and debates around women's liberation.

But the impact of this period of militancy and political radicalisation over women's oppression is still seen today within the working class movement. The fight for women's rights, whether equal pay, access to abortion or childcare facilities, is embedded in working class consciousness and refracted through trade union organisation. Of course women still experience sexism despite these commitments, but women as working class fighters made their mark and they leave a powerful lasting legacy.

8

The renaissance of feminism today

The Women's Liberation Movement (WLM) in the US was a product of a period of mass social resistance and upheaval. In Britain it grew up at a time of militant workers' struggles and political protests including against the Vietnam War. As the women's liberation movements fragmented they became untethered from their roots in active struggles—in fact their very decline was a symptom of the decline of the wider struggles.

The separation of theory and practice had consequences for the further development of theory. The movement's decline meant debates about women's oppression were now more likely to be taking place in the rarified conditions of academia where many of the leading activists gravitated. Feminism became more likely to be seen as a set of ideas rather than a cause to take action over. Debates generated today by the recent renaissance in interest in the politics of women's liberation often look to theoretical developments of this period for insight into contemporary dilemmas. The second wave Women's Liberation Movement remains the key reference point for activists and academics, even when they seek to offer an alternative vision.

Many of the different threads of post second wave feminism were already becoming visible during the period of the WLM. Alice Echols points to early signs of the emergence of what was to become cultural feminism in the American WLM in the early 1970s. She notes a shift from "a political movement dedicated to eliminating the sex-class system" to a "countercultural movement aimed at reversing the cultural evaluation of the male and the devaluation of the female"—ie prioritising ideas and representations over the systemic material structures of oppression.[337]

These developments did not happen in a political vacuum. In Britain the election of a Tory government in 1979 with Margaret Thatcher as the first woman prime minister led to a series of devastating attacks on some of the best organised sections of the working class. The 1980s were dominated by these bitter struggles against Thatcher and that caused a problem for some feminists. They struggled to explain how a woman could be leading this assault on ordinary people. Thatcher was sometimes referred to as a "man in drag"—as if being a woman was incompatible with representing ruling class interests.

Others were critical of what they saw as the women's movement "disowning" Thatcher. Feminist writer Natasha Walter argued Thatcher was "the great unsung heroine of British feminism" and saw criticisms of her as an "inability to accept worldly female power". For Walter it was cathartic for women to be able to celebrate "their ability not just to be caring...but also to be deeply unpleasant, to be death dealing, to be egotistic".[338] A minority agreed and took the view that Thatcher had "her own brand of feminism" and that her love of power "made it legitimate for us to love it too".[339]

Thatcher's neoliberal project led to the privatisation of huge swathes of public assets and a culture of celebrating competition and greed. It was against this background that the media began to talk about "post-feminism"—a mythical world in which women now had achieved everything, supposedly making the fight for women's rights some sort of quaint anachronism.

The idea that women were getting ahead by aping men was expressed visually in the fashion of "power dressing", a term coined by a US writer in the 1970s in a book advising men. The ridiculously large shoulder pads in power suits for business women even came as standard for a time in T-shirts and nightwear. It was as if all that kept women from being treated equally was their diminutive stature, and with a slice of foam in their clothes they could assert themselves on wider society.

The "post-feminism" argument developed into an assertion that women's problem was now that they had too much liberation. By the 1990s this became a serious right wing ideological backlash against many of the gains made by women in the 1960s and 1970s. The media constantly pumped out stories about women risking their fertility as they pursued their careers, and letting their body clocks time out. This told women they were trying to buck their biology, which wasn't compatible with being equal in the workforce.

US feminist Susan Faludi's 1992 book *Backlash* spelled out the scale of attack from the right wing who wanted to push back women's rights. She also looked at the move away from radicalism by some high profile feminists who now sought to distance themselves from the WLM.[340] Faludi describes Betty Friedan's descent into denunciations of women for trying to make it in a man's world. Friedan dismissed those marching against sexual violence as "kind of wallowing in that victim-state".[341]

A number of high profile women writers were closely associated with the ideas of post-feminism, including Katie Roiphe, Naomi Wolf and Camille Paglia. They argued to replace 1970s "victim feminism" with what was sometimes called "power feminism". Roiphe's most controversial work was on rape and sexual harassment, which was becoming a major issue on US campuses. In *The Morning After* she looked at student culture at the Ivy League Princeton University in New Jersey and claimed that feminists were creating a "victim" culture where young women felt themselves in constant danger of male violence. Camille Paglia argued that it was women's responsibility to protect themselves from "primordial male sexuality".[342] The media featured Paglia's "dismissal of date rape as feminist nonsense".[343] Wolf rightly rejected Roiphe's and Paglia's views on rape and pointed out that they belittled and dismissed the very real problems suffered by victims of sexual assault.

Women who had reached top positions in business were often enthusiastic post-feminists. The emphasis was on proving how strong women could be in the neoliberal world.

The third wave

The idea that women should reject "victimhood" was mirrored in some of the ideas that came to the fore under the banner of the "third wave" of feminism. This developed alongside post-feminism and took up some of the "we don't need extra support we can do anything we want" attitudes but from the point of view that "feminism" in some form was a good thing and was still needed.

It was in many ways an explicit rejection of second wave feminism, which was seen as solely representing white middle class women who had now found their place in society. Instead the third wave was to be about anti-racism, queer politics and identity. Rebecca Walker, the daughter of feminist author Alice Walker, coined the term when she wrote a piece in the US feminist magazine *Ms* in early 1992, declaring, "I am not a post-feminism feminist. I am the Third Wave".[344]

Third wave feminism was pluralistic, it generated websites and 'zines and influenced music scenes including, for example, the Riot Grrrl movement, as well as rock and hip hop.[345] It didn't claim to have a unitary project and proclaimed itself to be less prescriptive than second wave feminism, which was, according to British writer and journalist Natasha Walter, "associated with man hating and with a rather sullen kind of political correctness or Puritanism...the movement is seen as intolerant".[346] The new feminism was sold as fun and sexy, apparently to distance it from the dungaree-wearing, unshaven women of the 1970s—a stereotype lifted straight from the right wing media. US feminist Jessica Valenti wrote, "Is there anything wrong with being ugly, fat or hairy? Of course not. But let's be honest. No one wants to be associated with something that is seen as uncool and unattractive".[347]

It is true that the WLM in the US did come from a narrow class base that was predominantly, though not exclusively, white. Ultimately it was unable to relate to the day to day problems of the mass of working class women. Yet the third wave did not offer a real solution either.

This became a feminism that decided it could subvert sexism and reclaim language, so women wore T-shirts with "slut", "bitch" and "porn rocks" emblazoned on them, websites such as Bitchphd and Angryblack appeared, as well as magazines *Bitch* and *Bust*. And they were often successful in reaching a market—"*Bust* distribution rose from 1,000 to 32,000 in its first five years".[348] The US website aimed at younger women Feministing.com, originally set up by Valenti, has as its logo "an image of a silhouetted seated female with an exaggerated physique (notably very large breasts)". They claim they are subverting the classic sexist "mudflap girl" image because the woman is raising her middle finger.[349]

Feminism became whatever or whoever you wanted it to be. For example, the feminist pressure group the Fawcett Society ran a campaign in 2006 with photos of high profile individuals wearing their "This is what a feminist looks like" T-shirts. They included the Tory Theresa May. Anna Bird of the Fawcett Society defended this some years later saying, "There's nothing inherently leftwing or rightwing about feminism as we would define it: it's about women having equal power and influence over the course of their lives".[350] Walter said that "living feminism" in Britain meant some organisations "hold parties with champagne and canapés, others hold demonstrations with banners."

This anything-goes "new" feminism that came from breaking off the "shackles" of the 1960s and 1970s meant you might be a feminist who makes porn films or one who protests against them; you could make cupcakes or quilts; you might accept that biology determines our gender attributes or believe socialisation plays the dominant role—this all became a matter of choice. Every woman's choice was elevated as empowering and by definition feminist. This took little account of the context and limitations within which women make choices—"in many third wave texts...an emphasis on inequality and power structures is seen as old fashioned and irrelevant... Indeed much of the emphasis...is on being sexy and pleasure seeking".[351]

Periel Ashenbrand, creator in 2000 of the bestselling T-shirt with the slogan "The only bush I trust is my own" (in reference to then US president George W Bush) and author of the book by the same name, was lauded as a voice for a new generation.[352] She boasted in an interview that she enjoyed going to lap-dancing clubs: "I think it's better if the girls give me a lap dance than some fat, balding, sweaty guy. It's fun. It's sexy. I think you can be a strong, sexy woman and still be a feminist".[353]

Former professor of feminist theory at Yale Divinity School, Jan Breslauer, generated headlines for declaring that her cosmetic surgery to have her breast size increased was a feminist choice. She wrote in

Playboy, "This boob job is empowering." She continues "I know the party line on breast augmentation that women who have surgery are the oppressed victims of a patriarchal culture...[but] feminism is about having control over life and one's body".[354]

The alternative to such statements is not to attack the women, self-professed feminists or not, for getting cosmetic surgery or going to strip clubs. It is to explain a world that turns women into sex objects and leads some to see conforming to or celebrating that objectification as rebellion. But for most of the high profile voices of the third wave such analysis simply wasn't their project. Third waver and *Manifesta* author Jennifer Baumgardner, looking back on the period, writes, "Third Wave feminism was portable, you didn't have to go to a meeting...where the Second Wave radicals believed in the mass movement and the liberal feminists believed in creating women's institutions to influence men's, a Third Waver might say 'Every time I move, I make a women's movement'."[355]

State co-option of feminism

Most controversially, the malleability of feminist ideals allowed them to be used by the ruling class to justify the wars in Afghanistan and Iraq. Politicians argued in 2001 that the Western invasion and occupation of Afghanistan was going to open the door to a new era of liberation for Afghan women—girls' schools would be opened and democracy installed. But bombing one of the poorest nations on the planet is no way to liberate it. As in any war the most vulnerable suffer the greatest hardships; instead of liberation the war brought Afghan women poverty and violence.

Muslims in the West also face persecution in the name of feminism and liberation. In France some feminists joined the campaign for the hijab (headscarf) to be banned in schools in 2003, with notable exceptions including Christine Delphy, who spoke out against the law.[356] The ban was passed and then followed in 2011 by a ban on wearing the niqab (face veil) anywhere in public, which has seen Muslim women prosecuted—and persecuted in the streets.[357] In January 2015 an Islamist group murdered 12 journalists at the Paris offices of *Charlie*

Hebdo—a magazine which had become notorious for its "satirical" cartoons attacking Islam and the prophet Mohammed. Delphy has written that since those events the situation for Muslims has deteriorated even further. Politicians have declared that France is "at war" and it was implicit that "the enemy was inside our walls". This has meant that "women wearing a headscarf are little by little being excluded from jobs in the public sector, and now in the private sector as well—in the name of their emancipation".[358]

Nina Power, author of *One Dimensional Woman* (2009), comments on the ruling class using feminism to justify repression and war: "One of the most profound and disturbing recent shifts in geopolitical discourse is the co-opting of the language of feminism by figures who ten or 15 years ago would have spoken out most vociferously against what feminism stands for".[359] US Marxist feminist Hester Eisenstein calls this "Madeleine Albright feminism" and points out the distance travelled by a feminism that originally came out of a militant anti-war movement against US imperialism.[360]

The imperialist propaganda from past centuries that portrayed the Western powers travelling the globe "civilising savages" would be recognised as racist and rejected. Yet over the last decade there has been a collapse of some feminist thought into a narrative that supports the idea of the superiority of western "enlightenment", "modernity" and "feminism" over what is dismissed as "medieval" Islam. In France CNDF, a major feminist coalition, blocked women wearing the hijab from coming into meetings and also tried to stop them taking part in International Women's Day demonstrations. As Delphy writes, Muslim women are being judged as "unworthy of fighting for women's rights".[361]

Delphy writes that she opposes this "because the 'women's cause' has been instrumentalised in a shameful way, and continues to be so, by the imperial war...we will not win our oppressors' indulgence by giving them our support, following them along other paths of oppression and othering. Would we even want to? We don't need their indulgence—we want justice".[362]

Whether it's Western troops in Afghanistan or Iraq, or the right of women to wear the veil, Islamophobia has become mainstream.

Liz Fekete, whose work has done much to expose the rise of Islamophobia and the use of feminism to justify it, points to the inherent contradiction:

> The most divisive measure to compel Muslims to assimilate into the dominant culture is, despite all the rhetoric about "women's rights", targeted against Muslim women, with the support of other women. What an irony!... Muslim women, though, such feminists argue, are too passive or enslaved... So the state has to act as the liberator.[363]

Michele Barrett has referred to "an undeniable inflection of straightforward female chauvinism in much feminist writing".[364] She is reflecting on the resurgence of an essentialist view of gender, which declares women and their choices in some way naturally or morally superior to men. Such chauvinism can also be said to be at work when the behaviour and life choices of some women are seen as less valid than the (usually) Western white middle class women who are in a position to pass judgment on others.

Barrett acknowledges the lack of diversity in much second wave writing—although Marxist feminist Lise Vogel has pointed out elsewhere that there were other voices in the movement, "for example, the well-known collection *Sisterhood is Powerful* dealt with differences among women by publishing, among other pieces, Fran Beal's 'Double jeopardy: to be black and female', Jean Tepperman's 'Two Jobs: women who work in factories', Martha Shelley's 'Notes of a Radical Lesbian' and Zoe Moss's 'It Hurts to be alive and obsolete: the ageing women'."[365]

The reality is that representatives of the third wave in the US have hardly been any more diverse than the movement they critique. The authors of *Manifesta*, which attempted to pull together the ideas of the new generation, describe the development of their ideas through a long series of dinner parties, admitting "Obviously, this random sample of friends (who live in New York City and mostly work in the media) can't represent all women".[366] Walker, who so confidently declared, "I am the Third Wave" in 1992, attended Yale University and had the means in her early 20s to set up a foundation based on her political project, the Third Wave Action Cooperation.

Marxism and Women's Liberation

Identity, intersectionality and privilege

The issue that dominated the debate after the decline of the WLM was how to understand different experiences of oppression instead of seeing women's experience as homogenous. The rise of identity politics, which concentrated on each individual's personal experience of oppression, reflected an acceptance that "women" or "black people" and so on were not homogenous groups. But it dragged some elements of the movement into a set of politics solely based on individual identity.[367] Naomi Klein wrote that when she was at college the dominance of identity politics meant that "our criticism was focused on the representation of women and minorities within the structures of power, not on the economics behind the power structures".[368]

This meant ever more divisions among the oppressed and sometimes even a hierarchy of oppression. Some feminist authors have termed this "oppression privilege" where "identity politics had been twisted into an essentialism that assumed that those from subordinated communities had 'biological' or 'natural' access to knowledge or ideas that people from dominant groups could never have".[369] Identity politics was all about the experience of the individual, it concentrated on differences among people and not the common ground or interests that could unite people in struggles to successfully challenge their oppression.

The concept of intersectionality, currently enjoying a renaissance, is a development of identity politics. It is a recognition that oppressions are not simply experienced as a list of multiple sufferings that you add up—sometimes referred to as an "additive" approach. Intersectionality argues that different oppressions work simultaneously and "interlock" in specific ways. If you are a black woman you experience racism and sexism but not simply as two separate problems; the racism you face may also be "gendered" because of preconceptions about black women's sexuality. Today when young feminists declare themselves to be "intersectional" it signals that they want to be inclusive and appreciate that racism, sexism, homophobia, and so on "intersect" with each other and become more than the sum of their parts.

Activists have confronted the problem of how different oppressions interact right back to the 19th century. Journalist Ida B Wells, who had been born a slave, took up the struggle for votes for women in the late 19th century while at the same time leading campaigns against racist violence and lynching. In the 1960s and 1970s the question of multiple oppressions, some called it "double-" or "triple jeopardy", was raised by black women who argued the WLM didn't properly represent them.[370]

Interestingly, however, an influential statement by the Combahee River Collective black feminists in 1977, which many see as the first formal expression of an intersectional view, also stated a commitment to socialist politics and Marxism.[371]

> Black, other Third World, and working women have been involved in the feminist movement from its start, but both outside reactionary forces and racism and elitism within the movement itself have served to obscure our participation...
>
> We realise that the liberation of all oppressed peoples necessitates the destruction of the political-economic systems of capitalism and imperialism as well as patriarchy. We are socialists because we believe that work must be organised for the collective benefit of those who do the work and create the products, and not for the profit of the bosses... Although we are in essential agreement with Marx's theory as it applied to the very specific economic relationships he analysed, we know that his analysis must be extended further in order for us to understand our specific economic situation as Black women.[372]

They also criticise the moves that some feminists were making towards lesbian separatism, questioning whether it "is an adequate and progressive political analysis and strategy, even for those who practice it, since it so completely denies any but the sexual sources of women's oppression, negating the facts of class and race". Although they themselves faced splits over issues of sexuality so were not immune to the divisions of the time that they argue against.

The Combahee statement also refers to "privilege": "We do not have racial, sexual, heterosexual, or class privilege to rely upon, nor do we have even the minimal access to resources and power that groups who possess anyone of these types of privilege have".[373] Privilege theory has experienced a revival in recent years among academics and activists, sometimes in conjunction with an intersectional approach. The theory will be examined in more detail below.

Feminist and law professor Kimberlé Crenshaw first named intersectionality in 1989. It came out of a legal case taken out by black women who had been laid off by General Motors. The company argued it couldn't be sued under sex discrimination legislation because not all women were affected, nor could it be sued under race equality laws as many black workers were not laid off. Crenshaw pointed out that General Motors only recruited black women after 1964; before that black men had been employed on the shop floor and white women in the office jobs. So when after 1970 lay-offs were carried out on the basis of seniority the black women lost out specifically because they had been discriminated against in previous years as black women—something the law didn't recognise.[374]

She likened the situation to ambulances coming to the scene of an accident at a crossroads and leaving because the direction of the driver responsible for the victim's injuries hasn't been identified. This metaphor sees an oppressed person as the point of intersection of oppressions, coming from many different directions and discrete sources. It doesn't allow for a single, common source for all those oppressions—the system of capitalism itself.

Black feminist Patricia Hill Collins's use of the term "matrix of domination" to describe the multiple interlocking impacts of oppressions doesn't solve this. She sees every individual as part of the matrix, only, "each one of us derives varying amounts of penalty and privilege from the multiple systems of oppression that frame our lives". This sometimes leads her to focus on individuals changing themselves. She quotes the late Audre Lorde's statement that "the true focus of revolutionary change is never merely the oppressive situations which we seek to escape, but that piece of the oppressor which is planted deep within each of us". She goes on to assert that "change starts with self, and relationships that we have with those around us must always be the site for social change".[375]

The individual woman and her experience of oppression has often been the spurring issue for the politicisation of activists. But as British writer Gary Younge has argued, "Identities are a great place to start—they're about how we got here, what makes people want to be part of a certain politics. But it's a terrible place to finish".[376] Intersectionality may be a useful concept to break from the idea that all women are a single category with the same experiences and needs, but it remains useful only at the level of description and recognition. It takes the struggle no further forward in analysing where oppression comes from or how we can challenge it. Simply declaring a commitment to intersectionality is not a strategy for confronting systemic oppression.

The overlap with the recent revisiting of privilege theory is clear. Privilege is seen as something the system confers on an individual, so making that individual responsible for the oppression of others. Of course oppression is not an abstract theoretical confection, it has real material effects, often articulated through the human actions of individuals as opposed to the "system". It's vital to address and oppose the prejudices and behaviour of anyone acting in an oppressive way. But this view of explaining discrimination and prejudice is deeply problematic. It is, as Esme Choonara and Yuri Prasad argue, "potentially corrosive to debate and actually risks letting oppressive behaviour off the hook. If someone speaks or behaves in a racist or sexist way, it is surely better, and more educative for all concerned, to challenge them by explaining that what they do or say is racist or sexist, rather than attributing it to an automatic expression of their 'privileged' gender, race, sexuality and so on".[377]

Although many privilege theorists do not go beyond the level of interpersonal relationships the approach does often point the system as the root of oppression. But individuals are now rendered helpless agents of oppression and the politics of personal narratives come to dominate and shape the debate. The theory relies on the idea that if you are white or male, for example, you gain privilege simply by being perceived as being part of a "dominant" section of society. So a working class white man supposedly benefits from the privilege of being white in a racist society. The logic of this emphasis on identity is that it implies a unity of interest across gender and race where none exists. It also puts the blame and responsibility for oppression onto individuals and ignores how divisions of race and gender are built into the structures of society.

So its project is to make "privilege" visible, for example by choosing to look at inequality from the perspective of the one who is "helped"—hence the fascination in academia with whiteness and masculinity in recent years. So the fact that women are paid less on average than men is turned into what one academic called "the 'masculinity dividend'—the unearned benefits that accrue to men, just for being men".[378] This makes men's pay something that is received at the expense of women's pay; it sees men, specifically male workers, as benefiting from the lower pay of women. This ignores the reality that many men and women live together and are worse off as a household because of women's lower pay. It also overlooks the fact that male, and female, bosses who employ workers take home more income than their employees, whatever their gender.

This has dangerous practical conclusions. In a battle for equal pay men can be told that they will have to be paid less in order for women's pay to be raised—this was the idea behind the "feminist incomes policy" pushed by some British feminists in the 1980s. But it has not just remained at a theoretical level. Such ideas were used to give progressive gloss to an attack on male workers' pay in a series of equal pay disputes in the early 2000s in Britain. Public sector workers were seeking pay equality under the "single status" agreement of 1997. Low paid male manual workers were told that in order for women to get more, they would have to accept less. The employer was able to use the notion that men were gaining at women's expense to level down, rather than fighting for the government funding required to level up.

Although some proponents say this approach "does not blame individuals...we receive privileges whether we want to or not...we may not be consciously heterosexist, however, heterosexuals receive privileges in our society that LGBTQ people do not".[379] Its logic is that the individual is the problem. As one theorist sees it, "men's silence is what keeps the system going".[380]

The symbol of the "invisible knapsack", as popularised by feminist writer Peggy McIntosh in 1988, has come to represent how people should "check their privilege".[381] She describes the need for men, or whites, to unpack "an invisible weightless knapsack of special provisions, assurances, tools, maps, guides, codebooks, passports, visas, clothes, compass, emergency gear, and blank checks." This concept is now mainstream in many US educational programmes, anti-racism and women's studies. There is a Knapsack Institute at Colorado University for teachers and other education professionals to be trained in the privilege theory approach in their classes.

Choonara and Prasad show the inherent elitism of this approach:

> We are all seen to be inescapably bound to innate bias and oppressive ideas except the theorists themselves who have been able to reach a degree of enlightened self-awareness...despite superficially appearing to be rooted in material reality, privilege theory actually collapses into idealism... That is why for privilege theory the key focus is education and awareness.[382]

Privilege theory sees oppression as a systemic but unchanging feature of human society with no escape route, no possibility of change, except by the "privileged" being made aware of their "privilege". But the reality is racism does not benefit white working class people (see more in Chapter 2). Objectively anything that divides our side weakens us. For a worker to be racist actually means damaging their own interests whether they believe that to be the case or not. Fighting against racist and all other oppressive ideas is important on principle. It also means the less our side is weakened by divisions of race, gender, religion and so on, the better able it is to fight those at the top of society who are the actual beneficiaries of oppression.

If you follow the logic of privilege theory to its conclusion, like all theories that see personal identity as the critical factor, it entrenches divisions and fragmentation within the working class. But at the same time it presupposes a unity of interest among all white men, for example, which would mean that all women should organise separately. But of course it follows that because women come from many different circumstances then black women, lesbians and working class women, for example, would also need to organise themselves separately, and so on.

Socialists support the right of oppressed groups to organise separately if they choose to—but we also believe we are strongest when united against the real enemy, the ruling class which seeks to divide us.

The cultural turn

The ideas that have become dominant since the decline of the movements of the 1960s and 1970s are marked by a common rejection of Marxism or any other "grand narrative" that attempts to understand the system as a whole and how to change it. Nancy Fraser writes that feminist theorists of the 1970s moved from "locating gender relations on the terrain of political economy" to in the 1990s "joining the larger exodus of intellectuals from Marxism, [when] most feminists took the 'cultural turn.'" This saw gender purely as "an identity or a 'cultural construction.'" And so gender studies is today "largely a branch of cultural studies".[383]

Marxist feminist Teresa Ebert has written that these developments meant a shift away from the materialism of Marx to "reinscribe a Hegelian model that regards society as the effect of the movement of ideas".[384] Marx argued that the approach of German philosopher Georg Hegel was to turn society on its head. He mocked, "Once upon a time a valiant fellow had the idea that men were drowned in water only because they were possessed with the idea of gravity. If they were to knock this notion out of their heads, say by stating it to be a superstition, a religious concept, they would be sublimely proof against any danger from water".[385] Marx gave the light hearted example to make a serious and still revolutionary point—ideas do not create the material world, the material world shapes us and our ideas.

This political trajectory away from class and Marxism was bound up with the rise of postmodernist and post-structuralist ideas, which had an immense impact on academic thinking. It had implications for feminist theorising in particular, as it coincided with many feminists' retreat from activism into the arena of academia. This affected both the form and the content of political writing. One writer described the process as the feminist ideas that came out of the "social ferment" of the 1970s losing their "material anchor".[386] Another writes that the "radical vision" of many of those active in the 1960s and 1970s was "thwarted, not by outright suppression, but rather by more subtle processes inherent in the institutionalisation and intellectualisation of academic knowledge".[387]

Much of the third wave's challenge to the idea that any movement or set of demands could represent all women became entrenched in identity politics and multiple divisions. The different political and theoretical strands that were always part of the WLM—such as Marxist feminism or radical feminism—were eclipsed by politics according to identity. "Africana feminism, Black feminist thought or the women of colour and ethnicity perspective... This shift...was itself misleading, since it lumped together women of colour or ethnicity, ignoring their own diversity of political persuasions".[388]

At the same time there was a drive towards completely deconstructing and rejecting the notion of identity, including even declaring the concept of "women" invalid. This, as some feminists have pointed out, raises the question of whether there is a need for any struggle for gender equality if gender can indeed be completely deconstructed.

The assertion that gender was simply "performed" was the response of theorists such as Judith Butler to the essentialism of the feminists who argued that all women as a sex had a common experience and cause. Butler's book *Gender Trouble*, published in 1990, was part of a broader rejection of the idea that gender is simply a binary biological fact. The anti-essentialist view showed how gender is shaped by our socialisation and argued that we all have tendencies that might be seen as "masculine" or "feminine" regardless of our sex. Such ideas, taken up and developed into what became called queer theory, were a useful challenge to biologically determinist views of gender expressed by some feminists. Butler pointed out that the repudiation of heterosexuals by some radical feminists past and present was itself a form of "essentialism", which queer politics rejected.[389] But the logic for some, although this was not the case for Butler herself, became a complete rejection of any structural basis for inequality, discrimination and oppression rooted in the broader system.

Writing in 2009, nearly two decades later, the mother and daughter feminist writing duo, Woodward and Woodward, wrote that the impact of these ideas was such that in academic circles putting woman in scare quotes had become the orthodoxy. This, they argued, meant that using the word woman "constitutes a new form of radicalism".[390] Butler has written about her own concerns over where her ideas were taken by some theorists.[391] In response to those post-structuralists who might write the lived experience of women out of their theory there is a turn among some feminists to the politics of women's bodies. These do not look to revere the child-bearing capability of women as mothers, which characterised some of the 1980s feminists. Instead they point to how often women's oppression is experienced as precisely a struggle for control of their own bodies. The Woodwards coin this view of women's bodies as political battlegrounds as a "corporeal turn".[392] Naomi Wolf's biography of the vagina in which she refers to the vagina's "emotional sensitivity" being damaged by oppression could be seen as an extreme, and somewhat surreal, example of this turn.[393]

Is there a fourth wave?

The third wave was not really a "wave" in the sense that the WLM was—there was no major upsurge in struggle for women's rights or liberation and no major gains for women that weren't, in reality, fallout from the second wave. The fourth wave is similarly a mere ripple. But the term has been used by a new layer of feminists to differentiate themselves from the superficiality that dominated much of the third wave. Baumgardner has said one differentiation is the mode of communication—the third wave was "zines and songs" but the fourth wave, said to have started around 2010, is all about blogs and twitter.[394] The internet certainly has enabled multiple writers and activists to share ideas and take part in arguments—websites such as the F Word, the Women's Room and Everyday Sexism have played a significant role in the politicisation of a new generation.

But there have also been occasions when anger has spilled out into street protests and demonstrations. The Slutwalks in 2011 are a prime example. A Toronto police officer at a student safety event told women students that they could avoid sexual assault if they didn't "dress like sluts". This led to thousands marching first in Toronto and then in solidarity across the world, including in Britain. It showed the level of rage that lay just beneath the surface against women being blamed for rape and sexual assault and at the general treatment of women in today's society.

There were arguments within the left and among feminists about the demonstrations embracing and attempting to subvert the derogatory term "slut". But it was right that many socialists joined the protests despite misgivingings about attempts to reclaim sexist terms.

There has been a move away from the third wave tendency to laugh off or take up sexist stereotypes as ironic. The Woodwards write, "The assumption that anything called irony is subversive has become so well established it is no longer critical. It has become increasingly hard to differentiate between the subversion of popular culture and the way in which the rhetoric of liberation is adopted to try and sell things to young women".[395] Feminist writer Lynne Segal has warned of the dangers of leaving "the goal of expanding personal liberation to a commodity consumer culture eager to expand its markets, whatever its sometimes 'dissident' or, playful or progressive moments".[396] Chapter 9 will look in more detail at how both these "waves" have dealt with the particular intensification of sexism around the commodification of women's bodies, often referred to as "raunch culture" or the "pornification" of popular culture. These developments have been important drivers behind the activism and writings of a new generation taking up issues of women's oppression.

Social reproduction: the search for a grand narrative?

Recently there has been a resurgence of interest in developing serious theories of oppression and looking for materialist answers to questions that cannot be answered by an emphasis on cultural representations. This has once again involved going back to the second wave's theoretical roots as well as re-examining the role of the family—a task which Marxists have a particular interest in engaging with.

Chapter 4 laid out the Marxist view of the family as the institution that shapes women's oppression in class societies and in capitalism specifically. Current debates about the role the family plays in women's oppression have been framed in terms of "social reproduction theory". This is an attempt to move away from the "dual systems" approach of many socialist feminists, which saw the sphere of the privatised family and the sphere of commodity production and exploitation as separate and parallel. This rooted women's oppression in the interpersonal relationships within individual families and patriarchy rather than looking at the social context and function families fulfill in the system as a whole.

A newly republished book by Lise Vogel, originally written in 1983, is an attempt to provide an alternative to this division as the title, *Marxism and the Oppression of Women: Toward a Unitary Theory*, suggests.[397] Social reproduction can simply mean the reproduction of capitalist structures and ways of organising—the self-perpetuation of the system. But in the context of feminist theory it refers to the connection between the privatised reproduction of labour power in the working class home and the accumulation of capital. Marx defined labour power as a unique commodity, "the aggregate of those mental and physical capabilities existing in a human being, which he exercises whenever he produces a use value of any description". On the one hand you have production of things, commodities, by human waged labour, and on the other you have the reproduction of the "producers"—the workers whose labour power generates surplus value.

Vogel argues that women's oppression in class societies is rooted in their "differential position" in the "generational replacement process". She identifies families as "the historically specific form" in which this usually takes place".[398] She points to three processes that make up the reproduction of labour power:

> First a variety of daily activities restore the energies of direct producers and enable them to return to work. Second, similar activities maintain non-labouring members of subordinate classes—those that are too young, old or sick...or out of the workforce for other reasons. And third, replacement processes renew the labour force by replacing members of the subordinate classes who have died or no longer work.[399]

By laying out the processes in this way she wants to free them from the common assumptions about biological roles in "heterosexual family-contexts".

She argues that although "biological differences constitute the material factor in the differential position of the sexes in a society" sex differences can't be seen in isolation from the social relations in any society. So women's ability to bear and breastfeed children does not inevitably lead to oppression, "the social significance of divisions of labour and of individual differences is constructed in the context of the actual society in which they are embedded".[400] She identifies that even when women work it is this responsibility in the home that hampers them, so while women may also be "direct producers, it is their differential role in the reproduction of labour power that lies at the root of their oppression in class society."

The strengths of the social reproduction approach are that it is seeking a materialist understanding of women's oppression rather than leaving it in the realm of ideas and symbols, and it looks at the family as functioning within the system as a totality. Social reproduction theory sees domestic labour in the home as serving the interests of capital, not those of men.

As Vogel writes, it's easy to see why in the "atmosphere of chronic tension within private family households, women's oppression may appear to be solely an oppression by men, rooted in a transhistorically-antagonistic sex division of labour and embodied in the family." But she is clear, "Nonetheless it is responsibility for the domestic labour necessary to capitalist reproduction—and not the sex-division of labour...that materially underpins the perpetuation of women's oppression".[401] The revival of Vogel's contribution to the debate about the roots of women's oppression is a welcome development as it shifts the arena from idealism and puts privatised reproduction at the centre of the debate. However, some social reproduction theorists reject an understanding of the family being a specific institution in which oppression is located and can sometimes dismiss Engels' *Origin of the Family* as merely historical description, rather than offering a theoretical understanding of where women's oppression originated.

The debates about the important role of domestic work in capitalism have led some feminists to assert that its role in replenishing labour power means that it is actually creating surplus value—that is, that women in the home are being exploited. The argument pursued by Mariarosa Dalla Costa and Selma James, among others, was that because only waged work was seen as valuable or "productive" under capitalism, so housework should be paid. This was a flawed attempt to

Marxism and Women's Liberation

use a Marxist framework to tie work in the home into an understanding of the system as a whole.

But this was to misunderstand Marx's labour theory of value and his understanding of privatised reproduction. Marx's labour theory of value is not about whether the work undertaken is valuable or productive according to how arduous it is or even how vital it might be for human survival. Marx defined exploitation as the process through which workers sell their ability to labour, their labour power, as a commodity to a boss who pays a wage. This wage will be as little as the boss can get away with at any given time, and will depend on a whole number of factors—the balance of class forces, workers' confidence or lack of it, general expectations in society about what constitutes an average standard of living, and so on.

What is being bought and sold is a worker's ability to labour, not the actual work. Because exploitation is a social relationship between worker and boss and between bosses who compete with each other, the crucial question is not even how much value a single worker produces. The concept of "socially necessary labour time" has to be recognised—the average time needed to produce a given commodity in society at any one time.

But just because domestic labour in the home is not directly producing surplus value that does not mean that Marxists don't recognise its contribution to the ability of the ruling class to make profits. This is the accusation put by Italian feminist writer Silvia Federici. She writes that Marx's analysis of capitalism was "hampered" by his view that only commodity production created value and his "blindness to the significance of women's unpaid reproductive work in the process of capitalist accumulation".[402] Yet a Marxist analysis precisely recognises the economic and ideological role the family plays, the role of women in privatised reproduction of labour power or, for the ruling class family, the means to pass on wealth. This view also exposes the damaging and soul destroying impact of the isolation women can experience within the family.

Federici has claimed that housework was "invisible and unvalued" until the struggles of the 1960 and 1970s, which "disclosed the centrality of unpaid domestic labour in capitalist economy, reconfiguring our image of society as an immense circuit of domestic plantations".[403] Yet not only has the nature of women's work in the home been a central question of debate among socialists and feminists for over 100 years, the comparison with plantations and the connotations with slavery obscure the contradictions of work in the family. "Domestic labour" can be experienced as simultaneously a terrible burden and as part of trying to make life better for people you love.

The theme of women's work in the home has been a constant. US socialist Josephine Conger-Kaneko wrote campaigning leaflets in 1913 declaring that women's labour in the home was to ensure "your husband may be an efficient worker...for the employer to pile up immense profits".[404] The German revolutionary Rosa Luxemburg said in a speech on women, "this kind of work is not productive in the sense of the present capitalist economy no matter how enormous an achievement the sacrifices and energy spent, the thousand little efforts add up to." She says, "this sounds brutal and insane" but "corresponds exactly to the brutality and insanity of our present capitalist economy".[405] Marx is making a similar point, Heather Brown argues, when he shows he understands the importance of women's work in the home by putting inverted commas around unproductive when referring to such labour.

Lenin and Trotsky, two key leaders of the Russian Revolution, took the question of work in the home, which was a heavy physical burden in early 20th century Russia, seriously as a material obstacle to women playing their full part in society and in the revolution. Lenin described women's position as a "domestic slave, because petty housework crushes, strangles, stultifies and degrades her, chains her to the kitchen and the nursery, and she wastes her labour on barbarously unproductive, petty, nerve-racking, stultifying and crushing drudgery".[406]

The Bolsheviks in Russia looked to social solutions (see Chapter 12) which rejected the idea that privatised domestic work is inevitable—something that calls for wages for housework don't challenge. The demand for wages for housework is not a solution, nor a way of understanding the problem. In fact it can lead to entrenching the very divisions we are trying to eradicate—that housework is "women's work" and will remain so. The responsibility for the upbringing of society's next generation should be carried by society. There should be a wide ranging welfare state, proper maternity and paternity pay, child benefit and so on—and these are demands by the whole class, for the whole class, because the question of how we care for our children, the elderly, the ill, is not a "woman's question".

In the history of feminist theory and practice there is a tension between seeing gender as the key divide that unites all women and an understanding of the class divisions in society that shape women's lives. Any theory that sees sexism and oppression as somehow operating independently from capitalist society will lead away from an effective struggle for liberation. Oppression is not simply a cultural invention that can be wished away by changing ourselves, nor is it simply about gender roles within individual families.

The recent upsurge in feminist theorising and activity shows the anger that exists about women's oppression among both young and old. For many new activists the idea that women's oppression is inextricably linked to the whole nature of the capitalist system makes sense. The political tradition of Marxism offers a way forward that not only explains the world in which discrimination seems endemic, but can offer a way to change it.

9

Why sexual liberation is important

What is sexual liberation and how can we achieve it in a world that treats women and their bodies like pieces of meat? Everywhere we look women's sexuality is associated with some of the most sexist stereotypes of women and their bodies. The images in everything from mainstream advertising to porn—and sometimes it's difficult to see the difference—show women displayed as passive sex objects in ever more explicit poses, "images that would have once been seen as shocking are no longer even noticed, and have become part of the invisible landscape of television, magazines and the city itself".[407]

The relentless seepage of values, images, behaviour and fashion from the world of selling sex for money into mainstream culture and society has come to shape perceptions of what sexual freedom is. In the 1990s it seemed that sexual liberation for women meant being comfortable in a lap dancing club and in 2011 *Fifty Shades of Grey*, a novel about an abusive relationship, was declared to be sexually liberating women and became an international bestseller.

Sexual violence

Recent years have also seen the extent of sexual violence and abuse in society, both current and historic, being revealed. Figures for rape and sexual violence against women show that although more women may be reporting attacks to the police convictions are still shockingly low. As highlighted in Chapter 1 some police forces have been found to be disproportionately "no criming" rape allegations; in some cases up to a third of complaints are dismissed in this way. The average "no crime" rate for rape was 10.8 percent, compared to 3.4 percent of overall police recorded crime.[408]

This means that statistics about the proportion of reported rapes that result in a conviction underestimate the true extent of the gap. Media coverage also distorts the reality of the issue. Most recently the spotlight has been on institutional abuse of children and young people involving networks of abusers—obscuring the fact that most cases of child abuse happen within families and children know their abuser in 90 percent of reported cases.[409] The vast majority of all rape and assault cases involve someone the woman knows. Government figures from 2013 reported that, "Around 90 percent of victims of the most serious sexual offences in the previous year knew the perpetrator".[410]

Figures from the Office for National Statistics (ONS) published in October 2014 show 22,116 recorded sexual offences in the year to June 2014. This is up by 29 percent on the year before and is the highest number ever recorded. Some of this figure is due to the large number of historic cases reported but John Flatley, head of crime statistics at the ONS, confirmed that "73 percent of the rise is due to current offences".[411] It is difficult to be precise about the exact impact of different factors behind the rise, but the greater the public awareness of the issue the more women will feel they can demand such assaults are taken seriously as crimes.

Prejudice that blames women for rape is still shaping public opinion, and police and political responses. A study by Amnesty International showed that "more than a quarter of respondents believed a woman was totally or partially responsible for being raped if she wore certain types of clothes, while an even higher proportion (30 percent) thought it was her fault if she was drunk, one in 12 thought a woman was to blame if she had numerous sexual partners".[412] Police poster campaigns constantly target women, calling on them to "drink sensibly", "get home safely" or not to leave a friend alone. West Mercia police faced protests in 2015 when they used the slogan "don't let a night full of promises turn into a morning of regret". They said they used the same slogan in posters that depicted men and women drinking. Yet what all these have in common is that they imply that a women is exercising choice about whether she is raped or not and blame her for making wrong choices if she is assaulted.

The only question is whether a woman has consented to sex—not what she was wearing or if she had been drinking, or if she said yes to a coffee. Women are still often put in the position of having to prove they made it clear they did not want sex, despite many attempts to switch the onus of responsibility off the victim. While rape figures rise, rape and sexual violence is trivialised in popular culture. Jokes about rape are even known as "rape-banter". This is not just in lads' mags, but in the mainstream. One comedian, Nick Page, refused to take his spot in a showcase at the Edinburgh Festival in 2012 after listening to a string of three comedians making jokes about rape. After complaints Amazon had to remove from its website the sale of a "rape simulation" game called Rapeplay, which "allowed players to rape any female character in the game and get other male characters to join the attack".[413]

Jimmy Savile's widespread and shocking sexual abuse of children and young people was only brought out into the open after his death. Savile was close to Margaret Thatcher, the royal family and senior police officers. He was regarded as untouchable. His exposure has brought out many other cases of abuse, which are now being investigated. A series of court cases, sometimes against high profile figures, into historic rape and sexual harassment and abuse have taken place. The ruling class establishment was enmeshed in so many of the scandals that the first two chairs of a new committee to investigate the way sexual abuse allegations were handled had to stand down because of their connections with politicians of the era in question. The third chair, New Zealand judge Lowell Goddard, had to be brought in from the other side of the globe to ensure she was not connected to any of the figures involved.

Some commentators have blamed 1960s "permissive" attitudes for the scandal of high profile celebrity abuse cases. But institutional and other forms of child abuse did not start in the 1960s. And sexual liberation is about choice and control—it is the exact opposite of abusive behaviour. In fact, the opening up of repressive ideas about sexuality, and women's sexuality in particular, has over time made it easier to challenge oppressive behaviour. Abusers were taking advantage of the fact that many young women and girls, as well as boys, did not feel able to report the abuse for fear of not being believed—a fear that was well founded.

Marxism and Women's Liberation

The struggle for sexual freedom

Part of the women's liberation struggle of the 1960s and 1970s was centred round questions of sexuality and sexual freedom. This wasn't seen as some frivolous optional extra; it was essential to any vision of liberation. Women reacted against the imposed ignorance faced by their mothers and grandmothers about their bodies and their ability to express their own sexual desires. The availability of contraception and access to safe and legal abortion were important material gains that opened up possibilities for freer heterosexual sexual activity without the anxiety of an unwanted pregnancy. The whole period threw up new choices about how to live and love. The birth of the gay liberation movement was another expression of this new confidence and refusal to stick to old norms.

Every struggle and mass social upheaval shows that when the social mores and repressive architecture of law and tradition and ideology are shaken, so too are the assumptions about and controls over sexuality. This was the case in Russia in 1917, Germany in the 1920s and Spain in 1936. As Engels wrote, "with every great revolutionary movement the question of 'free love' comes in to the foreground".[414] Even during the First and Second World Wars in Britain and the US the ripping up of women's traditional roles for the war effort had an impact on people's sexual activity. Many married women had relationships while their husbands were away. This partly explains official estimates that the number of married women having abortions, still illegal at the time, doubled during the war, as did the divorce rate after the war was over.[415]

Sex before marriage was not a new phenomenon by any means but the impact of war and the numbers of women going out to work expanded the opportunities and desire to have sexual relationships. Because of the lack of access to birth control, especially to the unmarried, the evidence of greater sexual activity is seen vividly in the figures of what were referred to as "illegitimate" births—these had been around 4 to 5 percent of all live births but the rate shot up during both world wars, and by 1945 a third of all births were to unmarried women.[416]

Sexuality is intrinsic to being human. It feels like it is a private and personal part of our lives, and often tied up with issues of personal identity, and it is hard to see how it can be so deeply affected by the society in which we live. Yet, like every other part of what makes us human, our sexuality does not develop in a sealed vacuum.

Today we see the commercialisation of sex and sexuality on an unprecedented scale. In particular this means the commodification of women's bodies—apparently it is not sex that sells, it is sexism. The sexualisation of girls is happening at younger and younger ages, even babies are not immune—you can buy soft red "stiletto high heels" for babies and romper suits with "Daddy's little hottie" across them.[417]

Lap dancing clubs are big business—in Britain the yearly turnover is estimated to be £300 million. They are regularly used as "hospitality" for bankers and business men entertaining clients. To aid this practice 86 percent of lap dancing clubs in London provide "discreet receipts" which don't feature the name of the lap dancing club so visits can be claimed on expenses.[418] In fact so entwined with business have these clubs become that when one applied for a licence in Coventry a "leading business man" argued with the council that if "Coventry has aspirations to be a major business area, then it would have to have a quality adult entertainment area, and that would include a lap dancing club".[419]

The 1960s fight for sexual liberation seems to have enabled even more explicit sexist imagery and a colossal global market in porn. Winning more openness about sex was one of the real gains of the WLM. Women challenged repressive attitudes and taboos towards their sexuality and wanted to define themselves as more than mere appendages of men in every area of life. They wanted the right to express their own desires and be actors in their own lives. Both women and men wanted to be able to talk about sex openly and to break from the crushing morality of the past—a morality which of course the ruling class didn't subscribe to in their own lives.

For too long many women couldn't even name parts of their body and were taught that its natural functions were something dirty or shameful. Declaring the existence and importance of the clitoris was not just about women having better anatomical knowledge; it was a

Marxism and Women's Liberation

political act in a world where doctors reported women would say they had problems "down below". Alongside the prospect of unwanted pregnancies, this disconnect from their own bodies meant that for many women sex was not a source of pleasure, as voices of working class married women collected in the mid-1940s attest: "Husbands are valued in an inverse relation to sexuality: 'he's very good, he doesn't bother me much', 'he's not lustful', 'he wouldn't trouble you at all'."[420]

Going back to those bad old days is no alternative to the open commodification of women's bodies and sexuality today. Capitalism has shown its versatility by absorbing and co-opting the greater openness about sex and women's increased freedoms in order to turn them into profit. Despite the mass struggles and rebellions of the 1960s across the globe the system survived and the gains made have been warped through the prism of a society driven by profit. Marxist Nicola Field charted how newly confident LGBT people coming out of the 1970s movements were exploited by businesses for their previously unrecognised spending power in what became known as the "pink economy".[421]

So women's sexual assertiveness morphs into the infamous "Hello Boys" push-up bra billboard ad and pole dancing classes. This, the most commodified and commercial form of sexuality, became the new measure for freedom and it was deemed prudish and repressed to object.

One website punting its hen party packages is typical of the genre, using the language of liberation to sell its wares: "Pole dancing classes are all about freeing yourself from the restrictions imposed on you in your everyday life and empowering yourself".[422] It has become so mainstream that in 2009 South Devon College in Paignton invited a burlesque and pole dancing company to give a pole dancing exhibition to an audience of 1,000 14 to 19 year olds as part of a Be Healthy Week. One of the company's selling slogans was "Specialists in female empowerment".

Judith Williamson, one of the first feminist academics to identify the intensification of sexual commodification, particularly in advertising, called it "sexism with an alibi".[423] What she meant was that the "new" sexist objectification was sold as ironic harmless pastiche, because as women were supposedly liberated sexist imagery wasn't offensive but fun. US writer Ariel Levy in her 2005 book *Female Chauvinist Pigs*, argued that the new sexism, which she called "raunch culture", had hijacked the language of the liberation movements. She wrote, "This isn't free love. Raunch culture isn't about opening our minds to the possibilities and mysteries of sexuality. It's about endlessly reiterating one particular—endlessly commercial—shorthand for sexiness".[424]

Marx wrote about the effect of capitalism on humans' unique ability to consciously labour on nature. He showed how workers find they cannot survive unless they turn this attribute into a commodity and sell it to a boss. So this wonderful ability that could potentially improve people's lives must, under the social relations of capitalism, become something alien that had to be bought and sold if a worker is going to get the means, the money, to live.[425]

This is the same process that is taking place with human sexuality. Individuals' capacity to take pleasure in their sexuality is curtailed by living in a society that only values what can be bought and sold. This sexual commodification of women's bodies demeans women and men. It assumes that all men are sexually confident and predatory and that they desire and measure women in relation to their bra cup size.

Bodies

The objectification of women's bodies is not a new phenomenon; women have long been judged by their appearance in a way that men are not. Women's bodies are under constant scrutiny, they are criticised if their clothes are too skimpy, or too frumpy, or if they cover up too much by wearing a hijab or other religious dress.

This affects women of all ages. Older women who can't fulfill society's obsession with youth and glamour are stigmatised, even if they try to halt the years and wrinkles with cosmetic surgery. In fact if they do this they are often ridiculed for trying to be something they are not. Women MPs have been harangued in the media for allowing their grey roots to appear. Such is the pressure for high profile women that in the US in 2010 "of the 16 female US senators between the ages of 56 and 74, not one has visible grey hair, nor do 90 percent of the women in the House of Representatives".[426] Women television presenters have been sacked for being too old while older men appear on our television screens every night. Television presenter Kirsty Young has spoken out about the ageism that only affects women in television, saying, "I look forward to the day that Jon Snow hands over to a lady newsreader and she's as old as him".[427]

BBC presenter Miriam O'Reilly, aged 57, won an age discrimination case against the BBC in 2011 after she was sacked from the weekly programme *Countryfile* in favour of a younger woman, while John Craven remained. Craven, at 74, was still presenting the programme in 2015.[428] Historian Mary Beard faces a media onslaught when she appears on television because she doesn't conform to sexist stereotypes. She published the stream of abusive and threatening tweets and messages she received after just one appearance on the BBC's *Question Time* in 2013 to draw attention to the problem.

But it is not just women in the public eye who are affected by the obsession with women's appearance. Women and girls face an onslaught of images of women's bodies that are examined in forensic detail on magazine front pages every week. If a celebrity is snapped with a slight roll of fat over skinny jeans or a bikini it will be blown up with large arrows pointing to the offending area. At the same time other female celebrities appear to waste away and their exposed ribs and gaunt faces are similarly picked over. Interspersed with the gossip and celebrity magazines are numerous others devoted to diets and food, assumed to be the twin obsessions of every woman. No wonder 95 percent of women would change their bodies—the gap between reality and the photoshopped images of what women should aspire to is insurmountable.

In 1975 most models weighed 8 percent less than the average woman; today they weigh 23 percent less. "Compared to the *Playboy* centerfolds and Miss America winners from the 1950s, at least one-quarter of present-day icons meet the weight criteria for anorexia. Meanwhile, the average woman's weight has increased".[429] Some shops in Britain, including Gap and Top Shop, introduced "size zero" into their stores a decade ago. This US size equivalent to a British size four became the aspirational size for women, and has since been followed by the introduction of a "size double zero", equivalent to a British size two. In 2013 two major US stores, J Crew and Abercrombie & Fitch, launched yet another new size, "triple zero", for those women with a 23 inch waist—a body size more akin to a seven year old child than a grown woman.

The pressure for women, and increasingly young men, to fulfill society's current expectations of appearances can lead some to develop eating disorders. There is now a term, diabulimics, for diabetics who miss insulin shots in order to keep their weight down. The complex causes of anorexia and bulimia cannot be simply put down to a desire to be fashionably thin. Nevertheless the context in which women may experience such mental health problems is a world in which food is not a neutral issue of sustenance. Instead it comes loaded with cultural expectations. Women are infantilised by adverts and articles that associate eating chocolate and cream cakes with being "naughty" or are seen as objects of admiration for their discipline when they stick to tasteless crackers and salad.

No wonder the term "regime" is used to describe the process of being plucked, shaved, groomed and made up to meet society's expectations. But now "beauty regimes" go further than ever before and "make over" television shows don't just advise people on clothes and getting fit, they recommend and carry out cosmetic surgery. One feminist author describes the process over recent years as women being worked over by the "beauty-industrial complex".[430] This is an industry worth $160 billion a year.[431]

It's also an industry always looking for new markets. The editor of *Vogue*, Anna Wintour, and a raft of cosmetic companies got together to set up a "beauty school" in Afghanistan's Ministry of Women's Affairs in 2002 after the US invasion. Wintour was quoted as saying that it would "not only help women in Afghanistan to look and feel better but also to give them employment." Crass as this view of Afghan women's priorities when living under Western occupation was, the raw economic motives were revealed when one of the cosmetic business executives involved said it wouldn't be judged a success "if it did not create a demand for American cosmetics before too long".[432]

In 2013 the vast majority, 90.5 percent, of all cosmetic procedures were carried out on women. Research is now showing that some of the psychological issues that might bring women to see cosmetic surgery as a solution are not necessarily solved in the operating theatre—"studies beginning in 2007...found that the suicide rate among women who had received breast implants was twice the suicide rate of the general population".[433]

Breast "augmentation" is the most common operation, but now labioplasty and vaginoplasty are also popular. These are marketed to women who are "embarrassed" by their body parts and offer them a "designer vagina" that looks more like the photoshopped vaginas in modern porn. Those women feeling crushed by expectations of a sexist society are told they will be "empowered" if they allow surgeons to carry out major and sometimes dangerous surgeries to recast them to fit those expectations.

So as if it wasn't galling enough that the language of liberation is being used to try and convince us that strip clubs are liberating and fun, it is also invoked to encourage us to go under the surgeon's knife. One company boasts that their labioplasty procedure "will not only recreate more youthful and aesthetically pleasing external genital structures, but will also restore self-image and self-esteem!" Just so you are clear that it's not medical need that's driving this they say their surgeons "are trained to understand the artistic nature of the procedure; and desired results that women expect".[434]

It's estimated around 30,000 breast implant operations are carried out every year, almost all in private clinics. Of these around 4,500 are reconstructive surgeries done within the NHS for women who have had mastectomies after breast cancer. Some companies cut corners to maximise profits. In 2010 implants made by a French company had to be banned. The PIP implants were found to contain industrial-use silicone, most commonly used as stuffing for sofas, rather than medical-grade fillers. As many as 47,000 women in Britain are thought to have had these implants, which were also found to be more likely to split and leak, in private clinics.

The profits such companies are chasing are immense; government figures show the industry in Britain was worth "£2.3 billion in 2010, and estimated to rise to £3.6 billion by 2015".[435] The average bill for breast "enhancement" in a private clinic in Britain is £3,000 to £5,000. Websites such as Make Yourself Amazing market their invasive procedures with helpful payment plans to spread the cost.

Some feminists have compared the growing trend of cosmetic surgery in the West to the issue of female genital mutilation (FGM).[436] This is a procedure carried out mainly in 29 countries across Africa and the Middle East normally on pre-pubescent girls. It can involve removal of the clitoris or it can mean the removal of the outer labia and sewing up of the vagina's entrance, which then is cut open before sexual intercourse or childbirth. It is right to expose the hypocrisy of politicians and the media who like to portray the West as being free of women's oppression and cosmetic surgery as just another consumer choice. We have to expose the terrible pressures put on women to fit unattainable expectations—just because they can become internalised does not mean they are any less a product of a sexist society.

The practice of FGM also reflects deeply oppressive views of women and their sexuality. But the ruling class in the West uses the issue of FGM to stigmatise Muslims and has a top-down, state enforcement strategy which does not necessarily help the girls and women affected. Instead it can mean that girls may hold back from reporting their concerns to the authorities for fear of what will happen to their parents or families. The experience of Islamophobia can mean that those pressured to have FGM do not trust the authorities and have no one to turn to. When the UN's Rashida Manjoo reported on violence against women in Britain in 2014, she wrote that she was concerned "by legal and policy responses that are often limited to some harmful practices, such as early/forced marriages of young women and girls, or female genital mutilation, while ignoring all the harms emanating due to a sexist culture that exists in the country; and which impacts all women and girls".[437]

The issues of cosmetic surgery and FGM are related but are not equivalent. It belittles the reality of FGM to equate it with adult women getting cosmetic surgery, even though that is as a result of a sexist society's relentless pressure to look good. FGM is often performed with no anaesthetic by people, usually women, with no medical training. In different communities the age varies but in general it is carried out on young girls who may not have a full understanding of what is being done to them and what the long term consequences are for their health and sex life. Contrary to popular prejudice its roots lie in tradition, not religious doctrine. So although it is most prevalent in countries with large Muslim populations, most of the world's Muslims do not practise it and it is also practised by some Christian communities. It reflects the pressure on some communities to ensure their daughters can get the security of marriage that may be the only way of ensuring her future. It is seen as a way of proving to a prospective husband the purity of the bride and a way of preventing her having casual sex outside marriage.

One 2013 Unicef study reported that pressure to conform was cited as the most common reason for FGM. It estimated that more than 125 million girls and women alive today have been cut. Some estimate that as many as 65,000 women in Britain have undergone some form of FGM, which would be the highest number in Europe. However, this is simply projected from census figures of women from countries where FGM is practised and so cannot be relied on as a true picture. For example some families may have moved away precisely to avoid their daughters undergoing the custom.

Western strategies to address FGM have been misplaced at home and abroad. A US religious organisation ran a fundraising campaign to build what was called a "Pleasure hospital" in Bobo Dioulasso in Burkina Faso. Its slogan was "adopt a clitoris". It claimed it was to be a unique hospital where women could come to have some sort of reparative surgery in attempt to reverse their FGM procedure.[438] Yet there are many existing local hospitals that offer such surgery—they are limited only by chronic lack of resources which a more sensitive campaign shaped by local needs could have addressed.

Porn and prostitution

One of the reasons that vaginal cosmetic surgery in the West is on the increase is because of the prevalence of porn. Easily available images can begin to shift what is seen as "normal". Pornography is not a new phenomenon. What has changed is the ease of access to millions of pornographic images and films on the internet. This has transformed the industry. While previously porn was accessed in sex shops and under the counter and strip clubs were in seedy back streets, porn is now part of mainstream cultural consumption. One study in 2004 found that "pornographic sites are visited three times more than Google, Yahoo! and MSN search engines combined".[439]

More than half of nine to 19 year olds who go online at least once a week have seen pornography online, including a quarter who have received pornographic junk mail by email or instant messaging. Of teenagers, 68 percent say they have watched porn online.

This means that the debate among feminists and socialists about pornography is very different than it was during the 1970s when radical feminist Robin Morgan famously argued, "porn is the theory, rape is the practice".[440] Today debates include those who argue for feminist porn, or even simply porn made by women, as well as "organic fair trade porn" in which performers are said to be treated with more respect than in the mainstream version. Feminist writer Caitlin Moran writes of the need for "free range" porn and worries about what present day porn teaches boys. She says she want them to have a chance to see "something that shows sex as something two people do together, rather than a thing that just happens to a women when she has to make the rent".[441]

Rhiannon Lucy Cosslett, co-founder of the feminist online magazine *Vagenda*, is representative of the attitude of many younger feminists to porn today. She told *Guardian* columnist Zoe Williams, "It feels unnatural to be completely against pornography, having grown up in a culture that's so saturated in sex. I remember being a teenager when Christina Aguilera had just done her 'Dirrty' video; that to my mother was pornographic, but that to me was normal." She associates anti-porn with being critical of other people's desires and of women who work in porn.[442]

Arguments about porn and the wider "sex industry" represent a sharp faultline among feminist activists and writers today. Positions range from those who want to criminalise men who buy sex, or those who want to decriminalise prostitution to those who believe it is just like any other job. Cosslett's comments express a view that is gaining prominence—that criticism of porn, lap dancing clubs or prostitution are in effect an attack on the women who do the work. This argues that because women who work as prostitutes, for example, are already stigmatised in society it is wrong to pose prostitution as a problem. Instead it should be seen simply as a job women choose to do and we should restrict ourselves to enabling women to ensure their safety and economic security. Any other view is denounced as being "whorephobic" and denying women who define themselves as "sex workers" their own agency.

This emphasis on choice echoes some of the post-feminist arguments of the 1980s and 1990s. The new generation of feminists would not accept that women's oppression is a thing of the past, but they do argue that in order to prove you are on the side of women you must support any choice they make. This is deeply problematic. It means every woman's choice is assumed to be free without any pressures, whether economic, social or physical. As Caroline Criado-Perez, who suffered horrendous online abuse for suggesting at least one woman should be portrayed on bank notes, wrote, "No feminist denies that women have a right to choose. But some feminists refuse to pretend that right is already being exercised. To refuse to analyse the structures that force women into very particular choices for fear of seeming like we are condemning the women rather than the structures is to give up the fight in the face of wilful misunderstanding".[443]

We have to look beyond seeing sex work as an issue of individual "choice". For socialists it is impossible to analyse prostitution and other aspects of an industry based on turning women's bodies into commodities without taking into account alienation under capitalism and the general position of women in society. Such discussions took place throughout the 1980s.

Porn reproduces the most sexist portrayals of women, as well as the crudest racist stereotypes. For example Asian women will be portrayed as passive and black women as dangerous and voracious. As US feminist writer bell hooks argues, "Within racist and sexist iconography the black female is stereotypically portrayed as experienced and impure".[444] It also reproduces warped stereotypes of men and leads to distorted conceptions about penis size, sexual performance and what women want in sexual relationships. There are men who take part in prostitution, but they are a minority. Estimates are that between 10 and 15 percent of those working in prostitution are men.[445]

As Jane Pritchard wrote, "The scale and nature of prostitution and sex work have been and are conditioned by the poverty, polarisation and dislocation endemic to global capitalism. However, prostitution is not just another dimension of exploitation, but has to be understood in the context of women's oppression".[446]

US restaurant chain Hooters, which has opened a branch in Britain, bases its whole ethos on leering at the breasts of the female staff. The contract for women working in Hooters reveals they have to accept objectification and possibly even harassment while they serve up chicken wings in a job that would not even be termed as part of the "sex industry". It states, "I hereby acknowledge and affirm that the Hooters concept is based on female sex appeal and the work environment is one in which joking and innuendo based on female sex appeal is commonplace... I also expressly acknowledge and affirm I do not find my job duties, uniform requirements or work environment to be intimidating, hostile or unwelcome".[447]

Those who argue that prostitution is a job like any other argue that there is no difference between the alienation involved in the transaction of any worker selling their labour power as a commodity and the selling of sex. But as Mackay writes, "being a builder does not involve making one's body sexually available to one's employers, the same is true of journalists, academics, waiters, etc".[448]

Selling labour power is different to a woman's body, and her capacity to have a sexual relationship, itself becoming the commodity. Sexual exploitation is one of the most extreme expressions of women's oppression and alienation. Sex has become a valuable currency in our society—and for some women it may be their only currency. A look at what leads many women to work in prostitution reveals conditions in which many feel they have very limited options. Those who argue that all women are exercising real choice about how they solve the problems they face are ignoring the material reality of their lives.

A recent overview of studies shows that homelessness and drug addiction are the "two most significant factors which prompt engagement in on-street sex work." In one study in Bristol two thirds of women interviewed described themselves as homeless or living in insecure accommodation; all described themselves as having problems with drug addiction. Other studies point to the numbers of survivors of abuse—in one study two thirds of women who worked in prostitution said they had experienced "physical, sexual or emotional abuse during childhood".[449] Estimates also indicate that around 70 percent of women working in prostitution have been in care at some point as children.

This is confirmed by a number of the cases in recent years in Rochdale, Rotherham and elsewhere involving child sex exploitation. These showed that abusers targeted vulnerable young people in care and groomed and coerced them into prostitution. Some of the young women had been removed from their family homes after surviving abuse but were not given the support they needed.[450] People in authority repeatedly dismissed young working class women as "choosing" to live chaotic lives. Instead they should have recognised that their short lives had been so bereft of genuine love and affection they accepted the attentions of predatory men as real relationships.

To simply talk about individual choice means ignoring the major forces that shape everyone's lives. Most people have very limited control over where they live or what job they do. Attacking the nuclear industry, for instance, does not mean you are criticising the people who work within it, but it is possible to assert that in a socialist society the nuclear power industry and its connection to the creation of nuclear weapons should not exist.

The exchange of money can distort any ordinary relationship between individuals. Some grandparents' generous financial help with grandchildren may give them unwelcome clout as to how they are brought up. A man is encouraged to believe that if he has "forked out" for dinner then he can make an assumption that the woman will "give" something in return. Money pollutes and distorts everything it touches, every part of human lives. But the selling of sex, which is mainly the sale of women's bodies, involves the alienation and distortion of an aspect of our humanity that not only can be the source of great pleasure but can also inform some of our most important relationships.

It's right that women working in the sex industry should have every opportunity to get organised and to keep themselves safe. Women who work on the street are most at risk of experiencing violence—it is estimated that they are 60 to 100 times more likely to be murdered than women who do not work as prostitutes.[451] All such women should have the right to join trade unions and demand to be treated with respect, and not be criminalised or harassed by the police. But we should be under no illusions that trade union membership, which is currently very minimal, will transform their situation. Women are vulnerable not only to attack by the men who buy sex, and the pimps who profit from them, but also by the state. Women who have been trafficked risk being deported if discovered by the authorities, and we have seen that even children who have been groomed by sexual predators cannot expect protection from the police.

The revulsion many feel about the sexist and dehumanising impact of mass produced porn has led some to argue that porn and prostitution are by definition violence against women and a specific "instrument of oppression".[452] It was this view that led two high profile feminists, Andrea Dworkin and Catharine MacKinnon, to work alongside right wing organisations in the US in 1983 to argue in a controversial legal case that porn was a civil rights violation. Their proposals were eventually quashed as being unconstitutional and their action, and the allies they made, generated much criticism among the majority of feminists, including other anti-porn campaigners.[453] Although, contrary to common understanding of their action, they did not call for state censorship of porn, nevertheless their attempt to use state intervention to combat porn was a dangerous precedent. More recently radical feminist Julie Bindel has allied with right wing groups around a campaign to ban lap dancing clubs.[454] Invoking the powers of the state in this way is a mistake. It ignores the fact that it is the state, in the form of the police and courts, that is responsible for the everyday harassment and punishment of the very women it is being asked to help.

Pornography is one symptom of women's oppression, not its root cause. Women were oppressed long before the mass production of even the earliest pornographic photographs and printed materials. Censorship of pornographic materials is not a solution, if it were even possible today. It can appear tempting to call for banning of specific forms of, for example, pornography that involves violence. But once you give the police, civil servants, judges or any part of the state the power to police our sexuality they will use those powers to ban literature and images they find "depraved". That can mean LGBT literature or perhaps explicit advice on safe sex will be targeted. Pornography that features child abuse is already covered by other legislation.

The way laws against porn can be used was seen when "in 1984 the Obscene Publications Act (1959) was used to raid the Gay's the Word bookshop and seize hundreds of books as part of the moral backlash under Margaret Thatcher's Conservative government".[455] Before that Radclyffe Hall's story of lesbian love, *The Well of Loneliness*, was banned for years even though, as one anti-censorship feminist writer points out, "the nearest lovers in that book get to an explicit act is the deathless sentence, 'and that night they were not divided'."[456] There is a history of laws brought in supposedly as progressive legislation only to be used against those who challenge the state. The anti-stalking law has been used against environmental campaigners and the Public Order Act, originally posed as legislation to stop fascists marching, was regularly used against anti-capitalist and other protests. The state is not a neutral benevolent force and should not be encouraged to gain even more powers over any part of our lives, public or private.

Censorship and state control has always been about controlling access for the working class. The 1960 trial over the publication of D H Lawrence's novel, *Lady Chatterley's Lover*, was not about banning the book, which had long been in print in hardback. It was about whether it could be published in paperback, so that for the first time "servants and wives" might be able to buy it. Similarly archaeologists excavating the famous Roman site at Pompeii in southern Italy from the 18th century onwards confiscated the many sexually explicit wall paintings and statues, which had been popular at the time when the volcano lava enveloped the town. They locked them in a secret collection that was closed to women and children. In 1816 a very expensive illustrated French catalogue of the exhibits was published. Many copies were confiscated or destroyed by the French authorities but it became a collectors' item for those who could afford it.[457] The British Museum also had such a room, the Secretum, which originated as a place to keep materials and objects judged by Victorian curators as too sexually explicit for the public eye, although selected gentlemen could apply for entry.

There is no contradiction between opposing porn and demanding more freedom of sexual expression. In fact the dominance of porn has a very repressive influence on sexual expression that doesn't fit its narrow formulaic representations of sex. A counter to the dominance of porn is to enable more openness about sexuality and human relationships in all their diversity. This is especially necessary in schools where sympathetic, explicit and wide ranging discussion of all aspects of sex is too often completely missing. As a socialist pamphlet written by revolutionary Clara Zetkin in 1905 put it, "Tell your children the truth about sexual matters!"[458]

Sex education

While the media regularly features prurient shock stories on the rampaging sex life of teenagers and the wide use of porn, very little is said about the problems young people face learning about sex in a society where sex is everywhere but is also deeply repressed. Sex education is currently only compulsory in local authority maintained secondary schools, though in February 2015 a government select committee proposed that sex education should be made compulsory in all schools. Young people are being let down by being denied the opportunity to learn about sex and all its facets in a situation of empathy and openness, free from moralism and the pervasive view of sex as something to buy, sell or bargain with.

In the US sex education was dominated by programmes promoting abstinence—funding for such programmes amounted to $1 billion dollars between 1996 and 2006.[459] As the author of *The*

Lolita Effect wrote, "girls can't understand or explore the options they might have in sexual situations if their desires are always framed as dangerous and harmful (while they're simultaneously being encouraged to attract boys' sexual attention)".[460] Women are taught how they should contain men's desire but not how to cultivate their own. In the US the teenage pregnancy rate was at its highest when abstinence-only sex education was at its peak. Today it has reached historic lows for many reasons, including better comprehensive sex education in more schools and greater use of contraception.[461] But researchers have concluded that "programmes that exclusively promote abstinence outside of marriage have been proven ineffective at stopping or even delaying sex".

Sex education has long been a political battleground, in particular around LGBT sexuality. The notorious clause 28 (see Chapter 4) passed in Britain in 1988 was all about enforcing narrow and reactionary ruling class ideology about sex, gender and the family on working class school students. At the same time the Tories also removed "teaching relating to contraception, abortion, HIV and AIDS from the compulsory science curriculum".[462]

Modern right wing panic about young people being attracted to homosexuality if they learned it wasn't "deviant" recalls the discussion in 1921 over a proposal to criminalise lesbianism. The director of public prosecutions, Lord Descart argued against making sexual acts between women an offence of gross indecency saying, "You are going to tell the whole world that there is such an offence, to bring to the notice of women who have never heard of it, never thought of it, never dreamt it. I think that is a very great mischief".[463]

The reality is that even as late as the Second World War women had thought of it, had dreamt about it but some didn't have a name for it or didn't know others felt the same. One woman from upstate New York reported that during the war when she "went off harvesting with the land army she saw two women kissing. On being told they were lesbians, she realised, 'for the first time I had a name for myself'".[464] Historically there have been regular moral panics about the lives of the "lower orders". The sexual activity of the working classes was something to be controlled. Attitudes to sexuality have been tied since the rise of class society and the family to specific gender roles and those who don't conform have faced isolation, discrimination and even prosecution.

The gay liberation movement was born out of resistance to police repression and the criminalisation of anyone challenging the dominant gender or sexual roles.[465] At the time of the Stonewall riot in 1969 after a police raid on a working class gay bar in New York, Laura Miles writes that, "Wearing less than three items of gender-appropriate attire meant a person could be subject to arrest. Such codes were used to harass gender variant people such as crossdressers and drag queens and were one of the causes of the pent-up frustrations and anger that triggered the watershed Stonewall rebellion and other acts of resistance in the 1960s".[466]

Today, although huge strides have been made by campaigners, more than half of LGBT school students have experienced direct bullying in and outside school.[467] Girls are encouraged to measure themselves by their sex appeal from an earlier and earlier age. Although the old double standards still apply—boys who are sexually active prove they are real men, but young women are under pressure to be sexually pure at the same time as sexually available and sexually active young women can still find themselves denounced as "sluts".

Is sexual freedom bad for women?

Some feminists have even argued that what we are seeing today shows that sexual freedom has not helped women, that in the 1960s men were simply able to have more sex with less responsibility and women were used. Italian feminist Silvia Federici writes, "Sex is work for us, it is a duty. The duty to please is so built into our sexuality that we have learned to get pleasure out of giving pleasure, out of getting men aroused and excited".[468] Germaine Greer blames her "promiscuous" past for her inability to have children and advocates chastity. More recently feminist anti-porn campaigner Julia Long makes a direct link between the opening up of the 1960s and the porn industry, which she claims "was characterised by a profoundly male supremacist counter-culture which lionised misogynist writers, such as Norman

Mailer and William Burroughs... In this way the sexual revolution and its masculinist heroes framed male sexual use of women as revolutionary, opening up the gateway for the expansion of pornography in the 1970s".[469]

Feminists Barbara Ehrenreich and Deirdre English have challenged these views. They remember "the sexism was there but women were actually having more sexual experience of different kinds and enjoying it. Women were experiencing more sex that was not for procreation and claiming the right to it as well as paying a lower social and emotional cost".[470] The argument that sexual freedom only benefits men plays into longstanding reactionary myths, which so many activists in the 1960s were keen to shatter, that women do not actually enjoy sex, have no desires of their own and only have sex to please men. Sheila Rowbotham writes of this argument being raised as far back as the 1890s when women were struggling to access usable effective birth control and safe abortion.[471] Some reformers felt they needed to talk in terms of the need for "voluntary motherhood" instead of "free love" as they were worried about losing their respectability.

Other women activists have been more open about contraception being vital to enable women to enjoy sex more freely.[472] In response to those claiming that calls for contraception were simply to please men, one free love advocate of the 19th century, Amy Linnett, insisted, "The desire for sexual relations was mutual and not confined to men...contraceptives meant that a woman could 'please herself' sexually." She pointed to one reason others were suggesting otherwise—"perhaps the fact that I am not yet 30 instead of 70 has something to do with the feelings in this matter." Rowbotham points out that though "the idea of a woman's right to experience pleasure had been part of 19th century radicalism, it was still an explosive desire for a woman herself to articulate in the 1890s".[473]

Today when it seems like the price for sexual freedom is inexorably greater objectification the right has used the opportunity to play on people's fears. Tory prime minister David Cameron campaigned over the sexualisation of children, but his agenda is not progressive. He and fellow Tories wanted to clamp down on sexual freedoms we have won; he is looking for votes from those who want to deny abortion rights and see women as demure housewives and walking incubators. Similarly in the US right wing authors such as Carol Platt Liebau wail about how the "sex obsessed culture damages girls" but they see sex and not sexism as the main problem.[474]

Morality and class

The ruling class has long feared and demonised the sexuality of the masses and working class and black women have faced particular constraints. Women are told they are by nature pure and must be morally responsible to maintain that purity. Those with feelings of sexual desire or who are sexually active have been denounced as "loose" and depraved. One 1946 *British Medical Journal* article on "The Unstable Adolescent Girl" showed all the fears and prejudices of the establishment "under the guise of 'objective social research'... This urged attention to what it defined as a serious social problem...that of the 'good time girl', 'unamenable to discipline and control'." It is notable that this report even saw the maturing of young women's bodies as a threat—"These unstable girls often showed 'precocious physical development, especially in the breast and hips'."[475]

A conference on "Lax Conduct among Girls" run by the archbishop of Canterbury in 1933 discussed whether "the availability of contraceptives should be seen as a problem or a solution".[476] The separation of procreation from sex was both feared and welcomed; this goes to the heart of the contradictory ideology over working class women's sexuality and procreation. Attitudes to birth control have often been bound up with reactionary and eugenicist desires to control the "over breeding" of the poor.

Imperialist and Liberal politician Lord Rosebery expressed ruling class worries at the poor over-breeding at the start of the 20th century saying, "in the rookeries and slums which still survive, an imperial race cannot be reared".[477] But it wasn't just reactionary lords who held such views. Birth control campaigners such as Marie Stopes and Margaret Sanger echoed such views about the poor.[478] There was concern that only the educated middle class would make use of birth control while the poor would continue to breed.

Stopes complained that "society allows the diseased, the racially negligent, the thriftless, the careless, the feeble minded, the very lowest and worst members of the community, to produce innumerable tens of thousands of stunted warped and inferior infants".[479] But others saw access to birth control as part of a wider struggle for a more egalitarian society—such as Bolshevik Alexandra Kollontai in Russia and Stella Browne in Britain, who said, "birth control is women's crucial effort at self-determination" but also said it connected to "workers' control".[480]

Now birth control is readily available in Britain and, although still overly restricted, legal abortion is accessible. Even this limited access to abortion was fought by sections of the ruling class and is regularly targeted today with moral panics and scare stories that try to undermine it.

Separating sex from procreation is a precondition for sexual liberation. Because women's oppression is shaped by their role in the family as a mother and carer, controlling our fertility is a fundamental principle. But even for women who can access contraception and safe abortion, sexual liberation seems as far away as ever. Sexual freedom is not a luxury that can wait till we change the world. Society objectifies women's bodies but capitalism's distorting of sex affects women and men. The ability of women and men, LGBT or straight, to express our sexuality in any way we choose without repression, without fear is tied up with how the system works. Every day we are bombarded with images and ideological propaganda as to what sort of relationships we should aspire to. Women are still told we need to seek out and attract a stable mate, who will be a good father and offer security. Those who do not conform, who choose to be single, not have children or live outside accepted family and personal relationships are patronised, pitied or worse. It is hard to imagine how we might live in a world where our personal lives were not constricted by society's expectations.

Engels wrote that what is written about sexual relations in a socialist society is "limited for the most part to what will disappear. But what will there be new?" What follows is a famous passage that shows such an understanding of the impact of inequality and oppression on women that it can reach across the ages from the Victorian era to a world of Hooters bars and internet porn. But it's also a passage infused with a spirit of optimism about the possibilities of the future and how changing the world can transform us and even our most intimate relationships. On the question of what will be new he writes:

> That will be answered when a new generation has grown up: a generation of men who never in their lives have known what it is to buy a woman's surrender with money or any other social instrument of power; a generation of women who have never known what it is to give themselves to a man from any other considerations than real love, or to refuse to give themselves to their lover from fear of the economic consequences.
>
> When these people are in the world, they will care precious little what anybody today thinks they ought to do; they will make their own practice and their corresponding public opinion about the practice of each individual—and that will be the end of it.[481]

10

Trading places:
can we win under capitalism?

Capitalism is driven by the search for profit. Everything else, including women's oppression, is in some way a by-product of this central dynamic. So alternative ways of reproducing the current and next generation of workers—bringing up and looking after children—and caring for other dependents could technically be envisaged under capitalism. Lise Vogel has pointed out some alternatives: "Labour camps or dormitory facilities can also be used to maintain workers, and the workforce can be replenished through immigration or enslavement as well as by generational replacement of existing workers".[482]

We have seen examples of the extremes of workers being used as dispensable units of labour power whether during slavery in the American South, in Europe under the Nazis and in apartheid South Africa. Vogel was not suggesting labour camps and dorms are a more pleasant alternative to nuclear families but simply that the form that the reproduction of labour power takes in modern capitalism is not the only one. Such alternatives are not just part of history but are seen today across the world. In fact for the millions of migrant workers who travel across the globe, often in dangerous circumstances, to find work to survive, family life is a luxury they can't afford.

This is true for the millions of workers in "special enterprise zones"—one of neoliberalism's innovations allowing businesses to avoid the laws and taxes of the host countries—whether in China, South East Asia or in various parts of Africa and the Middle East. Here workers live, sleep and eat in camps on company property sometimes in horrendous conditions. At least one million workers live in squalid, overcrowded labour camps in the Gulf state of Qatar, building the infrastructure for the 2022 football World Cup. When a major earthquake hit Nepal in early 2015, killing over 8,000 people, Nepalese migrant workers on construction sites in Qatar were barred from taking leave to return home for the funerals of family members who had been killed.

Yet the family and women's role in it has not been superseded even in these examples of some of the most repressive and brutal conditions of capitalism. Many migrants are only working in those conditions so that they can send money home to families they rarely see. In turn women are largely responsible for the families left behind. This was true of the miners in the Marikana mine in South Africa, where police shot and killed 34 strikers during a dispute in August 2012. Many miners were forced to live far from their families as it was the only way to earn enough money to support them.

So even when the needs of capitalism splits families across and within continents, the family is still, albeit with changes, the dominant form of social organisation. All aspects of society are structured around the assumption that people will bring up children in some form of family and that women will be mainly responsible for that work. In Britain this includes everything from the size and forms of housing to the welfare system and schooling.

The family is not technically essential to capitalism but, as Marx and Engels put it in the *Communist Manifesto*, "family relations are entirely subordinated to property relations". The family serves such a useful role in the system that there is no pressure, except in extraordinary circumstances, to look for alternatives. As explored in Chapter 4, alternatives to the family are hugely costly to the system. As capitalism lurches from crisis to ever deeper crisis the prospect of massive resources being pumped into services such as free childcare in order for women to be able to play an equal role in society is remote indeed.

Socialisation of domestic labour in wartime

The ruling class's attachment to the family is purely pragmatic, and its resilience as an institution stems not only from what it delivers to the system but also because for many people it can offer a place of

Marxism and Women's Liberation

solace and love. The ruling class has made attempts to socialise women's domestic labour when it needed to. This was seen in Britain and the US during the First and Second World Wars.

Propaganda was unceremoniously switched to calls for women to fulfil their patriotic duty and go out to work, even if that meant leaving their children. This wasn't a smooth process; some in the ruling class were more worried about the impact of women's role in society being changed than by the need for more war workers. Civil servants and politicians raised ideological objections about encouraging women to neglect their domestic duties and cited legal obstacles to doing certain jobs and long hours because they went against women's natural roles and attributes. But over the course of the war these obstacles were systematically challenged and many overturned out of sheer necessity.

The mobilisation of women war workers during the First World War forced the state to face up to what to do about the domestic responsibilities women carried. The Sunderland Suffrage Society reported on a strike by carriage cleaners on the Great Western Railway against their long hours. Many of the workers were widows and had sole responsibility for their homes. One commented, "It's not fair to argue that a woman cannot do as much work as a man from the fact that she cannot do twice as much".[483] For the first time caring for children, cooking and shopping for a family, all of which had been previously seen as belonging solely to the private domestic world of the home, were discussed by civil servants and were the subject of government regulation.

The purpose of these material alternatives to women's individual role in the family was not to liberate women, but to win a war and make the system stable and efficient all the better to make profits in future. But nevertheless the experience of having greater financial independence and being freed from responsibility for every aspect of the home was a liberating one for many. Even before the First World War many women had worked in industry—in coalmines, cotton mills and potteries. But the role that women played during that war as workers meant that their lives and expectations would never be quite the same again. Up to two million women moved into previously male-only industrial jobs. They replaced the ever-greater numbers of men being sent to fight in the bloody trenches of the Somme and Passchendaele. The work women did was dirty, sometimes dangerous and usually on a lower wage than the male workers had received. In six months in 1916 as many as 41 munitions workers died from TNT poisoning. A doctor gave evidence at the inquest of one, a 16 year old girl, and tried to play down the problem saying "only a small class were susceptible to TNT poisoning, and this was the class of those under 18".[484] Before the war some 1.7 million women were domestic servants, more than worked in any other occupation. For these women war work was a revelation. Even the low wages were higher than they had ever earned before and they had more independence than live-in servants ever experienced.[485]

The state had to provide services to make the 24-hour shifts in munitions factories possible, including canteens and nurseries. The Arsenal factory had a workplace nursery and mothers who worked the night shift got an extra childcare allowance. By 1917 there were more than 100 day-nurseries across the country. In west London munitions factories were built on the fields of the Royal Agricultural Show Ground at Park Royal. The biggest employed 7,000 workers, most of them women. A nursery was opened in February 1917, "designed to provide a home for the children of munitions workers living in Willesden, whilst their parents are busy helping to win the war. It has been furnished by the Ministry of Munitions and the Willesden Urban District Council, and is open every day and night, including Saturdays and Sundays".[486] Such a level of state provision was unknown before. In a reflection of the government's priorities, it is significant that this was only provided to women working in the armaments industry.

The sections of the ruling class who worried about the impact of pulling unprecedented numbers of women into the workforce and into jobs previously only done by men had their worst fears fulfilled. Every aspect of life was affected. Clothes changed to accommodate manual work—trousers and shorter skirts appeared. Women even wore shorts and showed their knees in the workplace-based women's football teams that sprouted up across the country. The games became

Marxism and Women's Liberation

so popular that by the end of the war they could attract audiences of tens of thousands.

No metal could be worn in the munitions factories so this meant no corsets. Long hair could get caught in machines so women started wearing it short. Already by 1917 such women were denounced in the press as "flaunting flappers". So although the ruling class needed them, they didn't like the new found confidence this was giving working class women. Much was written about the risk to public morality of the new freedoms women were relishing. The *Daily Mail* in 1915 pointed to what they coined the "Dining Out Girls"—working women in London who had the confidence and the money to eat out alone: "Formerly she would never have had her evening meal in town unless in the company of a man friend".[487] The government appointed welfare inspectors—the forerunners of the first women police officers—to try to control the morality of women workers. These mainly middle class women patrolled parks and alleys chasing away couples trying to find some privacy. But they faced resistance and resentment.

Assumptions about women's limitations were shattered. Now bosses pushed women to the limits of endurance in the name of the war. Protective legislation was abolished. The same ruling class that had stubbornly refused women the right to vote now lauded women's ability to serve the war effort. As soon as the war ended the government wanted to put the clocks back. It did give a limited number of women the vote (see Chapter 6) but, backed by much of the trade union leadership, it forced hundreds of thousands of women out of their jobs. By the autumn of 1919, 750,000 fewer women were employed in industry. Accommodation for single women, canteens and day nurseries were quickly shut down.

In deals that had been agreed with trade unions women's employment had been only "for the duration". Some fought hard to stay employed. The clock could not be turned back entirely. Women had found new independence. They had shown themselves and the rest of society that they could do jobs that before the war would have been unthinkable. They had seen that the government could organise state provision for them and their children when it needed to. Above all they had experienced in greater numbers than ever before being part of the collective force of the working class. In fact many jobs traditionally done by women became unionised after women's experience of war work. Barbara Drake's major study of women and trade unions in 1920 recognised this was one of the most important consequences of the war. She wrote that most of all what women workers learned, "which they did not intend to forget" was "the power of organisation and...the value of their labour".[488]

This experience was only eclipsed by the mass mobilisation of women during the Second World War when 75 percent of new workers were married women. Eventually 3 million married women and widows were employed during that war; this was almost double pre-war figures. Once again women were told that the war effort not their family was the priority and once again at the end of the war women did not want to lose their new found independence. One US study interviewed women as they took up jobs at the start of the war and found that 90 percent said they wanted to give the jobs up when the war was over; when the war ended up to 85 percent declared they wanted to stay in work.[489]

The number of nurseries mushroomed from a handful before the war to a peak in 1943 of around 1,450 local authority day nurseries with places for up to 71,806 children.[490] Women workers were assumed to be the worst absentees. It was some time before the government acknowledged that many women had to take time off to travel long distances to shops and queue for scarce rationed goods. Some factories introduced a "shopping hour" so that women could officially leave early to do essential shopping. Others employed professional "shoppers" for the women or obtained passes for their employees to go to the front of the queues at selected shops.

In 1944, 170 million meals were eaten outside the home each week both in factory canteens and in the 2,000 government-funded "British Restaurants", which served 600,000 cheap meals a day. In schools increasing numbers of children received school dinners and free milk.

Just as in 1918 the same process of pushing women out of the workforce took place in 1945 when the war finished. In both wars women were told they were there just "for the duration" in what were "men's jobs". In some cases, for example on the railways, many jobs women did were named after the man who did it before going to fight. Everything was done to ensure women never felt they were entitled to the job.

But it wasn't long before the post-war boom saw such an expansion of the system that the need for women's labour power became greater than ever before. This led to a limited level of socialisation of women's domestic role, helped by the innovations delivered by new technology that lightened the burden in the home.

From the post-war boom through to today the ruling class has wanted only to make changes sufficient to allow women to generate surplus value in the system without the ruling class having to provide an alternative to the family. Full equality will not be delivered while this, the material basis for women's oppression, remains. The deep and long term crises of capitalism are actually increasing the domestic burden on working class and poor women. This is true in Britain and the rest of the West but it is even more glaring globally. So for example in Kenya, poverty and oppression means that women's burden is such that they "can burn up to 85 percent of their daily calorie intake just fetching water".[491]

Is this an argument that change is not possible under capitalism or that reforms cannot be won? Absolutely not. In fact history has shown that struggles for reforms can deliver real material changes that can save lives, as in the case of the legalisation of abortion rights.

The limits of reformism

The aim of winning reforms through parliament motivated some feminists to look to the Labour Party as a vehicle for change. Many moved into Labour in the 1980s and fought for it to take up the issues of women's rights. These activists were also committed to a fight for better standards of living for the working class as a whole. Yet time and time again the Labour leadership has been found wanting, even though many of its members and voters are committed class fighters. What history shows is that the ruling class did not willingly hand over any of the gains that women have won in the last century. Every new right, every pay rise, every legal protection achieved by women or the working class as a whole has taken a battle.

Such victories are important, but they are limited, and they can be taken away when the balance of class forces shifts in favour of the ruling class. So the five years of David Cameron's Tory coalition government from 2010 saw a dramatic fall in living standards of millions of working class people. Pay and pension rights won in past struggles were ripped away. The slashing back of much of the welfare state, again won by previous generations, has resulted in an increase in the burden carried by working class women in particular.

The 1967 Abortion Act has faced attack since its very inception and was never extended to Northern Ireland. Cameron's government gave new confidence to anti-abortionists to try to attack the rights it gave women, so far without success. But the bigots are constantly on the look out for opportunities to challenge women's right to access abortion, even if they don't have the confidence to confront it with open opposition to legality.

In fact they are learning that they have to couch their attacks using the language of women's rights. So when anti-abortionists try to insist on extra grilling—or "counselling"—of women who ask for abortion they claim it will "empower" women to make the right choices. This is a sign of their weakness but it also means they are not giving up and we have to be vigilant over every private member's bill or amendment that anti-abortionists try to push through under the radar. A generation of women has grown up with abortion rights and, despite their limitations both in law and in practice depending on local provision, we have to be ready to fight to defend and extend them.[492]

When it comes to wider legislation on equality, new laws, although welcome, do not guarantee change. The equal pay act has been in place since 1970 (although bosses were given five years to implement it) but 45 years on it has not resulted in equal pay. Similarly race discrimination is outlawed but is still endemic as black and Asian people are disproportionately unemployed, stopped and searched by police, imprisoned and so on.

So we have to fight each and every day for every improvement we can, however small. Revolutionaries never declare "wait till the revolution" and everything will be alright. The fight for reforms even within the system is important, both for what it achieves and for the struggles it generates. These can open up wider questions about the nature of society and can undermine the sense that the system is the way it is because it's the natural order of things and must be accepted.

Every reform, every victory is important, but there is a danger if we only focus on what can be won within the confines of the system. The logic can end up leading to demands that simply mean a different distribution of the limited crumbs working class people receive from the table of the rich and powerful. So a political strategy for women's equality that doesn't seek to ultimately challenge the power of the state or ruling class can end up posing the way forward as taking from ordinary men. This position has been expressed by some feminist theorists from the second wave through to today.

So for example in a roundup of changes women need around parenting and the home feminist authors Catherine Redfern and Kristin Aune write that, as well as co-operation between individuals and workplaces and the state, "men need to be willing to drop some hours of paid work to take up care for their families".[493] But to regard "paid work" as some sort of male perk that they should relinquish shows little regard for the reality of working class families' struggle to survive. Working hours in Britain are some of the longest in Europe. For many workers long shifts are the only way to earn enough to live on and to work fewer hours would be the dream of many, if it didn't mean a drop in precious income.

This echoes the feminist writers examined in Chapter 8, who said men were "not facing up to the fact that they would have to give up power and privilege, and even be inconvenienced, if women were to move towards liberation".[494] For these women the loss of tens of thousands of jobs in the 1980s in mining, on the docks, in the printing industry, to name but a few, was written up as a feminist achievement because these were mainly jobs done by men.[495]

Such solutions suggest that we should be content with improving the lives of one section of the working class at the expense of another. The majority of men do not have "power and privilege". If we say that working class men have to pay the price for greater gender equality then we are swallowing the lies of the ruling class that say there is only so much to go around. It is to target the wrong enemy and limit our potential for success. Instead we should be looking to wrench reforms from the clutches of the rich and powerful, who maintain their dominance in part by keeping us divided. Working class men have everything to gain from any part of the working class improving their conditions and extracting more from those at the top.

This is where the whole question of looking to gender equality within capitalism hits a rock, because gender equality leaves women fighting to be equal to men in a society where not all men are equal. So which men are we fighting to be equal to—Richard Branson or a hospital porter? This doesn't mean that gender equality is not a worthy goal, whether class society is abolished or not. Women should be in equal numbers across society, whether it's high court judges, MPs, managing directors or cleaners and nurses.

Those in positions of power will use any means to resist change. They sometimes come up with the most desperate assertions in their desire to find an explanation, other than systemic oppression, to explain women's limited numbers in powerful positions. For example a takeover battle between mining firms Anglo American and Xstrata led to former Anglo boss, Graham Boustred, expressing all his bile about a woman, Cynthia Carroll, being in charge of the company. He attacked her performance, saying, "Do you know why it's so difficult to find a female CEO? It's because most women are sexually frustrated. Men are not because they can fall back on call girls, go to erectile dysfunction clinics. If you have a CEO who's sexually frustrated, she can't act properly".[496]

Boustred cannot be dismissed as just a chauvinistic hangover from an earlier time. The ruling class is not interested in equality; its existence depends precisely on the enforced inequality of class society.

Different initiatives have been launched internationally to try to make the institutions at the top of society reflect the fact that women are 50 percent of the population. The Norwegian government made it compulsory for listed companies to have at least 40 percent women on their boards in 2003. They were given five years to comply. Now women make up 42 percent of the boards of these companies and of those many are non-executive directors and not part of the day to day running of the companies. In a defence of the impact of the policy Norwegian academic Agnes Bolso perhaps does not help the perception that it is limited when she says, "Greater female representation seems to make meetings a little more pleasant, the preparation material is tidier and more comprehensive, and the processes more formal".[497]

Successive British governments have balked at making any legal requirements on gender balance for businesses. Instead they have appealed to bosses' desire to maximise profits by pointing to all the expertise they are missing out on by ignoring half the talent pool. In Britain in March 2015 new legislation made the publication of gender pay audits compulsory for companies that employ more than 250 people. This came after years of businesses saying they would abide by a voluntary code that only a minority adhered to. In an attempt to address the lack of women on the boards of FTSE-100 companies a group of British women executives formed the 30% Club in 2010. Its goal was to have 30 percent women on such boards by the end 2015.[498]

It would be a great advance if we had a world where women were found in every role and position right across society. But not because women are in some way intrinsically better, nicer, more competent or more progressive than men. If there were more women at the top of capitalist society would it mean that we would be under less threat from the dangers of climate change, world poverty or war? No, such gender equality is desirable simply because it would reflect a less sexist society.

But even if such a society was possible who could be satisfied with a world that looked the same as today but with more Theresa Mays, Angela Merkels and Sheryl Sandbergs sharing in the exploitation of the majority of women and men? The battle we face is for something more fundamental, it is for liberation. Women's liberation cannot be won while capitalism remains; it is incompatible with the exploitation, imperialist war and grinding poverty that are at the heart of the system.

Women's oppression is enmeshed in every fibre of class society and distorts every sphere of our existence. That's why women's liberation is only possible if we rip capitalism up. It is within class society that the very roots of women's oppression are formed. Is such fundamental change possible? It can sound like utopian rhetoric when you look around at how entrenched every aspect of the system is in our day to day lives. But when you look at the phenomenal struggles that have challenged the system even in only the last few years another picture emerges. That is a picture of a world where the poor and exploited can and do resist, and it also shows the extraordinary and brutal lengths to which rulers will go to hang onto power.

If we are to win such struggles it means looking to mobilise where we are strongest, as a class.

Why class offers agency

We are not women arrayed in struggle against men but workers who are in struggle against the exploiters.
—Eleanor Marx[499]

Class shapes every aspect of our lives—where we live and go to school, our health, when we die and of what—yet there are constant arguments about whether it even exists. This thing that may no longer exist is, however, endlessly discussed in the media. Working class people are dismissed as "chavs" and people living in poverty are demonised as feckless scroungers. The dominance of public school boys in the Cabinet or on Oscar shortlists is pointed out and the class snobbery of business woman Katie Hopkins is condemned. Hopkins gained minor celebrity status as a contender in *The Apprentice* TV series and declared that she would not want her children to play with anyone called Charmaine or Chardonnay because those names showed they were "lower class".

Such prejudice leads some to say that working class people are discriminated against in a similar way to other oppressed groups; this is sometimes referred to as "classism". The term is seen as acknowledging poor and working class people's lack of opportunities and the bigotry they face. Of course working class people do have fewer opportunities in life and such bigotry does exist. Working class people are continually dismissed and patronised as thick and capable of only the most mundane work. But foul as such ideas are, they do not create class differences, they simply try and justify them.

Another view is that class is something that people define themselves or that it is mainly about lifestyle and culture. One study carried out by the London School of Economics with the BBC made the headlines in 2013 when it claimed to have discovered that there were seven different classes in Britain. It declared society was using a "Victorian system" that did not recognise that the "traditional working class" is dying out and was "a 'throwback' to an earlier phase in Britain's social history".[500] They came to this conclusion on the basis of research which mapped people's class position on the basis of asking what they ate, what music they listened to and where they went on holiday. This both plays to the oldest stereotypes of class and also sees class as a purely subjective issue—your class position is solely what you perceive it to be.

This brings us to the key questions: what is the basis for class division and why is this so important in the struggle for women's liberation?

The mainstream view is that class is purely about status and economic inequality. Of course economic inequality is a product of class division in society. But in the *Communist Manifesto* Marx was disparaging about those, including those on the left, who saw class as just being about poverty and wealth. He wrote that defining the working class as simply the "most suffering class" robs workers of their agency. In Marx's view, workers did not need pity or charity; they had the power to change the world. That is what makes class so important to any theory of liberation. Understanding class exposes who has both an interest in and the ability to change things.

Marx saw class not as a static category to which people are allocated but as rooted in a dynamic social relationship within the system. This relationship is between those who own and control the means of production and those who have to sell their labour power—their ability to work—in order to live. It does not depend on subjective feelings about where you stand in some pecking order, but is an objective social relationship between the exploited and exploiter.

From this fundamental relationship flow all the trappings of class which change over time. Today manual workers may wear designer clothes, eat in restaurants and have foreign holidays, all of which would have marked them out as middle class a few decades ago. What people regard as the minimum necessary to maintain an average standard of living is very different today from what it was only a decade ago.

Marxism and Women's Liberation

To understand class in this way means looking at the system and society as a totality, a unity of opposites, with an inherent contradiction at its heart. The minority of people who own and control the wealth are driven to extract as much surplus as possible from the majority, who are forced to work to live. For the ruling class does not make profits just by owning factories and businesses. Those buildings, offices and production lines, however high tech, are themselves the product of human labour and on their own do not make profit. It is the human intervention that is the source of profit.

The capacity to consciously labour on nature and to shape the world is something that is at the centre of what makes us human. But this intrinsic attribute has to be converted into a commodity to be exchanged for cash if a worker is to survive in the system (see Chapter 2).

Under capitalism the only thing worse than having to turn your capacity to labour into a commodity to sell, is being unable to turn your labour power into a commodity to sell. Those who are unemployed or unable to work for different reasons are treated as useless by the system. They are derided and expected to live on meagre benefits and be grateful. Capitalism only values the ability to generate a surplus. Workers' lives, their health, their hopes and fears, their desire for education, art and culture are of no consequence to employers or the ruling class in general. They just want you to turn up on time and deliver what they need and take care of the rest of your life yourself.

But inherent in this process is the creation of a class of people that enables the whole system to function. The ruling class is entirely dependent on workers not just to generate their profits and add to their wealth, but also to provide the food they eat, the homes they live in, the roads they and their products are transported on and the health care they need. Absolutely nothing works within capitalism without human labour.

Contradiction of class

Class is not a box to which you are allocated. It only exists as the antagonistic, exploitative relationship between a minority of society and the majority. This explains why struggle is intrinsic to capitalism.

This can be a low-key, day-to-day push and pull over hours, pay, working conditions or time off, or it can explode into seismic struggles that challenge the very right of bosses to rule.

When Marxists argue that class is not just another "ism" it is because there is much more to class that the experience of suffering. Oppression can generate militant resistance, which can win gains, but struggles solely based on opposing oppression can face limitations of scale and politics. The contradiction of class is that the experience of exploitation can be gruelling, relentless and soul destroying, but being exploited also offers the possibility of powerful collective resistance. As Martha Gimenez wrote: "While racism and sexism have no redeeming feature, class relations are, dialectically, a unity of opposites; both a site of exploitation and, objectively, a site where the potential agents of social change are forged".[501]

Out of date?

We are told that such a view of class may have fitted during the period of the industrial revolution or when Marx was writing but the world looks very different now. The decline of major industries such as coal, steel and shipbuilding are cited as being the end of the working class as Marx knew it. This narrow view sees the working class as synonymous with male manual workers at a particular moment in the expansion of capitalism. This is echoed by many feminist writers, who describe women workers today as "feminising" the working class or state that women should "take history into their own hands and not wait for liberation through others, such as workers", seemingly dismissing the existence of women workers.[502]

This stance does not recognise that capitalism is always transforming itself and the nature of the work in a drive for new markets and increased profits. This was true even during Marx's lifetime. He wrote: "All old established industries have been destroyed or are daily being destroyed. They are dislodged by new industries, whose introduction becomes a life and death question".[503]

This process has only intensified and accelerated since Marx's time. He wrote that capitalism "stripped of its halo every occupation hitherto honoured. It has converted the physician, the lawyer, the priest, the poet, the man of science, into its paid wage labourers".[504] This "constant revolutionising of the means of production" has been a feature of capitalism since its birth and continues today. Call centres, "dark" supermarkets and vast warehouses of goods for home delivery for online shoppers did not exist 20 years ago. But the workers in them are exploited in the same way as their predecessors in the mills or factories of the 19th century. Teachers and lecturers, who used to be seen as belonging to professions that brought a level of autonomy and prestige, have become very much part of the working class.

Where do women fit in the working class?

There are many myths and much confusion on the left and among some feminist writers about where women fit in the working class. It is worth repeating that there have always been women who have worked outside the home. The model of the nuclear family in which a male worker's wage supports his wife and children has never been the experience for much of the working class.

This book has concentrated on Britain and the US, but understanding the role of women in the working class is impossible without looking at the figures internationally. If you look around the globe, all the statistics show that the number of women in the working class has never been greater. For example, the proportion of women in work in Latin America and the Caribbean has risen by 35 percent since 1990.[505] Worldwide, women make up at least 40 percent of the workforce, according to the World Bank, and at least 55 percent of all adult women are in waged work.

In Britain today 66.7 percent of women (14.1 million) are in waged work, more than ever before. More women are working full time than ever before (8.1 million) and 6 million work part time. The wages women earn are more likely to be low, but are vital for them and their dependents. The labour power they put into the system is also vital for the national economy in Britain. Lone parents make up a quarter of all families and 90 percent of lone parents are women. Even in families with two parents working, women's income is significant.

Women's income represents over half the family income in 21 percent of all working couples.[506]

But despite making up half the workforce today, it is still common for women workers to be seen as marginal to the working class and doing only transitory or precarious jobs. Natasha Walter has written: "Yes, women are working more. But they often work on the fringes of the economy—in 'atypical' jobs".[507] Yet the evidence shows that trends for the overall employment rate of women and men have been converging since 1971. Nina Power writes that when people refer to the "feminisation" of labour it is "at once descriptive (work is generally more precarious and communication-based, as women's jobs tended to be in the past) and an expression of resentment (women have stolen proper men's jobs! It's their fault—somehow—that we don't have any industry anymore!)". But she then asserts: "There are more women in work, and work itself has become more 'female'."[508] She is right about the moral panic sometimes generated by the greater numbers of women in the workplace, but once again there is an underlying assumption that women workers are not part of the working class proper.

Between 1971 and 2011 there was an upward trend in the proportion of women in employment and a downward trend in employment rates for men.[509] Over the last 15 years there has been a narrowing of the gap in employment rates for women with and without dependent children, from 5.8 percentage points in 1996 to 0.8 percentage points at the end of 2010. Women don't go out to work to top up a man's wage, to get a few luxuries—what used to be sneered at as "pin money". Nor are they a "reserve army of labour"; that is, a section of the class that is pulled into the workforce only at times of crisis and then discarded.

Despite the difficulties women with children face, they are not automatically thrown into a vortex of instability and marginal work. The majority of adult women work. As many as 77 percent of women return to work within 18 months of the birth of a child.[510] A labour force survey shows that for women with children under one, the mean length of time they have been with their current employer is over six years. A survey by the Department of Work and Pensions showed that since 2002 there has been a dramatic rise in women returning to the same employer after maternity leave: in 2002, 41 percent moved to a new employer, whereas in 2007 only 14 percent did. Staying with the same employer can mean retaining precious pay and skill levels that women are often forced to forego after having children.[511]

Part-time work is predominantly done by women workers and though pay for part-time working women is actually higher than that of part-time working men, part-time hourly wage rates are at least 37 percent lower than full-time hourly rates.[512] But it doesn't automatically follow that these part-time jobs are precarious. Women take on part-time work mainly to accommodate childcare responsibilities. Many would like to work more hours, but are held back by the lack of affordable childcare or more flexible full-time contracts. Recent research by the Fawcett Society found that 28 percent of women surveyed worked fewer hours than they would like.

The fact that women are still expected to carry the bulk of the responsibility for domestic labour, even when they work outside the home, means that being part of the workforce in such numbers is a contradictory situation for women. Having a job creates an extra burden in already stressed lives. But the other side of the contradiction is that by being part of the workforce, part of a collective, women gain power and possibilities for resistance that do not exist in the isolation of the home.

Feminist writers such as Silvia Federici, who campaigned for wages for housework in the 1970s, do not recognise this distinction. Federici writes that work outside the home "not only increases our exploitation but simply reproduces our role in different forms. Where ever we turn we can see that the jobs women perform are mere extensions of the housewife's condition in all its implications".[513] She goes on to argue that: "in the paid workforce, as in the household, women are assigned to, indeed ghettoised in, distinctively feminine, service oriented, and often sexualised occupations".[514] She gives examples of such jobs as being, "secretaries, domestic workers, salespersons, prostitutes and flight attendants".[515]

Many such jobs do reflect and perpetuate sexist stereotypes of women's abilities and role in society and the family, although they do not represent the sum total of the range of jobs women now do.

Women workers predominate in some parts of the service and public sector in part because these were expanding at the time when large numbers of women were being pulled into the workforce in the post-war boom. Many of these jobs, for example in care work, are undervalued under capitalism even though they often involve looking after the needs of some of the most vulnerable in society.

But even in jobs that do reflect such sexist stereotypes, women workers, alongside men, have class power. In such a job workers can use management's need for workers to conform to stereotypes to fight back. For example, in 1999 female flight attendants working for the airline Cathay Pacific "threatened to take industrial action in a dispute over pay and conditions by refusing to smile at passengers for one hour every flight".[516] Academic Deborah Cameron rightly pointed out that the company's advertising of smiling, willing Asian women also played to racist stereotypes.

We can and should complain about sexist airline adverts that virtually imply the female cabin crew will be a businessman's sex slave for the duration of his flight. But it is significant that, whatever the advertising clichés, these very same women have the power to bring an airline company to a halt. This was seen in a bitter dispute over conditions with British Airways in 2011 when flight attendants did more than refuse to smile, they refused to go to work.

The nature of waged work is to bring workers, women and men, together and the logic is to organise collectively. An individual worker is unlikely to win a pay rise by making an appointment with their boss and asking nicely. Most workers would not get past reception, let alone get a hearing. The history of the labour movement has been one where the most significant gains have been made through union organisation and workers wielding their most powerful weapon, industrial action.

"A woman's place is in her union"

Government figures published in 2014 showed that women workers in Britain were more likely to be in a union than men for the 12th year in a row. This is the case irrespective of whether women are working part or full time and whether they have permanent or temporary jobs.[517] The proportion of women workers in a trade union in 2013 was around 28 percent compared to 23 percent of men. Britain saw the biggest ever strike of women workers in history on 30 November 2011 when 2.6 million public sector workers, the majority of whom are women, walked out over cuts in their pensions.

"The relative declines in the proportions of women and men in a trade union since 1995 has been much weaker for women. The rate of female trade union membership has decreased from 29.7 per cent in 1995 to 28.3 per cent in 2013, whereas for men, the rate has fallen from 35 per cent in 1995 to 22.9 per cent in 2013".[518] Research also shows that women, and young workers under 24 years old, have most to gain from being in a union. Figures measure what is called the "union premium"; that is, "the percentage difference in average gross hourly earnings of union members compared with non-members." This premium is higher for women—around 30 percent—compared with 8 percent for men. "The wage premium was 38 per cent for those aged 16-24, compared with 13 per cent for those aged 25 to 34".[519]

US feminist writer Hester Eisenstein found similar trends in the US, albeit within the much smaller proportion of workers who are trade union members there: "Even as the nation's unionisation rate has declined, the female share of union membership has expanded rapidly. In 2004, 43 percent of all the nation's union members were women—a record high." She suggests that such figures mean that: "with close to 7 million women covered by union contracts, organised labour arguably is the largest working women's movement in the country".[520]

The existence of trade union organisation is not on its own enough to ensure that working conditions and pay will be maintained, let alone improved, as years of Tory attacks on working class living standards have shown. What is critical is the strength of rank and file organisation. Where that is lacking, workers are reliant on the union leadership's willingness to lead a fight and take on the employers or the government.

The leadership of the trade union movement in Britain is still accurately described as "male, pale, and stale". This is true even of unions that have a majority of women members. At the time of writing, only one in four union general secretaries are women, although women represent around 49 percent of union members. But with women's representation on the TUC General Council and TUC Executive Committee both running at 42 percent, it must be said that the gender balance far exceeds the 29 percent of MPs in Westminster, for example.

Militancy, consciousness and confidence

There are two aspects to class power: the objective reality of the position and strength of the working class, and the subjective feeling workers have of their ability to fight.

The ruling class not only owns the means of production (factories, offices, businesses), they also own and control the mental means of production. In 1911 socialist Helen Keller wrote that these included: "the nourishers of intellectual life, the press, the church, the school".[521] Today the media is extremely diverse—including websites, TV channels and newspapers, print and online—while the education process is being increasingly privatised and shaped by the needs of capital rather that the needs of students. That is why Marx wrote that: "the ideas of the ruling class are in every epoch the ruling ideas, ie the class which is the ruling material force of society, is at the same time its ruling intellectual force".[522]

But if that was the whole picture then you would not be reading this book and the mass of ordinary people would always swallow the ruling class propaganda in Rupert Murdoch's right wing rags. The situation is not that simple or stable. Marx also wrote that: "the history of all class societies is a history of class struggle." The very process of exploitation creates a tension in society that means that ruling class ideas are sometimes undermined or challenged by workers' lived experience.

Capitalism forces workers together in ever greater concentrations in order to exploit their labour power. The pressure of competition means bosses constantly attempt to extract more from workers. This in turn forces workers to try and defend themselves the only way possible—collectively—regardless of their ideas about class, race or anything else. Socialist and historian Hal Draper explained that workers' resistance was a product of their class position not in some way intrinsic to their nature. He wrote that there is "no evidence that workers like to struggle any more than anyone else, the evidence is that capitalism compels and accustoms them to do so".[523]

Karen Gearon was one of 12 Dunnes Stores workers in Ireland who went on strike in 1984 for almost three years after refusing to handle products from apartheid South Africa. She told RTE (the national broadcaster) that before the strike: "We were basically concerned about our own little life or little social circle and we would get paid on Friday, go out to a pub, some discos and blow the money, then go back into work on the Monday and just basically do your job and that was it." Yet their fight gained international attention and support and in 1987 the Irish government banned the sale of goods from South Africa until the apartheid regime fell.

So workers who have perhaps gone along in life without challenging the status quo, and even workers with reactionary ideas, can be pulled into struggle. How many times have you heard the refrain from strikers on a picket line: "I'm not a militant but..." and they go on to explain why they could not stomach a particular attack or injustice. Once workers are pulled into any struggle or resistance, the potential for seeing the true nature of the system opens up; class struggle is the most effective way of pulling back the veil that hides the reality of capitalism. During the Russian Revolution workers reported that the Bolsheviks always told them: "it is not we who will persuade you, but life itself".

This is how the working class moves from being, as Marx noted, a class "in itself" to becoming "a class for itself". This means it becomes conscious of its own interests and power and is ready to lay bare the real division in society in order to end it once and for all. However, even in times of low struggle, individuals can be won to socialist politics and to opposing capitalism by the force of ideas and argument or their individual experience. For example, many families of people killed in police custody have become determined activists as a consequence of dealing with their own personal tragedy and fight for justice.

Mass social movements also have the potential for profound politicisation. The worldwide anti-capitalist movement won a whole generation to the idea that the system was to blame and this still shapes much of politics today from student activism to campaigns against climate change. Arundhati Roy, Naomi Klein and Susan George were among the many leading activists and writers in that movement. The explosion of rage against the Iraq war brought two million people onto the streets in Britain in 2003. Such mass protests shaped national politics and the anti-war message resonated with public opinion. The Arab revolutions (see Chapter 12) inspired resistance internationally. The Occupy movement took up the idea of taking over public squares as a form of protest, education and organising resistance. But the measure of lasting success of all these struggles is how much they connected to struggle involving the organised working class.

The mass of ordinary people will not be won individually to challenging oppression and fighting for change. But the working class is unique in that within it there is an organic drive for unity and to overcome divisions. This is rooted in workers' material conditions and is not reliant on winning everyone ideologically first.

Marx argued that mass working class struggle was not just the only way capitalism could be destroyed, but also the only way for "production on a mass scale of communist consciousness". He wrote that: "revolution is necessary not only because the ruling class cannot be overthrown in any other way, but also because the class overthrowing it can only in a revolution succeed in ridding itself of all the muck of ages and become fitted to found society anew".[524]

The muck of ages—sexist ideas about women's capabilities, racism and homophobia—corrodes the unity needed for mass struggles to win. Millions of workers hold some of these ideas in day-to-day life under capitalism. When socialists argue that the working class is the vehicle for change, this is not because they have an idealised view of workers. It is because socialists see what the working class—women and men—can become.

Women have come to the fore with every upsurge of working class struggle. The bread riots of the 17th and 18th centuries saw women seize grain at markets or bakeries: "with knives stuck in their girdles to force corn at their own rates".[525] The eruption of New Unionism (see Chapter 6) saw hundreds of thousands of working women, often in the direst circumstances, standing up to the bosses and the state.

The 20th century saw women at the heart of struggles across the globe. Women workers ignited the Russian Revolution of 1917. The great workers' struggles in the US included the historic strike of 10,000 mainly immigrant women at Lawrence textile mill in 1912. Throughout both world wars women workers in Britain wielded their new-found collective power and elsewhere women fought in liberation struggles that shattered the hold of the British Empire. Women were a part of the worldwide revolts of the 1960s, including the victorious national liberation struggle of the Vietnamese against US imperialism. Britain's Great Miners' Strike showed that even a strike that involves only male workers has the ability to politicise the whole working class. In the end women in the mining communities played a pivotal role in the strike, including confronting police on picket lines. The 21st century has already seen women play a central role in the mighty revolts that toppled tyrants during the Arab revolutions (see Chapter 12).

Class power

In Britain the lack of militancy and low level of struggle in recent years should not be used to undermine a class perspective. The bigger picture shows that the general tendency of capitalism is also its greatest contradiction. To function it must create a growing working class, but that class has the potential power to overthrow the system. It is not about specifics of time and place. In Marx's time the working class existed only in a pocket of Western Europe. His insight was to understand the process of capitalism, which means that his analysis actually fits better today than it did when he was alive.

We have seen the process of globalisation accelerate and fulfil Marx's assertion that "capitalism nestles everywhere". This has led to women becoming even more integrated into the global working class with more than 200 million women being pulled into the workforce in the last 15 years. In China alone millions of peasants have been driven off the land to join the mass workforces selling their labour power in enormous new factories. In India the millions employed in the textile industry work in conditions eerily similar to those of women workers at the start of the 20th century in the Lower East Side of Manhattan in the US.

Marx called the working class the "gravedigger" of capitalism. He saw the working class as having the potential power to win much more than better pay and conditions from bosses within the confines of the system. Such economic struggles make a difference to the quality of working class life. But class power can go beyond economic issues and also be wielded for political goals.

The ruling class wants to keep economic and political issues separate and denounces even limited attempts by trade unions, for example, to make their views heard in parliament through the Labour Party. Tory politicians condemn them, claiming they are straying into territory where they do not belong. In February 2015 the *Daily Mail* attacked the TUC for taking a position against a proposed amendment that would curb abortion rights.[526] The TUC was quite right to make a stand in defence of a woman's right to choose. There is no separation between the economics and politics of capitalism. A government imposing austerity is at the same time following a political agenda and inflicting an economic attack.

It is entirely right that millions of workers should have a say in who represents them in parliament and how. Workers have fought for this right. But the real power in society does not reside in parliament, it is held by those who own and control the means of production. They are backed up by politicians from all sides and, most importantly, by the forces of the state: the laws, legal system and police. This power cannot be challenged by changing the party of government; ultimately the power of the ruling class can only be fundamentally challenged by mass class struggle.

The working class is not some outside force that will come to the rescue of women or fight on behalf of women. It is made up of women and men. It is black and white and Asian. It is LGBT and straight. It is the class of the majority for the majority.

Every setback or advance for the working class is felt most keenly by the oppressed and this is as true for women as any other oppressed group. When the working class is on the rise, women's position in society is improved. When it is defeated, most severely at times of dictatorship or fascism, women's rights are crushed. This was seen in Spain where women won important political rights as well as access to abortion and birth control in the Republic of 1931. Women and men fought together to defend the Republic after a fascist coup in 1936 by General Franco. After a bitter civil war, Franco was victorious in 1939 and women lost all the gains they had made. The fascist state made divorce, abortion and contraception illegal; women were rewarded for having babies and barred from economic independence.

The experience gained by workers, women and men, from taking action, from defying the structures we are told are immovable and inevitable, moves the sphere of struggle from the individual to the collective. When workers mobilise collectively, they develop class consciousness and the confidence to fight for even greater gains. But a genuine challenge to the system is more than just a series of big or even general strikes. It means a level of social struggle that shakes society to its roots. John Reed said that the Russian Revolution convinced him of workers' magnificent potential to change the world. He wrote: "The masses of the workers are capable not only of great dreams, but that they have in them the power to make dreams come true".[527]

Women and revolution

Women have been the dynamo of the revolution. You feel how the revolution has changed people, they have become mighty and courageous. They don't feel inferior to anyone.

—Mahienour El Massry, revolutionary socialist, Egypt

Revolutions throw everything that seems solid up in the air. When the mass of ordinary people taste the possibility of freedom from the crushing drudgery of everyday life under capitalism, anything is possible. Revolutions are nothing if they are not also festivals of the oppressed. They are a chance for all those who have the most to gain from the struggle to become the subjects of history.

The ruling class expends an enormous amount of effort promoting the myth that any attempt at a radical change of society is dangerous and will lead to chaos and violence. Marx described this ideology as the ruling class's "selfish misconception" that induces it to "transform into eternal laws of nature and of reason, the social forms springing from your present mode of production and form of property" even those that are constantly changing. He pointed out that this misconception has been shared "with every ruling class that has preceded you".[528]

It suits the ruling class's economic and political needs for women and men to believe that there is no alternative to the way we live. The process of encouraging us to fulfill the social roles mapped out for us is central to understanding not just gender but the whole of society. The maintenance of class rule relies, most of the time, on the fact that we learn to conform and feel we have no control over forces much greater than ourselves that appear to shape society. The ruling class want us to accept that some are born to rule—those who go to public school and

Oxford and Cambridge—and some are born to be ruled—everybody else. We are taught that we must take responsibility for the problems we and our families might face, whether that be poverty, unemployment, mental health issues or disability. We are told that putting an X on a ballot paper once every five years is the height of democracy.

All this ensures that the rich carry on getting richer while spinning the line that they are taking all the risks and so should reap the benefits. Workers are compelled to sell their labour power and stay on the treadmill of everyday life under capitalism because that is the only way to get by. Class power is maintained in this way in social democratic countries, without guns being held to workers' heads.

It is only when people decide they do not want to conform or can no longer bear the conditions in which they live and rebel that the ruling class reveals its willingness to resort to the use of force. They would rather not; it raises the stakes and exposes the fragility of their hold if they have to summon police officers or even the army to crack down on resistance. So the forces of the state are only mobilised at times of crisis, but they are there in the background ready to uphold the status quo. Even the term "status quo" is misleading: it implies that society is being maintained in some sort of natural equilibrium. In fact the status quo is enforcing the rule of the wealthy elite, ultimately at any cost. We have seen how the state upholds and helps shore up women's oppression through the structures of the legal system and the police.

Lenin wrote about the role of the state in his unfinished pamphlet *State and Revolution*—unfinished because his writing was interrupted by the 1917 October Revolution. He joked on the final page that it was "more pleasant to go through the 'experience of the revolution' than to write about it".[529] Despite the absence of the final chapters, which were lived out in the real life struggle, this is a clear and powerful account of why we have to get rid of the state if we are to win a new society.

Capitalism needs a state because the threat of violence is necessary to impose the will of a minority over that of the vast majority. When workers take power they will have to use force to impose their will, for a time, on remnants of the old ruling class who try to sabotage any revolution. But ultimately as a socialist society takes root, there will be less and less need for any separate state forces; the state as we know it with armed police forces and a professional military will "wither away" as the majority runs society in the interests of the majority.

Yet we are told that revolutionary events are simply anathema in Britain and that gradualism is built into our DNA. According to the racist stereotypes of the ruling class, revolutions are only made by the "hot heads" of Europe and elsewhere. This whopping great myth can be dispelled with just one example—the execution of King Charles I by his own people in 1649 during the English Revolution. The fact that history books refer to it as the English Civil War should not fool us into seeing it as anything other than the first European revolutionary uprising against the unlimited power of the monarchy.

Nothing has been gained by ordinary people, in Britain or across the world, without struggle. Male workers and women would not have won the vote without a fight. This is equally true of equal pay, maternity leave and any other reform or improvement in our conditions. The ruling class have always had to be forced to make concessions.

The US establishment now treats leading civil rights activist Martin Luther King as a national hero. He even has a public holiday in his name. Rosa Parks—who in 1955 refused to give up her seat at the front of a Montgomery bus to sit in the back, where black people were supposed to sit—is revered and often portrayed as an ordinary seamstress who was just too tired to stand up. But there was nothing inevitable about African Americans winning legal equality. The ruling class did not suddenly have an epiphany and realise it was immoral to deny people civil rights because of the colour of their skin, no more than they had abolished slavery by suddenly discovering it was barbaric.

In fact the US state resisted civil rights as long as it could get away with it. The FBI targeted King in order to smear him. Activists faced murder by racists and imprisonment by the state. As for Rosa Parks, she was a seasoned political activist who said years later in 1967: "I don't believe in gradualism" and declared: "The only tired I was, was tired of giving in."

The masses cannot nibble away at ruling class power until suddenly we have taken it from under the nose of the ruling elite without their noticing. Instead we will have to take power and it will take revolutionary upheaval to achieve it. But the experience of revolutions of the past raises many questions about whether they always produce tyrannical leaders and, if we won economic equality, whether there would have to be a second revolution to win equality for women.

What do revolutions look like?

Popular images of revolutions usually conjure up bombs, balaclavas and violence. The implication is that the majority of people are cowering at home waiting until the fighting is over. What can such battles possibly have to do with women's liberation?

In fact revolutions are about self-emancipation. They are not about a few well-informed and trained experts, or heavily armed guerrillas, going in to fight on behalf of the mass of ordinary people. They are not even single events. Revolutions are processes involving mass social upheaval pulling hundreds of thousands and ultimately millions of ordinary people, women and men, into the struggle. As Engels wrote: "the masses must be in on it themselves, must have already grasped what is at stake, what they are fighting for, body and soul".[530]

Revolutions can take months or even years. During that period there can be advances and retreats and there will be decisive moments that could culminate in the taking of power. French historian Albert Soboul wrote that: "Revolutions are not distinguished by their duration but by their content. Reform or revolution? It is not a question of choosing a longer or shorter route leading to the same result, but of specifying an end: to wit, either of the establishment of a new society, or of superficial modifications to the old society".[531]

The ruling class fears revolutions precisely because they pose a fundamental challenge to its whole right to rule. They know that people who go on strike or take to the streets on one issue can become emboldened, politicised and their anger and opposition can become generalised. The establishment tries to undercut that confidence by telling workers they are not equipped to run society. Draper referred to this attitude, which is sometimes shared by those sceptical about the potential of workers to fight: "you expect these wretches to make a revolution?"[532] When the Arab Revolutions erupted in 2011 former ambassadors and other pundits rushed to the television studios to tell us that the "Arab street" was not ready for democracy and needed a strong man at the top.

Telling ordinary people that they are not fit to take power is not a new tactic. Rosa Luxemburg wrote that working class people have always had to prove they were "mature enough for political freedom". As for the ruling class: "Only when God's Anointed on the throne together with the noblest Cream of the Nation felt the calloused fist of the proletariat on their eye and its knee on their breast, only then did belief in the political maturity of the people suddenly dawn on them".[533]

"Political maturity" is a product of struggle, it is the process of revolution that turns the working class, made up of individual women and men, into a conscious political body. Revolutions are not won because socialists have convinced the majority about the need for revolution. Marx argued: "Liberation is an historical not a mental act".[534] He meant workers' political consciousness is transformed by the actual struggle to change material conditions. The very experience of rising up and and taking control of their lives changes people in a way unimagined in the ordinary conditions of living under capitalism.

This is the process that means revolutionary change has the potential to liberate. Silvia Federici dismisses Marx as being wedded to a "technological concept of revolution". But for Marx revolutions were not simply about a new economic system being put in place; they were about the possibilities opened up for the emancipation of humanity.

Ideas that dominate when workers are ground down by the treadmill of mind-numbing jobs, scrabbling to survive, and alienated from their own humanity no longer fit as common sense. Racism, sexism and homophobia have grown out of a system that has to divide us to keep us under control. Any challenge to that system, to the material world around us, also throws the ideas that flow from it up in the air. Revolutionary times accelerate and intensify changes in political consciousness. In his work on the French Revolution Marx pointed out how the process of political growth of those involved was speeded up: "the different classes of French society had to count their epochs of development in weeks where they had previously counted them in half centuries."

Marxism and Women's Liberation

The experience of revolutions themselves proves Marx's assertion of their potential for liberation. History shows that a defining feature of every great social revolution is the rising up of the oppressed. Indeed, the very success of the struggle depends on women and other oppressed groups taking part and having a stake in it.

The Russian Revolution of 1917 was the best answer to the question about how to fight for women's liberation. It affected the lives of millions of women living in some of the most brutal conditions. Women had been active in the different strands of the revolutionary movement in Russia for years. Bolshevik women had faced imprisonment and exile for their political activity. Just as in Britain and the US, in Russia too women became a major part of the industrial workforce as men were taken from their jobs to fight in the First World War. Women made up 26 percent of the workforce in 1914, but by 1917 this had risen to 43 percent.[535] They took up a full range of jobs and such was the influx of women into the workforce that "scores of textile mills and even whole towns were now populated almost exclusively by women".[536] One Tsarist official had reported to his managers in January 1917 that working women were "a store of combustible material".[537] He was right.

Women workers marching on International Women's Day in 1917 sparked the February Revolution. On 23 February (8 March by the Western calendar) they "streamed out of their workplaces and homes, shouting for bread and an end to the war and as they passed factories and tenements they called on the people inside to join them... Police blocked the bridges into the city centre, so the women slid down the embankments along the river and walked across the ice".[538] They threw stones and snowballs at factory windows demanding other workers walk out and faced Cossacks armed with whips, but they were defiant. Within a week the Tsar had gone.

In his wonderful *History of the Russian Revolution*, Trotsky was open about the unexpectedness of women taking the lead: "The February revolution was begun from below, overcoming the resistance of its own revolutionary organisations, the initiative being taken of their own accord by the most oppressed and downtrodden part of the proletariat—the women textile workers".[539]

Women who had lived in the most oppressed conditions—in some areas it was legal for husbands to whip their wives—flooded into the revolutionary movement, which made their true liberation a priority. They had everything to gain from this momentous revolt from below calling for bread, peace and land—simple demands that could not be met without turning society upside down. The Bolsheviks won many of these militant working class women to their organisation, which went to great lengths to ensure women were part of the struggle.

Lenin argued: "The experience of all liberation movements has shown that the success of a revolution depends on how much the women take part in it".[540] When he arrived in Petrograd in 1917 he urged the Bolsheviks to organise political work among women, writing that it was idle to speak of socialism "unless women are drawn into taking an independent part, not only in political life generally, but also in daily social service obligatory to everyone".[541]

One history of the period calculates that almost half women members of the Bolsheviks were workers: "the percentage of working class women, both before and after 1917, is remarkable given their low levels of literacy and the demands the Bolsheviks made in terms of political education".[542] Women "go up to the cordons more boldly than the men, take hold of the rifles, beseech, almost command, 'Put down your bayonets—join us'", reported Trotsky of confrontations with Tsarist troops.[543] Women strikers would cart off uncooperative bosses in wheelbarrows. During the civil war that ensued as the fledgling workers' state fought for survival, women joined the Red Army and often took on dangerous spying operations against White Troops. The White army officers held them in contempt, describing women as an "imbecile element who by the rights of their destiny belong with the pots and the kitchen, not in politics which is absolutely alien to their understanding".[544]

Ruling class and bourgeois women were also scathing about the rising of the poor and they were fervent in their support for the imperialist war. A group of such women started a Women's Battalion and called for women to be drafted into the war effort in the months before the October Revolution. But as one historian writes, the war-weary poor and working people of Petrograd treated the battalion with contempt and "the Bolshevik anti-war propaganda gradually

Marxism and Women's Liberation

won popular support, at the expense not only of their revolutionary rivals, but of the liberals and feminists".[545]

One doctor and feminist Mariia Pokrovskaia showed how detached some of the bourgeois feminists were from the reality of the lives of millions of women. She expressed her disdain for the slogan of "bread, peace and land", saying that instead of "coarse material incentives" women should be fighting for "electoral rights, freedom of speech and a parliament." But issues of democracy and equal rights were indivisible from the demand for bread, peace and land; none would be achieved without a mass social revolution.

Millions of poor workers and peasants, particularly women, who had been illiterate and felt that their harsh lives were predestined by an unchangeable god, learned to read and write—more than 125,000 literacy schools were set up.[546] Ordinary people were involved in the big debates of the day and took part in taking control of their own lives. Thousands flooded to public squares to watch everything from poetry to Greek drama. There were "lectures, debates, speeches—in theatres, circuses, school houses, clubs, Soviet meeting rooms, union headquarters, barracks...in Petrograd, and all over Russia, every street corner was a public tribune".[547]

This description of the explosion of popular debate, a feature of every genuine mass revolution, echoes Alexandra Kollontai's recollections of the 1905 Revolution in Russia: "there was no corner in which one way or another, the voice of a woman speaking about herself and demanding rights was not heard".[548]

But the Bolsheviks knew that if women were really going to be able to play a role in building a new society, then the material basis for their oppression would have to be broken. Trotsky laid out what this meant: "The place of the family as a shut-in petty enterprise was to be occupied, according to the plans, by a finished system of social care and accommodation: maternity houses, crèches, kindergartens, schools, social dining rooms, social laundries, first-aid stations, hospitals, sanatoria, athletic organisations, moving-picture theaters, etc." What the Bolsheviks planned was no less than the "complete absorption of the house-keeping functions of the family by institutions of the socialist society".

The Revolution reached every corner of Russia. Within a year of the October Revolution, Alexandra Kollontai and other leading Bolsheviks organised the First All-Russian Congress of Working Women. Not everyone thought that this was a worthwhile venture. When the women applied for a hall of 300, they met some resistance. Kollontai wrote later: "We were told, 'don't bother it's not worth it you'll never get that many. Plan for 80 and no more.' In fact 1,147 delegates came". These women had to travel in sometimes treacherous conditions from across war-torn Russia, "many with children, dressed in sheepskin jackets, felt boots, peasant costumes, army greatcoats and the traditional Bolshevik red headscarves".[549] They cheered speeches from Kollontai and other leading women Bolsheviks as well as from Lenin, inspired to be part of a revolution that was committed to organising women.

The Bolsheviks also set up a special department for work among women, known by its acronym, Zhenotdel. When there was ink and paper available it also had a monthly paper, *Kommunistka*. Zhenotdel was led by Inessa Armand and then Kollontai and thousands of women signed up to take part in its work. Zhenotdel volunteers travelled thousands of miles from their homes to factories and villages to campaign for the Revolution. They used agit-trains or agit-ships, such as the *Red Star*, that travelled up and down the River Volga, to reach remote areas.[550]

They travelled with poster art and song and dance groups; they held meetings, showed films and plays; and they set up "reading cabins" with blackboards to teach literacy. They also travelled among Muslim populations in the East, often wearing hijabs so they could mix and work with veiled women. They sometimes faced heckling or complaints that change was too slow or food rations too meagre, but the main response from the thousands of women they organised among was enthusiasm for change, for an end to the old ways.

But the Revolution, and the powerful aspirations it generated, were attacked from without and within and crushed with Stalin's rise to power. Many of the core of the working class and the cadre of the Bolsheviks among them who led the Revolution were killed in the fighting against the Whites and the invading imperialist powers.

Others were taken from the factories to become commanders and commissars within the new state. The revolutionary forces became hollowed out.

The rise of the tyranny of Stalinism was not a result of the attempt at revolution, it was a sign the revolutionary wave started in Russia had been broken. The Russian Revolution could not sustain itself alone, it needed the victory of the German Revolution to survive. As Rosa Luxemburg wrote: "In Russia the problem could only be posed. It could not be solved in Russia".[551]

To entrench his power, Stalin murdered all the old Bolshevik leadership after the death of Lenin. The position of women deteriorated as Stalin increased his grip on the state and the growing bureaucracy. Peasants and workers suffered brutal conditions as the mass of ordinary people paid a terrible price for Stalin's drive to make the Soviet Union compete with the West. By the mid-1930s, efforts to restabilise Soviet society after the years of upheaval and hardship saw Stalinism put the institution of the family at the centre of Soviet ideology. The position of women as mothers was increasingly glorified in Soviet propaganda; women were given medals for having large numbers of children. Fulfilling this traditional role was seen as women's patriotic duty.[552]

This bitter defeat meant that when the women's movements of the 1960s exploded in the West, the real but short-lived achievements of the Russian Revolution had been erased from popular memory. Yet what Lenin said one year after the Revolution is still true today:

> Take the position of women. In this field, not a single democratic party in the world, not even in the most advanced bourgeois republic, has done in decades so much as a hundredth part of what we did in our very first year in power... We really razed to the ground the infamous laws placing women in a position of inequality, restricting divorce and surrounding it with disgusting formalities, denying recognition to children born out of wedlock, enforcing a search for their fathers, etc, laws numerous survivals of which, to the shame of the bourgeoisie and of capitalism, are to be found in all civilised countries.[553]

When Trotsky was asked was it true that in revolutionary Russia people could get a divorce just by asking, he replied that a better question would be "is it true there are still countries where this isn't the case?"

Lenin said they had a "thousand times the right to be proud" but despite all the changes the revolutionary government had implemented he had no illusions about the scale of the task they faced. He said they just cleared the ground of the "the lumber of the old, bourgeois laws and institutions" but were not yet building anything new to replace the old institutions that held women down.[554]

After Lenin's death, Trotsky, then in exile, wrote that he could see the Revolution's retreat from its ideals as "women were going back to doing their own washing instead of using the social laundries which had deteriorated so much that they tear and steal linen more than they wash it".[555] Here was a man who had led the Petrograd Soviet and the Red Army against the invading imperialist powers of the world, yet he understood the significance of these apparently small changes in the lives of working women and what they revealed about what had been lost.

Although the Russian Revolution took place almost a century ago and the conditions women lived under seem remote to us, it still holds powerful lessons for activists today. It shows the ability of ordinary people, even in the direst situation, to resist and build an alternative to capitalism and war. The 20th century was filled with examples of revolutionary upsurges and with each the position of women and all the oppressed was challenged. For example, during the German Revolution, which brought mass working class struggles to the heart of Western Europe between 1918 and 1923, revolutionary socialists put the need for women's liberation firmly at the centre of the struggle. But another important product of the politicisation of the period was serious agitation and organisation around sexual freedom and equality for LGBT people. The defeat of this revolution was to have tragic consequences that reached far beyond Germany's borders.

In 1936 Spanish workers rose up in an effort to stop fascist dictator General Franco. Every aspect of life was affected by the struggle. Rosa Vega, a schoolteacher in Madrid during the years of revolt, describes how she used to walk home late at night after preparing medical supplies: "It was so dark I often bumped into people on the streets. But never once was I molested or in any way made aware that I was a woman. Before the war there would have been remarks of one sort or the other—now that was entirely gone. Women were no longer objects, they were human beings, persons on the same level as men." One young socialist activist, Maria Solana, travelled from village to village to build support. Often the only woman, she would sometimes have to share beds with other youth, but "nothing would happen—absolutely nothing. There was a new sense of human relationships".[556]

We do not have to go back that far in history to see examples of the revolutionary process and its significance for the fight for women's liberation. The Arab Revolutions that erupted first in Tunisia and most importantly in Egypt, the most populous country of the region, in January 2011 reshaped the regional and world political map. The role of women was once again a central question. As the counter-revolution is tightening its grip it is important to remember that the revolutions had every monarch and dictator from Morocco, through the Gulf states to Iran trembling in their palaces. It was also an unwelcome shock to the ruling classes of the West who had been used to seeing the Arab masses as helpless pawns in their imperialist plans.

The Arab revolts confirm Lenin's description of the conditions necessary for revolution: "It is only when the 'lower classes' do not want to live in the old way and the 'upper classes' cannot carry on in the old way that the revolution can triumph." When Mohammed Bouazizi was attacked by police in Tunis in December 2010 while trying to scratch a living selling fruit he was not the first impoverished Tunisian to be brutalised. His act of protest and despair when he set himself on fire caused a national outcry. His individual act triggered a mass uprising that saw the end of the rotten tyranny of western-backed dictator Zine al-Abidine Ben Ali, who had ruled for over 20 years.

The wave of rage and solidarity saw the Egyptian Revolution explode in January 2011. It took just 18 days to end the 30-year dictatorship of Hosni Mubarak. He had been the puppet of Western imperialism and a poster boy for neoliberalism and his corrupt regime had inflicted torture and repression on any opposition, all backed by

US billions. Tens of thousands took to the streets in Cairo and across the country on 25 January 2011 in solidarity with Tunisia and against Mubarak. What turned this protest into a revolutionary situation was what happened at the end of the day. People did not go home. In the capital city of Cairo they occupied Tahrir Square, which became the epicentre of the revolution. Protesters knew what the stakes were, some held up homemade signs saying "Stay or die".

To witness the events in Tahrir Square was to watch a living, breathing experiment in collective organisation.[557] As revolutionary socialist Sameh Naguib recalls: "The space in Tahrir was not simply occupied physically but spiritually. Harassment against women disappeared, tensions between Copts and Muslims evaporated. People shared food, water, cigarettes. Songs, music, poetry and chants filled the air".[558] It showed a glimpse of the potential for humanity when everyone feels they have a stake in how society is organised.

Egyptian writer and activist Ahdaf Soueif described those inspiring days and what people were articulating: "They said we were divided, extreme, ignorant, fanatic—well here we are: diverse, inclusive, hospitable, generous, sophisticated, creative and witty." Tahrir was infused by a spirit of solidarity, humour and respect for difference that normal life under capitalism can crush from the human spirit. The sense of liberation was palpable. Three generations of one family were camping in front of a shop doorway, grandmother through to young children, with a handwritten sign saying: "Mubarak fuck off!". The sheer joy of being able to insult and mock a dictator who had ruled by fear was written across people's faces. The mood was captured by the typed sheet held up by one protester: "They want to scare us. He has ruined our lives. We only live once. This is it."

In a country where sexual harassment is endemic, women said they felt safe in Tahrir. They talked of the taboos they were breaking even by being out late at night in the city, let alone spending night after night camping out among thousands of strangers. One night, as thousands marched round the central reservation, a group of young women school students asked me if I was scared to be there alone. I said no, but asked were they? They replied: "No, Tahrir is the safest place in Egypt".

Women searched and covered checkpoints alongside men when trying to keep secret police out of the square. When Mubarak's thugs tried to smash the square occupation, women broke stones and rolled them in carpets to pass down to the frontline. This is not the image of women, in particular of Muslim women, which the ruling class wants us to see. Muslim women are rarely seen as being agents of their own liberation. Tahrir Square showed something different. There, women in full niqab, hijab or neither, Muslim, Christian, Jewish and of no faith, women of all ages enthusiastically took their lives into their own hands.

Mubarak fell on 11 February 2011 and after the rejoicing a military government took control. The ruling class tried to reassert its authority. The resurgence of sexual harassment on the streets after the opening of Tahrir was immediate. At protests, thugs targeted women. Gangs of men attacked women gathered in Tahrir to celebrate International Women's Day. In the following months and years several women suffered brutal sexual assaults and rape after being surrounded by gangs while on mass protests or demonstrations.

When soldiers were caught on video beating a woman on a protest in December 2011, the footage went viral. She became known as "blue bra woman" because during the beating the black abaya gown she was wearing over her jeans was pulled from her body. She became a symbol of what the state was willing to do to break women from being part of the revolution, to force them off the streets. It didn't work; days later more than 10,000 women marched through Cairo protesting in defiance.

Revolutionary socialist Gigi Ibrahim described the situation in the summer of 2013. "Before the revolution harassment by groups of men could be a problem in the streets. This was especially the case on holidays like Eid, when people were out in city squares and parks. But today group sexual harassment is being used as a weapon against the revolution."[559] Activists organised groups such as Tahrir Bodyguard and Operation Sexual Harassment that would respond to calls on protests. Women and men all wearing the same easily identifiable shirts would push through the crowd to pull women away from their attackers and once in a safe place give them any support they needed. Women refused to be intimidated off the streets.

The state tried to stigmatise women protesters by saying they were "loose women". The army strip searched and carried out what they called "virginity tests" on single women they arrested. These sexual assaults by army doctors were often carried out in front of male army officers. One woman who was arrested and assaulted the day after International Women's Day in 2011, was Samira Ibrahim. She did something no other woman had done before: she took the military to court. She lost the case and the military doctor went free, but the impact of her speaking out in public about her experience was immense. She said she did not regret bringing the case and refused to allow the military to make her feel shame about what she went through. She made the shame theirs.

The unity represented by the Revolution was its greatest strength. The attempts to whip up moral panic about women or sectarian hatred are about reimposing class rule. Such tactics have been repeated across the region by rulers desperate to hang onto power. Yemen's former dictator Ali Abdullah Saleh tried to undercut mass demonstrations involving thousands of women calling for his downfall by declaring it was "unIslamic" for women to protest. This only provoked even more women to take to the streets.

These examples, old and new, show the centrality of revolutionary events to women's liberation. The most recent examples are still unfolding, but the counterrevolution is on the offensive and victory remains elusive. We cannot point to a socialist society where equality and liberation has been achieved. Class struggle is an inevitable product of any system based on a minority living off the exploitation of the majority. But victory is far from inevitable. That depends on the role of the working class, the class with the power and the organic drive for unity within it, in the revolt as well as what sort of politics shapes and leads the struggles.

Revolutionaries argue for overcoming divisions, against racism and sexism, and for the biggest possible involvement of workers in leading the struggle, and they fight for a strategy to win. The fact that so many of the leading socialist women mentioned throughout this book were themselves members of revolutionary parties and organisations is no coincidence. From Eleanor Marx and Clara Zetkin to Rosa

Luxemburg, Alexandra Kollontai and Angela Davis we see women who were more than good activists; they saw that building our class into a socialist organisation was vital to win.

We have seen that the role of the working class is critical not just because it has the power but also because, as Marx argued: "All previous historical movements were movements of minorities, or in the interest of minorities. The proletarian movement is the self-conscious, independent movement of the immense majority, in the interest of the immense majority." And women are now more than ever part of that class around the world.

In Egypt the number of women workers in the industrial workforce has exploded since the early 1980s.[560] Sections of the public sector are dominated by women workers, "the education and health systems, along with the local and central government, would cease to function without their labour."[561] Women workers in the textile industry were at the centre of industrial struggles in the years leading up to the Revolution. After one strike in 2007 a male worker spoke to journalists from socialist newspaper *Al-Ishtiraki*: "We don't talk about 'women' and 'men' here. The women of Misr Spinning are braver than a hundred men. They are standing shoulder to shoulder with the men in the strike".[562]

Revolutions are the result of historic clashes between huge class forces in society, Marx described them as "locomotives of history".[563] But these forces are also made up of individuals. The ruling class understands this. During the German Revolution Rosa Luxemburg was seen as so dangerous to those wanting to break the revolutionary movement that they murdered her. Luxemburg made mistakes, one was not seeing the danger in trying to build independent revolutionary organisation during a revolutionary moment. Her murder took from the revolutionaries "their most able and experienced leader. Her successors were able and courageous—but they lacked her experience and her ability to cut through immediate impressions and grasp a situation in its totality".[564] The lesson is, individuals, organisation and ideas matter and they are all linked. The active intervention of organised revolutionaries in the struggle can make the difference between victory and defeat.

What would victory look like?

Plenty of people think that a fairer world where production will be for the needs of the many and not for the profit of the few would be a good thing. But many believe that a truly socialist society would never work and can be no more than a utopian dream.

The quick retort to this is, of course, that capitalism plainly does not work. All the wonders of 21st century capitalism are not providing the basic human needs of water, food and shelter for the population of the world. This is not because there are not enough resources. In fact the development of capitalism unleashed great and unprecedented productive powers. For the first time there was the possibility of plenty, a precondition for a socialist society. We now have enough resources around the globe potentially to feed, clothe and house all of humanity.

But the system that opened up an era of expansion of human possibilities is now holding humanity back. Tens of thousands die every day for lack of clean water or enough food because a tiny elite minority reaps all the benefits of the system's massive productive capacity. The forces of production are capable of providing everything we need but the social relations of production are, as Engels put it, a "positive hindrance". Instead of a world of plenty, ageing capitalism brings us war, famine and the prospect of the very planet we live on being destroyed by climate change. Is this really as good as it gets?

Socialism is not a complicated idea, in fact in contrast to the chaos of capitalism it is the most logical, efficient way to organise society. Just think what might be possible if all the wealth, talent and labour power that went into building nuclear and other weapons or that tried to sell us one brand of washing powder rather than another were invested in improving the lives of the majority of people.

We are not held back by physical limitations, quite the opposite, in fact "our biology makes us free"—humanity's ingenuity and creative and productive powers harnessed for the good of the mass of ordinary people make anything possible.[565] Once we are not pitted against each other in competition then the full fruits of human cooperation will be possible for the first time. We have to say to those who say it is impossible—if humans can fly cameras to Pluto and distribute coke to every corner of the globe, then providing clean water, food, contraception and safe abortions everywhere they are needed should not pose insurmountable hurdles.

Think what real democracy could look like if you had immediately recallable representatives from your workplace, college or community representing you instead of a series of overprivileged men, and a few women, with expense accounts.

True collective responsibility for society will mean everyone has a stake in it and open the possibility for the full blossoming of every individual. Anthropologist Eleanor Leacock wrote that, "the achievement of real cooperation is not at the expense of individual expression, but allows great latitude for it".[566] Imagine how women's lives would be transformed if society took collective responsibility for caring for the next generation rather than expecting the working class nuclear family to shoulder the burden.

Women's oppression will be the most difficult to uproot because it is the oldest and most deeply embedded oppression. The success of future revolutions will depend on the role that women play in the struggle and in the shaping of a new society. Change will not come overnight. There will be no programme or blue print. People who have been through the life-changing struggles of revolution will be better able to imagine and create new ways of living than any of us can attempt in the abstract today.

In a socialist society debates about how people will live and love will be played out in conditions of real choice. Gender will not be defined in proscriptive binary terms and women will not be penalised for having the ability to give birth

Looking to revolutionary change does not mean waiting for it. We cannot sit back in the hope that a great revolutionary moment will come along and simply sweep the system away. Every day we have to fight for every reform, oppose every expression of oppression, organise against every attack. These struggles can win real change.

If the bigots who want to push back abortion rights get away with it, then thousands of women will be forced to overcome more obstacles to access an abortion. So every protest and demonstration makes a difference, every activist who raises a motion in trade union or student meetings to win support for Abortion Rights, makes a difference.[567] Whether we campaign to defend nurseries or women's refuges from the cuts, or strike for equal pay or pension rights, or fight to stop sexist advertising, what we do now can not only win improvements today, it will also shape the struggles of tomorrow.

Because at the same time as throwing ourselves into resistance it is important to see how each and every struggle can, as Clara Zetkin put it, "revolutionise hundreds of thousands of minds". The experience of fighting back can build the confidence and organisation of our side for future and bigger struggles. Every lesson learnt out of defeat and victory can become decisive when the stakes are raised.

That is why fighting for socialist ideas and organisation every day within every struggle, however small, is vital. If we want to do more than run on an endless treadmill of defensive battles for generations to come then we also have to have a bigger vision in our sights—the possibility of a totally different society.

Capitalism pushes us apart and makes us think there is no alternative, that socialism is impossible. But our ability to overthrow the system, and with it the very roots of women's oppression, still lies in the fact that it also has to pull us together as a class in order to function. This is a contradiction that capitalism cannot escape, even in the 21st century. So in the words of Clara Zetkin, we fight and build and organise now so that one day "the working class in its entirety, without distinction of sex, shall be able to call out to the capitalist order of society, 'You rest on us, you oppress us, and see how the building which you have erected is tottering to the ground'."[568]

When the Egyptian people brought down one of the world's most entrenched dictators they inspired millions across the globe. Nothing can beat the experience of standing in Tahrir Square in January 2011. It was to witness real, living proof in the courageous acts of ordinary women and men that Zetkin's dream is within our reach. The fact that the military, backed by Western governments, has reasserted its power using brutal repression, shows the ruling class will stop at nothing to retain their system.

But the Revolution remains powerful testimony in our lifetime of everything that Marx fought for in his. When our class goes into battle whether in Cairo, Athens, Sao Paulo or London, we can shape our own history. We have the potential to win a socialist society, which means real women's liberation and with it the emancipation of the whole of humanity.

NOTES

1 YouGov Poll conducted by the Government Equalities Office, 2014.

2 Alison Wolf, *The XX Factor: How Working Women are Creating a New Society* (Profile Books, 2013), p111.

3 http://adage.com/article/cmo-strategy/marketing-matriarchy/293321/.

4 http://www.prowess.org.uk/ambitious-women-never-had-it-so-good.

5 *Daily Mail*, 23 July 2014, http://www.dailymail.co.uk/femail/article-2703345/The-MYTH-glass-ceiling-Think-women-raw-deal-work-In-ferocious-blast-pioneering-woman-boss-eats-sexist-pigs-breakfast-says-time-stopped-whining.html.

6 Centre for Women and Democracy, *Sex and Power 2014: Who runs Britain?* (Counting Women In coalition, 2014), p6.

7 TUC, *The Pregnancy Test: Ending Discrimination at Work for New Mothers* (TUC, 2014), p2.

8 TUC, *The Pregnancy Test*, pp2-3.

9 Crime Statistics, *Focus on Violent Crime and Sexual Offences, 2012/13* (Office for National Statistics, 2014), Appendix table 2.05. http://www.ons.gov.uk/ons/publications/re-reference-tables.html?edition=tcm%3A77-328149.

10 Joan Smith, *The Public Woman* (Westbourne Press, 2013), p110.

11 Martha Gimenez, "Capitalism and the Oppression of Women: Marx Revisited", *Science and Society Special Issue: Marxist and Feminist Thought Today*, vol 69, no 1, January 2005, p12.

12 Natasha Walter, *The New Feminism* (Little, Brown, 1998).

13 Finn Mackay, *Radical Feminism: Feminist Activism in Movement* (Palgrave Macmillan, 2015), p2.

14 Landry and MacLean give an insight into one consideration affecting feminist academics' engagement with Marxism in academia in the US: "The legacy of McCarthyism and red baiting in the US should not be underestimated, since it accounts to some extent for the many strategies of disavowal of anything Marxist we often find in US feminist work... whether the move to materialism constitutes a comparable evasion... remains to be seen." Donna Landry and Gerald MacLean, *Materialist Feminisms* (Blackwell, 1993), p32.

15 Michele Barrett, *Women's Oppression Today: The Marxist/Feminist Encounter* (Verso, 2014), pxv.

16 Alex Callinicos, *The Revolutionary Ideas of Karl Marx* (Bookmarks, 2004), p65.

17 Karl Marx, "The International Workingmen's Association 1864, General Rules" (October 1864), https://www.marxists.org/history/international/iwma/documents/1864/rules.htm.

18 https://www.marxists.org/archive/marx/works/1894-c3/ch48.htm.

19 Barbara Ehrenreich and Arlie Russell Hochschild, *Global Women: Nannies, Maids and Sex Workers in the New Economy* (Metropolitan Books, 2002), p39.

20 Alison Wolf, *The XX Factor*, p140.

21 Alison Wolf, *The XX Factor*, p337.

22 Rosa Luxemburg, "Women's Suffrage and Class Struggle" (1914) in Hal Draper, *Women and Class: Towards a Socialist Feminism* (Center for Socialist History, 2013), p290.

23 Eleanor Marx, "Women's Trade Unions in England" in Hal Draper, *Women and Class*, p308.

24 August H Nimtz, *Marx and Engels: Their Contribution to the Democratic Breakthrough* (SUNY, 2000) and Heather Brown, *Marx on Gender and the Family: A Critical Study* (Haymarket, 2013).

25 Shulamith Firestone, *The Dialectic of Sex: The Case for Feminist Revolution* (The Women's Press, 1971).

26 Clara Zetkin, *Selected Writings*, edited by Eric Foner (International Publishers, 1984), p108.

27 Clara Zetkin, *Selected Writings*, p108.

28 Martha Gimenez, "Capitalism and the Oppression of Women", p26.

29 Lindsey German, "Theories of Patriarchy", *International Socialism* 12, 1981.

30 http://www.theguardian.com/lifeandstyle/2009/jan/18/recession-murray.

31 Clara Zetkin, *Selected Writings*, p96.

32 http://www.hscic.gov.uk/article/3880/Eating-disorders-Hospital-admissions-up-by-8-per-cent-in-a-year.

33 http://www.transforminglives.co.uk.

34 Louise Phillips, *Mental Illness and the Body* (Routledge, 2006), p57.

35 Louise Phillips, *Mental Illness and the Body*, p57.

36 Stephen Jay Gould, *The Mismeasure of Man* (Penguin, 1992), p103.

37 Laurie Penny, *Meat Market: Female Flesh Under Capitalism* (Zero Books, 2011), p2.

38 Martha Gimenez, "Marxism and Class, Gender and Race: Rethinking the Trilogy", *Race, Gender and Class*, vol 8, no2, 2001, p22.

39 http://www.theguardian.com/uk/2005/jun/07/ukguns.features11.

40 Joan Smith, *The Public Woman*, p180.

41 Quoted in Manning Marable, "Peace and Black Liberation: The Contributions of W E B Du Bois", *Science and Society*, vol 47, no 1, 1983, p92.

42 V I Lenin, *What is to be Done*, https://www.marxists.org/archive/lenin/works/1901/witbd/iii.htm.

43 Eleanor Burke Leacock, *Myths of Male Dominance* (Monthly Review, 1981), p125.

44 http://www.jstor.org/discover/10.2307/2380818?sid=21105605745423&uid=2&uid=4.

45 Karen Sacks, "Engels Revisited", in Rayna Reiter (ed), *Towards an Anthropology of Women* (Monthly Review, 1975), p211.

46 https://www.marxists.org/archive/marx/works/1867-c1/ch07.htm.

47 Marx quoted in Thomas C Patterson, *Marx's Ghost: Conversations with Archaeologists* (Berg, 2009), p15.

48 https://www.marxists.org/archive/marx/works/1867-c1/ch07.htm.

49 Martin Empson, *Land and Labour: Marxism, Ecology and Human History* (Bookmarks, 2014), p16.

50 https://www.marxists.org/archive/marx/works/1883/death/burial.htm.

51 Chris Harman, "Engels and the origins of human society", *International Socialism* 65, Winter 1994, p88.

52 Karl Marx and Friedrich Engels, *The German Ideology* (Lawrence & Wishart, 1994), p64.

53 Friedrich Engels, *The Origin of the Family, Private Property and the State* (Peking Foreign Language Press, 1978), p4.

54 Karl Marx and Friedrich Engels, *The German Ideology*, p50.

55 https://www.marxists.org/archive/marx/works/1845/german-ideology/ch01a.htm.

56 https://www.marxists.org/archive/marx/works/1876/part-played-labour/.

57 Chris Harman, "Engels and the origins of human society", p101.

58 Steven Rose, R C Lewontin, Leon J Kamin, *Not in our Genes: Biology, Ideology and Human Nature* (Penguin, 1990), p286.

59 Chris Stringer, *The Origin of our Species* (Penguin, 2012), p113.

60 Rob Dinnis and Chris Stringer, *Britain: One Million Years of the Human Story* (Natural History Museum, 2013), p13.

61 The tens of thousands of children kept in large understaffed and underresourced orphanages and other state institutions in Romania have been the subject of studies on the impact of neglect. Romania's dictator

Nicolae Ceaușescu banned abortion and contraception in 1966 to boost population numbers but poverty meant many people had to give up their children. After Ceaușescu was toppled in 1989 as part of the wave of revolt against the Stalinist Eastern European regimes the conditions in the institutions were exposed. The children had severe communication and developmental problems as a result of growing up without verbal interaction or even regular eye contact with others. See for example Charles A Nelson, Nathan A Fox and Charles H Zeanah, "Tragedy Leads to Study of Severe Child Neglect", *Scientific American*, vol 308, issue 4, April 2013.

62 https://www.marxists.org/archive/marx/works/1857/grundrisse/ch01.htm. Marx's arguments on this question are explored in the opening chapter of Alex Callinicos, *The Revolutionary Ideas of Karl Marx*.

63 Thomas C Patterson, *Karl Marx, Anthropologist*, p46.

64 Morgan became an advocate of Native American rights, for example defending the Sioux stand against General Custer in 1876. For an interesting account of his life and assessment of his work see the 1984 essay by US anthropologist Elisabeth Tooker, https://www.lib.rochester.edu/index.cfm?PAGE=4040#5.

65 Eleanor Burke Leacock, *Myths of Male Dominance* (Monthly Review, 1981), p89.

66 https://www.marxists.org/archive/marx/works/1884/origin-family/preface2.htm

67 https://www.marxists.org/archive/draper/1970/07/women.htm

68 M Dyble, G D Salali, N Chaudhary, A Page, D Smith, J Thompson, L Vinicius, R Mace, A B Migliano, "Sex equality can explain the unique social structure of hunter-gatherer bands", *Science*, vol 348, no 6236, 15 May 2015, p796.

69 Thomas C Patterson, *Karl Marx,*

Anthropologist, p84.

70 http://web.archive.org/web/20010804020927/http://puffin.creighton.edu/jesuit/relations/.

71 http://puffin.creighton.edu/jesuit/relations/relations_14.html.

72 http://web.archive.org/web/20011215143225/http://puffin.creighton.edu/jesuit/relations/relations_15.html.

73 George Seaver, *David Livingstone: His Life and Letters* (Haroer, 1957), available at http://archive.org/stream/davidlivingstone001439mbp/davidlivingstone001439mbp_djvu.txt.

74 Eleanor Burke Leacock, *Myths of Male Dominance*, p239.

75 Eleanor Burke Leacock, *Myths of Male Dominance*, p 112.

76 Martin Empson, *Land and Labour*, p21.

77 Chris Stringer, *The Origin of our Species*, p143.

78 Empson looks at some of the possible environmental reasons the Neanderthals died out, leaving Homo sapiens as "the only humans on the planet". Martin Empson, *Land and Labour*.

79 Chris Stringer, *The Origin of our Species*, p221.

80 Kent Flannery and Joyce Marcus, *The Creation of Inequality: How our Prehistoric Ancestors Set the Stage for Monarchy, Slavery and Empire* (Harvard University Press, 2012), p3.

81 Thomas C Patterson, *Marx's Ghost*, p108.

82 Evelyn Reed, *Women's Evolution: From Matriarchal Clan to Patriarchal Family* (Pathfinder Press, 1975), p132.

83 Martin Empson, *Land and Labour*, p26.

84 Kent Flannery and Joyce Marcus, *The Creation of Inequality*, p559.

85 Kent Flannery and Joyce Marcus, *The Creation of Inequality*, p559.

86 Thomas C Patterson, *Marx's Ghost*, p110.

87 Thomas C Patterson, *Marx's Ghost*, p110.

88 Kent Flannery and Joyce Marcus, *The Creation of Inequality*, p563.

89 Karen Sacks, "Engels Revisited", p217.

90 Chris Harman, "Engels and the origins of human society", p136.

91 Heather Brown, *Marx on Gender and the Family*, p220.

92 Both Lise Vogel and Martha Gimenez have in the past pointed to the passage in the preface that led to some socialist feminists seeing Engels as legitimising a dual systems approach.

93 Heather Brown, *Marx on Gender and the Family*, p168.

94 Karl Marx and Friedrich Engels, *The Communist Manifesto* (Progress, 1977), p55.

95 Friedrich Engels, *The Origin of the Family*, p65.

96 Antonio Labriola, *Essays on the Materialistic Conception of History* (Cosimo, 2005), p155.

97 Leon Trotsky, *Women and the Family* (Pathfinder, 2009), p61.

98 Feminist magazine *Spare Rib* had an ironic "Don't Do It Di" campaign in 1981 in the lead up to the royal wedding of Prince Charles and Diana Spencer. The marriage famously collapsed after she had delivered the heir and spare.

99 Dugald Stewart quoted in Karl Marx, *Capital* vol 1 (Penguin, 1979), p616.

100 http://newleftreview.org/I/113-114/christopher-middleton-the-sexual-division-of-labour-in-feudal-england

101 Ivy Pinchbeck, *Women Workers and the Industrial Revolution 1750-1850* (Cass 1977), p1.

102 Ivy Pinchbeck, *Women Workers and the Industrial Revolution*, p168.

103 Ivy Pinchbeck, *Women Workers and the Industrial Revolution*, p249.

104 Ross Davies, *Women and Work* (Arrow Books, 1975), p44.

105 Ivy Pinchbeck, *Women Workers and the Industrial Revolution*, p261.

106 Lindsey German, *Sex, Class and Socialism* (Bookmarks, 1998), p25.

107 Heidi Hartmann, *The Unhappy Marriage of Marxism and Feminism* (Pluto Press, 1986), p15.

108 Ivy Pinchbeck, *Women Workers and the Industrial Revolution*, p269.

109 Louise A Tilly and Joan Scott, *Work, Women and Family* (Methuen, 1987), p196.

110 Clementina Black (ed), *Married Women's Work* (Virago, 1983), p7.

111 Chris Harman, "Women's Liberation and Revolutionary Socialism", *International Socialism* 23, Spring 1984, https://www.marxists.org/archive/harman/1984/xx/women.html.

112 carersuk.org.

113 http://www.salary.com/2014-mothers-day-infographics/.

114 http://www.ons.gov.uk/ons/dcp171766_300224.pdf.

115 http://www.ons.gov.uk/ons/rel/wellbeing/household-satellite-accounts/valuing-household-clothing-and-laundry-services-in-the-uk/rpt--household-clothing-and-laundry-services.html.

116 Studs Terkel, *Hard Times: An Oral History of the Great Depression* (The New Press, 1986), p162.

117 http://www.bbc.co.uk/news/uk-22610534. The BBC did a report for one month of deaths due to domestic violence.

118 http://www.nspcc.org.uk/preventing-abuse/research-and-resources/child-abuse-and-neglect-in-the-uk-today/.

119 http://www.bridesmagazine.co.uk/planning/general/planning-service/2013/01/average-cost-of-wedding.

120 http://www.telegraph.co.uk/women/womens-life/9817799/Hen-dos-every-girl-I-know-complains-about-the-cost.html

121 Alexandra Kollontai, *Selected Writings* (Alison and Busby, 1977), p258.

122 Michele Barrett, *Women's Oppression Today*, pxxxvi.

123 http://www.scu.edu/ethics/publications/other/lawreview/familyvalues.html#14f.

124 http://www.ons.gov.uk/ons/rel/

census/2011-census-analysis/how-have-living-arrangements-and-marital-status-in-england-and-wales-changed-since-2001-/summary.html.

125 http://thefeministbride.com/, http://www.catalystwedco.com/magazine/, http://www.theguardian.com/lifeandstyle/2014/jun/28/can-a-feminist-be-a-bride-laura-bates, http://everydayfeminism.com/2015/02/feminist-wedding/.

126 http://www.ons.gov.uk/ons/rel/vsob1/divorces-in-england-and-wales/2012/sty-13-facts.html.

127 http://www.ons.gov.uk/ons/rel/vsob1/birth-summary-tables--england-and-wales/2013/info-births-2013.html.

128 http://www.ons.gov.uk/ons/rel/vsob1/birth-summary-tables--england-and-wales/2013/info-births-2013.html.

129 http://www.ons.gov.uk/ons/rel/vsob1/birth-summary-tables--england-and-wales/2013/info-births-2013.html.

130 Jenny Chanfreau, Sally Gowland, Zoë Lancaster, Eloise Poole, Sarah Tipping and Mari Toomse, *Maternity and Paternity Rights and Women Returners, Survey 2009/10* (Department for Work and Pensions, September 2011), p7.

131 *Not Having it All: How Motherhood Reduces Women's Pay and Employment Prospects* (Fawcett Society, July 2009), p5.

132 http://www.nct.org.uk/sites/default/files/related_documents/ReturningToWork-Survey.pdf.

133 In a crass example of the casual sexism of the media the women MPs were called "Blair's Babes".

134 http://www.gingerbread.org.uk/content/365/Statistics.

135 http://www.gingerbread.org.uk/content/365/Statistics.

136 carersuk.org.

137 Marx and Engels, *Communist Manifesto*, p55.

138 Professor Hurlbert, Newcastle school of Psychology, quoted in Natasha Walter, *Living Dolls: The Return of Sexism* (Virago 2010), p145.

139 http://www.smithsonianmag.com/arts-culture/when-did-girls-start-wearing-pink-1370097/#DZbZxVDRr88T20c1.99.

140 Jo B Paoletti, *Pink and Blue: Telling the Boys from the Girls in America* (Indiana University Press, 2012), p101.

141 Jo B Paoletti, *Pink and Blue*, p95.

142 Steven Rose, *Lifelines* (Allen Lane, 1997), p280.

143 Quoted in Richard Lewontin, *It Ain't Necessarily So: The Dream of the Human Genome and Other Illusions* (Granta, 2000), p205.

144 Marian Lowe, "Sociobiology and Sex Differences", *Signs*, vol 4, no 1, *Women, Science, and Society*, autumn 1978, p118.

145 Richard Dawkins, *The Selfish Gene* (Granada, 1978).

146 Hilary and Steven Rose, *Alas, Poor Darwin: Arguments Against Evolutionary Psychology* (Jonathan Cape, 2000), p176.

147 Quoted in Deborah Cameron, *The Myth of Mars and Venus: Do Men and Women Really Speak Different Languages?* (Oxford University Press, 2007), p100.

148 John Marshall Townsend, Gary Levy, "Effects of Potential Partners' Physical Attractiveness and Socioeconomic Status on Sexuality and Partner Selection", *Archives of Sexual Behavior*, vol 19, no 2, 1990, pp149-164.

149 Krzysztof Kościński, "Assessment of Waist-to-Hip Ratio Attractiveness in Women: An Anthropometric Analysis of Digital Silhouettes", *Archives of Sexual Behavior*, vol 43, no 5, 2014, pp989-997. This study of 40 men concludes that such a "preference pattern mirrors the relationship between WHR and mate value, suggesting that the preferences are adaptive."

150 http://www.harpercollins.co.uk/9780007478361/men-are-from-mars-women-are-from-venus.

151 See Cordelia Fine, *Delusions of Gender: The Real Science Behind Sex*

Difference (Icon Books, 2010), Natasha Walter, *Living Dolls*, p195.

152 Jo B Paoletti, *Pink and Blue*, p101.

153 Steven Rose, *Lifelines*, p115.

154 Cordelia Fine, *Delusions of Gender*, p177.

155 Lise Eliot, *Pink Brain, Blue Brain*, p8, Eliot explains that a male's Y chromosome is by far the smallest of the 46 chromosomes and "constitutes about 60 genes; compare this to the approximately 800 genes on the X chromosome and some 25,000 in the total genome."

156 Louann Brizendine, *The Female Brain*, quoted in Lise Eliot, *Pink Brain, Blue Brain*, p9.

157 John Komlos and Benjamin E Lauderdale, "Underperformance in Affluence: The Remarkable Relative Decline in US Heights in the Second Half of the 20th Century", *Social Science Quarterly*, vol 88, no 2, June 2007, p283.

158 Kent Flannery and Joyce Marcus, *The Creation of Inequality*, p182.

159 Laura Miles, "Transgender Oppression and Resistance", *International Socialism* 141, Winter 2014.

160 Finn Mackay, *Radical Feminism*, p249.

161 Julie Bindel, "The Operation that can Ruin your Life", *Standpoint*, November 2009, http://www.standpointmag. co.uk/node/2298/full.

162 Finn Mackay, *Radical Feminism*, p256.

163 http://www.theguardian.com/ commentisfree/2009/feb/01/ davos-global-recession-gender.

164 http://dealbook.nytimes. com/2010/05/11/lagarde-what-if-it-had-been-lehman-sisters/?_r=0.

165 Judith Orr, "Lehman Sisters?" *Socialist Review*, March 2009, http://socialistreview.org.uk/334/ lehman-sisters.

166 Valentine M Moghadam, "Women, Gender, and Economic Crisis Revisited", *Perspectives on Global Development and Technology*, vol 10, issue 1, 2011, pp36-37.

167 http://www.theguardian.com/ business/2009/feb/15/gender-recession-credit-crunch. The round table discussion this article covers was headlined, "We can't go back to the old macho ways."

168 *Financial Times*, 16 January 2015, http://www.ft.com/cms/s/0/5482ac56-9d7a-11e4-8946-00144feabdc0.html?si teedition=uk#axzz3PaZThg01.

169 Lise Eliot, *Pink Brain, Blue Brain*, p7.

170 Gayle Rubin in Rayna R Reiter (ed), *Towards an Anthropology of Women* (Monthly Review, 1975), p180. She quotes the passage from Deuteronomy (22.5) in the *Bible* which declares that women who wear clothes "that pertaineth unto a man" and vice versa "are an abomination".

171 This experiment by Gleitman, Friedlund and Reisberg in 2000 is quoted in https://www.iser.essex. ac.uk/files/conferences/bhps/2003/ docs/pdf/papers/crespi.pdf.

172 Condry and Condry (1976) quoted in https://www.iser.essex.ac.uk/files/ conferences/bhps/2003/docs/pdf/ papers/crespi.pdf.

173 http://www.habsboys.org.uk/ Main-School-School-Rules.

174 http://www.parentdish. co.uk/2014/04/08/boy-15-threatened-with-exclusion-for-wearing-make-up-nomakeupselfie/#!slide= aol_1003921.

175 http://www.walesonline.co.uk/news/ wales-news/cardiff-schoolboys-turn-up-classes-5134447.

176 Lise Eliot, *Pink Brain, Blue Brain*, p136.

177 Lise Eliot, *Pink Brain, Blue Brain*, p121.

178 Jessica Valenti, *He's a Stud, She's a Slut and 49 Other Double Standards Every Woman Should Know* (Seal Press, 2008), p14.

179 From "The Causes of Sex Delinquency in Girls", 1936, quoted in Carol Dyhouse, *Girl Trouble: Panic and Process in the History of Young Women* (Zed, 2013), p107. Cyril Burt's ideas on IQ, which he claimed was inherited,

formed the basis for the 11-plus test and shaped educational policy for half a century in Britain. His research results, using identical twins, were subsequently found to be bogus and in some cases simply made up. See John Parrington, "The Intelligence Fraud", *Socialist Review*, April 1996, http://pubs.socialistreviewindex.org.uk/sr196/parrington.htm.

180 http://www.theguardian.com/uk-news/2015/jan/14/former-london-teacher-convicted-over-affair-with-teenager.

181 Judith Orr, "Rochdale: An anatomy of the sexual abuse scandal", *International Socialism* 135, Summer 2012.

182 Lise Eliot, *Pink Brain, Blue Brain*, p237.

183 Cordelia Fine, *Delusions of Gender*, p35.

184 Quoted in Carol Dyhouse, *Girl Trouble*, p68.

185 https://www.youtube.com/watch?v=_xjgI5oN8DM.

186 Polly Toynbee, *Guardian*, 18 August 1995.

187 Kaydee Summers, "Unequal Genders: Mothers and Fathers on Mountains" (2007), https://www.sheffield.ac.uk/polopoly_fs/1.71700!/file/10-Summers-article.pdf.

188 Quoted in Ivy Pinchbeck, *Women Workers and the Industrial Revolution*, p311.

189 Quoted in Nickie Charles, *Gender in Modern Britain* (Oxford, 2002), p110.

190 Anne and Bill Noir, *Why Men don't Iron: The New Reality of Gender Differences* (Harper Collins, 1999).

191 Warren Farrell, *The Myth of Male Power: Why Men are the Disposable Sex* (Finch, 2001).

192 Hanna Rosin, *The End of Men and the Rise of Women* (Viking, 2012), p79.

193 Kay S Hymowitz, *Manning Up: How the Rise of Women has Turned Men in to Boys* (Basic Books, 2011), pp102-103.

194 Kay S Hymowitz, *Manning Up*, p103.

195 "Valley of the Dudes", *The Economist*, 4 April, 2015.

196 https://www.gov.uk/government/statistics/gcse-and-equivalent-attainment-by-pupil-characteristics-2012-to-2013.

197 https://www.ucas.com/corporate/news-and-key-documents/news/ucas-publishes-2014-end-cycle-data-resources.

198 Women in Journalism carried out research into how young men were portrayed in the media and listed some examples: http://womeninjournalism.co.uk/hoodies-or-altar-boys/.

199 Emma Perry and Becky Francis, *The Social Class Gap For Educational Achievement: A Review of the Literature* (Royal Society for the Encouragement of Arts, Manufactures and Commerce, December 2010), p2.

200 http://www.genderandeducation.com/resources/pedagogies/singlesex-coeducation/.

201 Sara Delamont, *Sex Roles and the School* (Methuen, 1980), p11.

202 http://www.ons.gov.uk/ons/rel/subnational-health4/suicides-in-the-united-kingdom/2013-registrations/suicides-in-the-united-kingdom--2013-registrations.html.

203 Susan Faludi, *Stiffed: The Betrayal of Modern Man* (Vintage, 2000).

204 Steve Humphries and Pamela Gordon, *A Man's World: From Boyhood to Manhood, 1900-1960* (BBC, 1996), p173.

205 Laura King, *Family Men: Fatherhood and Masculinity in Britain* (Oxford University Press, 2015), p27.

206 Reproduced in Warren Farrell, *The Myth of Male Power*, p107.

207 http://www.theguardian.com/media/2009/may/20/asa-oven-pride-cleared-of-sexism.

208 Sheila Rowbotham, *Hidden from History* (Pluto Press, 1983), p13

209 Tony Cliff describes the radical groups that emerged during the period such as the Levellers, Diggers and Ranters, and their debates about women's position in society in *Class Struggle and Women's Liberation: 1640 to the Present Day* (Bookmarks, 1984), p14.

210 Sheila Rowbotham, *Women, Resistance and Revolution* (Penguin, 1972), p17.

211 Sheila Rowbotham, *Hidden from History*, p11.

212 Janet Todd, *Mary Wollstonecraft: A Revolutionary Life* (Weidenfeld & Nicolson, 2000), p219.

213 John M Merriman, *Massacre: The Life and Death of the Paris Commune of 1871* (Yale, 2014), p231.

214 August H Nimtz, *Marx and Engels*, p199.

215 Heather Brown, *Marx on Gender and the Family*, p118.

216 Clara Zetkin, *Selected Writings*, p50.

217 Clara Zetkin, *Selected Writings*, p31.

218 Sheila Rowbotham, *Dreamers of a New Day: Women who Invented the Twentieth Century* (Verso, 2010), p175.

219 Louise A Tilly and Joan W Scott, *Work, Women and Family* (Methuen, 1987), p189.

220 Sarah Boston, *Women Workers and the Trade Unions* (Davis-Poynter, 1980), p48.

221 Louise Raw, *Striking a Light: The Bryant and May Matchwomen* (Continuum, 2011), p219.

222 Barbara Drake, *Women in Trade Unions* (Virago, 1984), p27.

223 Letter from Engels to Laura Lafargue, 10 May 1890, https://www.marxists.org/archive/marx/works/1890/letters/90_05_10.htm

224 Barbara Drake, *Women in Trade Unions*, p28.

225 Barbara Drake, *Women in Trade Unions*, p30.

226 Jill Liddington and Jill Norris, *One Hand Tied Behind Us: The Rise of the Women's Suffrage Movement* (Rivers Oram, 2000), p122.

227 Jill Liddington and Jill Norris, *One Hand Tied Behind Us*, p175.

228 Marian Ramelson, *The Petticoat Rebellion: A Century of Struggle for Women's Rights* (Lawrence and Wishart, 1976), p148.

229 George Dangerfield, *The Strange Death of Liberal England* (Stanford, 1997), p153.

230 Paul Foot, *The Vote: How it was Won and How it was Undermined* (Viking, 2005), p226.

231 Jill Liddington and Jill Norris, *One Hand Tied Behind Us*, p19.

232 Helen Gordon Liddle, an extract from "The Prisoner" in Michael Rosen and David Widgery (eds), *The Chatto Book of Dissent* (Chatto & Windus, 1991), p140.

233 George Dangerfield, *The Strange Death of Liberal England*, p136.

234 Barbara Winslow, *Sylvia Pankhurst: Sexual Politics and Political Activism* (UCL, 1996), p67. The princess was an heiress to the Singer sewing machine empire, an open lesbian, a public housing advocate who built a housing project for the poor in Paris and a patron of the arts.

235 Sylvia Pankhurst, *The Suffragette Movement* (Virago, 1978), p517.

236 George Dangerfield, *The Strange Death of Liberal England*, p176.

237 Jill Liddington and Jill Norris, *One Hand Tied Behind Us*, p269.

238 http://www.parliament.uk/about/living-heritage/transformingsociety/electionsvoting/womenvote/overview/thevote/

239 Barbara Evans Clements, *Bolshevik Women* (Cambridge University Press, 1997), p107.

240 Quoted in Tony Cliff, "Clara Zetkin and the German Socialist Feminist Movement", *International Socialism* 13, Summer 1981, p69.

241 Elizabeth Roberts, *Women and Families: An Oral History, 1940-1970* (Blackwell, 1995), p117.

242 It is still one of the bestselling books of all time. Spock's view was a break from the rigorous routine and disciplinarian advice on child rearing that dominated before the war, but its popularity showed that bringing up children was something that parents, especially mothers, were increasingly expected to learn about in a world where the

extended family didn't always live in the same street.

243 Barbara Ehrenreich, *For Her Own Good: Two Centuries of the Experts' Advice to Women* (Anchor Books, 2005), p252.

244 http://individual.utoronto.ca/vicedo/vicedoca/Publications_files/Vicedo_BJHS.pdf.

245 Elizabeth Roberts, *Women and Families*, p138.

246 Carol Dyson, *Girl Trouble*, p128.

247 Louise A Tilly and Joan Scott, *Work, Women and Family*, p214.

248 Sara Evans, *Personal Politics: The Roots of Women's Liberation in the Civil Rights Movement and the New Left* (Vintage, 1980), p11.

249 Jonathan Eig, *The Birth of the Pill: How Four Pioneers Reinvented Sex and Launched a Revolution* (Macmillan, 2014), p312. The scale of uptake was shown by some unpredicted side effects: "Many women experienced unexpected breast growth—to the extent that the sale of C-cup bras increased 50 percent from 1960 to 1969."

250 Louise A Tilly and Joan Scott, *Work, Women and Family*, p168.

251 Edward Shorter, *A History of Women's Bodies* (Penguin, 1984), p191.

252 Jane Lewis, *Women in England, 1870-1950* (Wheatsheaf, 1984), p17.

253 Jane Lewis, *Women in England*, p17.

254 Lionel Rose, *Massacre of the Innocents: Infanticide in Great Britain 1800-1939* (Routledge and Kegan Paul, 1986), p88.

255 Jeffrey Weeks, *Sex, Politics and Society* (Longman, 1981), p259.

256 Jennifer Nelson, *Women of Color and the Reproductive Rights Movement* (NYU Press, 2003), p68.

257 Miriam Schneir (ed), *The Vintage Book of Feminism* (Vintage, 1995), p152.

258 Elizabeth Roberts, *Women and Families*, p128.

259 Julie A Matthaei, *An Economic History of Women in America: Women's Work, the Sexual Division of Labour, and the Development of Capitalism* (Harvester Press, 1982), p133.

260 *National Black Feminist Organisation Statement of Purpose*, in Miriam Schneir (ed), *The Vintage Book of Feminism*, p171.

261 Tanisha C Ford, "SNCC Women, Denim, and the Politics of Dress", *The Journal of Southern History*, vol 79, no 3), p625.

262 Sara Evans, *Personal Politics*, p39.

263 Sara Evans, *Personal Politics*, p61.

264 Aaron Cohen, *Amazing Grace* (Continuum, 2011), p43.

265 Kate Weigand, *Red Feminism: American Communism and the Making of Women's Liberation* (Johns Hopkins, 2001), p141.

266 Juliet Mitchell, *Woman's Estate* (Penguin, 1974), p94.

267 Martha Gimenez in Janet Sayers, Mary Evans and Nanneke Redclift, *Engels Revisited: New Feminist Essays* (Tavistock Publications, 1987), p39.

268 Anne Koedt, Ellen Levine, Anita Rapone (eds), *Radical Feminism* (Quadrangle, 1973), p320.

269 Sara Evans, *Personal Politics*, p120.

270 Sara Evans, *Personal Politics*, p120.

271 Kate Weigand, *Red Feminism*, p149; and see the powerful interviews with many different children of Communists in Judy Kaplan and Linn Shapiro (eds), *Red Diapers: Growing up in the Communist Left* (University of Illinois, 1998).

272 Betty Friedan, *It Changed my Life: Writings on the Women's Movement* (Victor Gollancz, 1976), pIII. Friedan writes in this memoir and collection of writings that "for me it began in the late 1950s…"—so skipping over the 1940s and early 1950s when she was a left wing journalist.

273 Daniel Horowitz, "Rethinking Betty Friedan and The Feminine Mystique: Labor union radicalism and feminism in Cold War America", *American Quarterly* 48.1, 1996, p3.

274 Alice Echols, *Daring to be Bad: Radical Feminism in America 1967-1975*

(Minnesota, 1989), p26.

275 Kate Weigand, *Red Feminism*, p156.

276 Judith Hole and Ellen Levine, *Rebirth of Feminism* (Quadrangle, 1973), p120.

277 Sara Evans, *Personal Politics*, p85.

278 Sara Evans, *Personal Politics*, p87. In her account of this incident Echols writes that many of the women in the group joined in the laughter and saw his statement as a parody of the movement. But even if this was the case it shows that the dismissive treatment of women was openly acknowledged rather than being challenged.

279 Judith Hole and Ellen Levine, *Rebirth of Feminism*, p112.

280 Alice Echols, *Daring to be Bad*, p120.

281 From Jo Freeman's own account, http://www.jofreeman.com/aboutjo/persorg.htm.

282 Alice Echols, *Daring to be Bad*, p65.

283 Alice Echols, *Daring to be Bad*, p51.

284 Alice Echols, *Daring to be Bad*, p52.

285 Alice Echols, *Daring to be Bad*, p52.

286 Alice Echols, *Daring to be Bad*, p12.

287 Sara Evans, *Personal Politics*, p214.

288 Alice Echols, *Daring to be Bad*, p92.

289 Judith Hole and Ellen Levine, *Rebirth of Feminism*, p420.

290 Miriam Schneir (ed), *The Vintage Book of Feminism*, p130.

291 Alice Echols, *Daring to be Bad*, p162.

292 Alice Echols, *Daring to be Bad*, p68.

293 Alice Echols, *Daring to be Bad*, p62.

294 Leslie B Tanner (ed), *Voices from Women's Liberation* (Signet, 1971), p366.

295 Leslie B Tanner (ed), *Voices from Women's Liberation*, p400.

296 Leslie B Tanner (ed), *Voices from Women's Liberation*, p411.

297 Alice Echols, *Daring to be Bad*, p246.

298 Leslie B Tanner (ed), *Voices from Women's Liberation*, p406.

299 Miriam Schneir (ed), *The Vintage Book of Feminism*, p160.

300 Miriam Schneir (ed), *The Vintage Book of Feminism*, p161.

301 Quoted in Alice Echols, *Daring to be Bad*, p105.

302 Alice Echols, *Daring to be Bad*, p105.

303 Alice Echols, *Daring to be Bad*, p176.

304 Alice Echols, *Daring to be Bad*, p96.

305 Alice Echols, *Daring to be Bad*, p71.

306 Michelene Wandor (ed), *Body Politic: Women's Liberation in Britain 1969-1972* (Stage 1, 1972), p91.

307 Interview in *Socialist Review*, October 2010, http://socialistreview.org.uk/351/when-history-was-made-dagenham.

308 Sheila Rowbotham in Michelene Wandor (ed), *Body Politic*, p95.

309 Rowbotham in Michelene Wandor (ed), *Body Politic*, p97.

310 Interview with author, *Socialist Review*, April 2010, http://socialistreview.org.uk/346/interview-sheila-rowbotham-women-who-dreamed-emancipation

311 Rowbotham in Michelene Wandor (ed), *Body Politic*, p98.

312 This was even the case in some consciousness raising groups. One account of a small women's group in London includes women reporting what they thought was valuable about their experience in the group, one woman, Judy, who had just split from her husband in week 15 of meeting said, "She'd valued the discussions we'd had about marriage and felt they'd help her understand. Jean said a therapy group could have had the same effect. Judy said she didn't know of any therapy groups which read and talked about Engels' *Origin of the Family*." Michelene Wandor (ed), *Body Politic*, p111.

313 Michelene Wandor (ed), *Body Politic*.

314 Sandra Allen, Lee Sanders and Jan Wallis (eds), *Conditions of Illusion: Papers from the Women's Movement* (Feminist Books, 1974).

315 Sheila Rowbotham, *A Century of Women: The History of Women in Britain and the United States* (Penguin, 1999), p415.

316 Judith Hunt and Shelley Adams, *Women, Work and Trade Union Organisation* (Workers Educational Association pamphlet, London, 1980), p15.

317 Anna Coote and Beatrix Campbell, *Sweet Freedom* (Blackwell, 1987), p32.

318 Tony Cliff, *Class Struggle and Women's Liberation*, p170.

319 Tufnell Park group of the London Women's Liberation Workshop in Michelene Wandor (ed), *Body Politic*, p103.

320 Rowbotham, in Michelene Wandor (ed), *Body Politic*, p100.

321 Anna Coote and Beatrix Campbell, *Sweet Freedom*, p165.

322 Sheila Rowbotham, Lynne Segal and Hilary Wainright, *Beyond the Fragments: Feminism and the Making of Socialism* (Merlin Press, 2013).

323 For a contemporary assessment of the original *Beyond the Fragments* see Peter Goodwin, "Beyond the Frangments", *International Socialism* 9, Summer 1980, p95.

324 Lynne Segal, *Slow Motion: Changing Masculinities, Changing Men* (Virago, 1990), p314.

325 Anna Coote and Beatrix Campbell, *Sweet Freedom*, p106.

326 Anna Coote and Beatrix Campbell, *Sweet Freedom*, p243.

327 Anna Coote and Beatrix Campbell, *Sweet Freedom*, p243.

328 Barbara Harford and Sarah Hopkins, *Greenham Common: Women at the Wire* (The Women's Press, 1984), p166.

329 Susan Faludi, "Death of a Revolutionary: Obituary of Shulamith Firestone", *New Yorker*, 15 April 2013, http://www.newyorker.com/magazine/2013/04/15/death-of-a-revolutionary?currentPage=all

330 Tony Cliff, *Class Struggle and Women's Liberation*, p176.

331 Anne Koedt, Ellen Levine, Anita Rapone (eds), *Radical Feminism*, p300.

332 Elizabeth Roberts, *Women and Families*, p63.

333 Hester Eisenstein, *Feminism Seduced: How Global Elites use Women's Labor and Ideas to Exploit the World* (Paradigm, 2009), p1.

334 Women and Work Commission, 2006.

335 Quoted in Hester Eisenstein, *Feminism Seduced*, p131.

336 Tony Cliff, *Class Struggle and Women's Liberation*, p167.

337 Alice Echols, *Daring to be Bad*, p6.

338 Natasha Walter, *The New Feminism*, pp172, 175.

339 Helen Wilkinson in Natasha Walter (ed), *On the Move: Feminism for a New Generation* (Virago Press, 1999), p31.

340 Susan Faludi, *Backlash: The Undeclared War Against Women* (Chatto & Windus 1992).

341 Susan Faludi, *Backlash*, p355.

342 Sarah Gamble (ed), *The Routledge Companion to Feminism and Post Feminism* (Routledge, 2001), p190.

343 Susan Faludi, *Backlash*, p353.

344 http://www.msmagazine.com/spring2002/BecomingThirdWaveRebeccaWalker.pdf.

345 Simon Reynolds and Joy Press, *The Sex Revolts: Gender, Rebellion and Rock 'n' Roll* (Serpent's Tail, 1995), p327.

346 Natasha Walter, *The New Feminism*, p36.

347 Jessica Valenti, *Full Frontal Feminism* (Seal Press, 2007), p1.

348 Susan Archer Mann and Douglas J Huffman, "The Decentring of Second Wave Feminism and the Rise of the Third Wave", in *Science and Society Special Issue*, vol 69, no 1, January 2005, p69.

349 Kath Woodward and Sophie Woodward, *Why Feminism Matters: Feminism Lost and Found* (Palgrave Macmillan, 2009), p30.

350 http://www.theguardian.com/politics/2012/jan/08/tory-women-mps-new-feminism.

351 Kath Woodward and Sophie Woodward, *Why Feminism Matters*, p169.

352 Perial Aschenbrand, *The Only Bush I Trust is My Own* (Corgi, 2006).

353 http://www.theguardian.com/books/2006/apr/09/society.

354 Quoted in Clair Snyder, "What is the

Third Wave?", *Signs*, vol 1, Autumn 2008. As Snyder goes on to write this is "a position that legitimises potentially everything a woman chooses to do as feminist."

355 Jennifer Baumgardner, *F'em! Goo Goo, Gaga, and Some Thoughts on Balls* (Seal Press, 2011), p250.

356 Hester Eisenstein, *Feminism Seduced*, p178.

357 Hilal Elver, *The Headscarf Controversy: Secularism and Freedom of Religion* (Oxford University Press, 2012), p119.

358 Christine Delphy, *Separate and Dominate: Feminism and Racism After the War on Terror* (Verso, 2015), pXV.

359 Nina Power, *One Dimensional Woman* (Zero Books, 2009), p11.

360 Hester Eisenstein, *Feminism Seduced*, p13.

361 Christine Delphy, *Separate and Dominate*, pp142-143.

362 Christine Delphy, *Separate and Dominate*, p35.

363 Liz Fekete, "Enlightened Fundamentalism? Immigration, feminism and the Right", *Race & Class* 48; 1, 2006, http://statecrime.org/data/uploads/2011/10/fekete2006a.pdf.

364 Michele Barrett, *Women's Oppression Today*, pxxlviii.

365 Lise Vogel, *Woman Questions: Essays for a Materialist Feminism* (Routledge, 1995), p105.

366 Jennifer Baumgardner and Amy Richards, *Manifesta: Young Women, Feminism, and the Future* (Farrar Straus Giroux, 2010).

367 Gary McFarlane in Brian Richardson (ed), *Say it Loud! Marxism and the Fight Against Racism* (Bookmarks, 2013), p102.

368 Naomi Klein, *No Logo* (Flamingo, 2000), p121.

369 Michael Kimmel and Abby L Ferber (eds), *Privilege: A Reader* (Westview Press, 2010), p218.

370 In a critique of intersectionality Delia D Aguilar points to newsletters published in the early 1970s by black feminists called Triple Jeopardy and subtitled "racism, imperialism and sexism", "Tracing the Roots of Intersectionality", *Monthly Review*, April 2012, http://mrzine.monthlyreview.org/2012/aguilar120412.html.

371 Miriam Schneir (ed), *The Vintage Book of Feminism*, p173. The group took their name from a daring and successful night raid at Combahee Ferry in South Carolina during the American Civil War. Escaped slave Harriet Tubman led union soldiers to rescue 700 slaves under heavy fire from slaveholders and Confederate troops.

372 http://circuitous.org/scraps/combahee.html.

373 Esme Choonara and Yuri Prasad, "What's wrong with Privilege Theory?", *International Socialism* 142, Spring 2014, http://www.isj.org.uk/index.php4?id=971&issue=142.

374 Kimberle Crenshaw, *Demarginalizing the Intersection of Race and Sex: A Black Feminist Critique of Antidiscrimination Doctrine, Feminist Theory, and Antiracist Politics* (University of Chicago Legal Forum, 1989), p139, http://philpapers.org/archive/CREDTI.pdf

375 Patricia Hill Collins, "Toward a New Vision: Race, Class and Gender as Categories of Analysis and Connection" in Michael Kimmel and Abby L Ferber (eds), *Privilege: A Reader*, p234.

376 Gary Younge, interview in *Socialist Review* (June 2010), http://socialistreview.org.uk/348/interview-gary-younge-contradictions-identity.

377 Esme Choonara and Yuri Prasad, "What's wrong with Privilege Theory?", p100.

378 Michael Kimmel and Abby L Ferber (eds), *Privilege: A Reader*, p6.

379 Michael Kimmel and Abby L Ferber (eds), *Privilege: A Reader*, p252.

380 Michael Kimmel and Abby L Ferber (eds), *Privilege: A Reader*, p120.

381 Peggy McIntosh, "White Privilege and

Male Privilege: a personal account of coming to see correspondences through work in women's studies" (1988), in Michael Kimmel and Abby L Ferber (eds), *Privilege: A Reader*, p13.

382 Esme Choonara and Yuri Prasad, "What's wrong with Privilege Theory?", p99.

383 Nancy Fraser, *Fortunes of Feminism: From State Managed Capitalism to Neoliberal Crisis* (Verso, 2013), p159.

384 Teresa E Ebert, "Materialising Feminism" in *Science and Society Special Issue*, vol 69, no 1, January 2005, p35.

385 Karl Marx and Friedrich Engels, *The German Ideology*, p37.

386 Delia D Aguilar, "Tracing the Roots of Intersectionality", http://mrzine.monthlyreview.org/2012/aguilar120412.html.

387 Susan Archer Mann and Douglas J Huffman, "The Decentring of Second Wave Feminism and the Rise of the Third Wave", p84.

388 Susan Archer Mann and Douglas J Huffman, "The Decentring of Second Wave Feminism and the Rise of the Third Wave", p61.

389 Rosemary Hennessy, Profit and Pleasure: Sexual identities in late capitalism (Routledge, 2000), p67. Finn Mackay takes to task those who criticise such groups as the Leeds Revolutionary Feminist group for their supposed exclusion of heterosexual women, saying that this did not mean "becoming a lesbian necessarily... in fact the group...clearly reassure heterosexuals that the lesbian bit is not compulsory, and that celibacy is always an option.", *Radical Feminism*, p67.

390 Kath Woodward and Sophie Woodward, *Why Feminism Matters*, p162.

391 Judith Butler, *Bodies that Matter* (Routledge, 1993).

392 Kath Woodward and Sophie Woodward, *Why Feminism Matters*, p160.

393 Naomi Wolf, *Vagina: A New Biography*

(Virago, 2012). See also http://socialistworker.co.uk/art/28999/Naomi+Wolf+reduces+women+to+vaginas.

394 Jennifer Baumgardner, *F'em!*, p251.

395 Kath Woodward and Sophie Woodward, *Why Feminism Matters*, p163.

396 Lynne Segal, *Straight Sex: The Politics of Pleasure* (Virago, 1994), p312.

397 Lise Vogel, *Marxism and the Oppression of Women: Towards a Unitary Theory* (Brill, 2013). Lise Vogel is herself a "red diaper" baby, she describes her parents' main concerns as she grew up as being "money and McCarthyism"—see Lise Vogel, *Woman Questions*, p6.

398 Lise Vogel, *Marxism and the Oppression of Women*, p135. She also points out that families are not the sole method of "generational replacement" as immigration and even labour camps have been used in the past, see p188.

399 Lise Vogel, *Marxism and the Oppression of Women*, p188.

400 Lise Vogel, *Marxism and the Oppression of Women*, p153.

401 Lise Vogel, *Marxism and the Oppression of Women*, p177.

402 Silvia Federici, *Revolution at Point Zero: Housework, Reproduction, and Feminist struggle* (PM Press, 2012), p92.

403 Silvia Federici, *Revolution at Point Zero*, p96.

404 Sheila Rowbotham, *Dreamers of a New Day*, p139.

405 Rosa Luxemburg, "Woman's Suffrage and Class Struggle", speech 1912, https://www.marxists.org/archive/luxemburg/1912/05/12.htm

406 https://www.marxists.org/archive/lenin/works/subject/women/abstract/19_06_28.htm.

407 Kath Woodward and Sophie Woodward, *Why Feminism Matters*, p124.

408 https://www.gov.uk/government/statistics/an-overview-of-sexual-offending-in-england-and-wales.

409 http://www.nspcc.org.uk/preventing-abuse/child-abuse-and-neglect/

Marxism and Women's Liberation

child-sexual-abuse/sexual-abuse-facts-statistics/.

410 https://www.gov.uk/government/statistics/an-overview-of-sexual-offending-in-england-and-wales.

411 http://www.ons.gov.uk/ons/rel/crime-stats/crime-statistics/period-ending-june-2014/stb-crime-stats--year-ending-june-2014.html.

412 Joan Smith, *The Public Woman*, p197.

413 Kat Banyard, *The Equality Illusion: The Truth About Women and Men Today* (Faber and Faber, 2010), p123.

414 Friedrich Engels, "The Book of Revelation" in *Marx and Engels on Religion* (1883), https://www.marxists.org/archive/marx/works/subject/religion/book-revelations.htm.

415 Steve Humphries and Pamela Gordon, *Forbidden Britain: Our Secret Past 1900-1960* (BBC Books, 1994), p57.

416 Steve Humphries, *A Secret World of Sex: Forbidden Fruit, the British Experience 1900-1950* (Sidwick & Jackson, 1988), p65.

417 Courtney E Martin, *Perfect Girls, Starving Daughters: The Frightening New Normality of Hating Your Body* (Piatkus, 2007), p298; and http://www.heelarious.com/baby-high-heels.

418 *Corporate Sexism* (Fawcett Society, 2009), p6, www.fawcettsociety.org.uk/documents/Corporate%20Sexism.pdf

419 Cordelia Fine, *Delusions of Gender*, p71.

420 Lesley A Hall, *Outspoken Women: An Anthology of Women's Writing on Sex, 1870-1969* (Routledge, 2005), p179.

421 Nicola Field, *Over the Rainbow: Money, Class and Homophobia* (Pluto Press, 1995), p50.

422 Natasha Walter, *Living Dolls*, p5.

423 Judith Williamson, "Sexism with an alibi", Guardian, 31 May 2003, http://www.theguardian.com/media/2003/may/31/advertising.comment

424 Ariel Levy, *Female Chauvinist Pigs: Women and the Rise of Raunch Culture* (Free Press, 2005), p30.

425 Istvan Meszaros, *Marx's Theory of Alienation* (Merlin, 1986), p35.

426 Alison Wolf, *The XX Factor*, p224.

427 http://www.standard.co.uk/lifestyle/esmagazine/desert-island-diaries-kirsty-young-on-grilling-celebs-and-being-mrs-soho-house-10069211.html.

428 Ellie Harrison, a 37 year old presenter on *Countryfile*, spoke out in early 2015 about her concerns that she now in turn might be replaced by a younger woman.

429 http://psychcentral.com/blog/archives/2012/06/02/why-do-women-hate-their-bodies/.

430 Susan J Douglas, *Enlightened Sexism: The Seductive Message that Feminism's Work is Done* (Times Books, 2010), p228.

431 Catherine Redfern and Kristine Aune, *Reclaiming the F Word: The New Feminist Movement* (Zed Books, 2010), p23.

432 Sheila Jeffreys, *Beauty and Misogyny: Harmful Cultural Practices in the West* (Routledge, 2005), p41.

433 David B Sarwer, "Cosmetic Breast Augmentation and Suicide", *American Journal of Psychiatry*, vol 164, no 7, July 2007, p1006, http://ajp.psychiatryonline.org/doi/full/10.1176/ajp.2007.164.7.1006

434 http://www.oceanclinic.net/labiaplasty-intimate-surgery/.

435 https://www.gov.uk/government/uploads/system/uploads/attachment_data/file/192028/Review_of_the_Regulation_of_Cosmetic_Interventions.pdf.

436 Sheila Jeffreys, *Beauty and Misogyny*, p83.

437 Rashida Manjoo, UN special rapporteur on human rights, report 2014, http://www.ohchr.org/en/newsevents/pages/displaynews.aspx?newsid=14514&

438 Susie Jolly, Andrea Cornwall, Kate Hawkins (eds), *Women, Sexuality and the Political Power of Pleasure* (Zed Books, 2013), p238. The hospital was originally backed by a vibrator company, Good Vibrations, who eventually pulled their support. It is

still not built as I write in early 2015.

439 Kath Woodward and Sophie Woodward, *Why Feminism Matters*, p124.

440 Sheila McGregor, "Rape, Pornography and Capitalism", *International Socialism* 45, Winter 1989.

441 Caitlin Moran, *How to be a Woman* (Ebury Press, 2011), p37.

442 http://www.theguardian.com/culture/2014/nov/01/ethical-porn-fair-trade-sex.

443 Caroline Criado-Perez, *Do It Like A Woman: And Change the World* (Portobello Books, 2015), p247.

444 bell hooks, *Outlaw Culture* (Routledge, 2006), p22.

445 Reuben Balfour and Jessica Allen, *A Review of the Literature on Sex Workers and Social Exclusion* (UCL Institute of Health Equity for Inclusion Health, Department of Health, 2014), p4.

446 Jane Pritchard, "The Sex Work Debate", *International Socialism* 125, Winter 2010, p168.

447 Quoted in Kath Woodward and Sophie Woodward, *Why Feminism Matters*, p106.

448 Finn Mackay, *Radical Feminism*, p217.

449 Reuben Balfour and Jessica Allen, *A Review of the Literature on Sex Workers and Social Exclusion*, p5.

450 Judith Orr, "Rochdale: An Anatomy of the Sexual Abuse Scandal".

451 Catherine Redfern and Kristin Aune, *Reclaiming the F Word*, p91.

452 Finn Mackay, *Radical Feminism*, p119.

453 Alison Assiter, *Pornography, Feminism and the Individual* (Pluto Press, 1991), p59.

454 Jane Pritchard, "The Sex Work Debate", p175.

455 Jane Pritchard, "The Sex Work Debate", p175.

456 Elizabeth Wilson, "Feminist Fundamentalism" in Lynne Segal and Mary McIntosh (eds), *Sex Exposed: Sexuality and the Pornography Debate* (Virago Press, 1992), p26.

457 http://www.atlasobscura.com/places/gabinetto-segreto.

458 Tony Cliff, "Clara Zetkin and the German Feminist Movement", p49.

459 Courtney E Martin, *Perfect Girls*, p105.

460 Gigi Durham, *The Lolita Effect: The Media Sexualisation of Young Girls and What We Can Do About It* (Overlook, 2008), p163.

461 http://www.guttmacher.org/gpr/17/3/gpr170315.html.

462 Lynne Segal, *The Politics of Pleasure* (Virago, 1994), p312.

463 Jeffrey Weeks, *Sex, Politics and Society*, p105.

464 Kevin White, *Sexual Liberation or Sexual License: The American Revolt Against Victorianism* (Ivan R Dee, 2000), p103.

465 David Carter, *Stonewall: The Riots That Sparked a Gay Revolution* (St Martin's Press, 2004), p30

466 Laura Miles, "Transgender Oppression and Resistance".

467 Stonewall, *The School Report 2012*.

468 Silvia Federici, *Revolution at Point Zero*, p24.

469 Julia Long, *Anti-Porn: The Resurgence of Anti-Pornography Feminism* (Zed Books, 2012), p15.

470 Kevin White, *Sexual Liberation or Sexual License: The American Revolt Against Victorianism* (Ivan R Dee, 2000), p55.

471 Jeffrey Weeks points out that "many doctors were advising women to space their births but refusing to tell them how. This is a particularly cruel irony because the 1911 census revealed doctors had the smallest families of all categories of occupations." *Sex, Politics and Society*, p45.

472 Sheila Rowbotham, *Dreamers of a New Day*, p85.

473 Sheila Rowbotham, *Dreamers of a New Day*, p86.

474 Carol Platt Liebau, *Prude: How the Sex Obsessed Culture Damages Girls* (Center Street, 2007).

475 Carol Dyhouse, *Girl Trouble*, p117.

476 Carol Dyhouse, *Girl Trouble*, p106.

477 Jeffrey Weeks, *Sex, Politics and Society*, p125.

478 Jonathan Eig, *The Birth of the Pill*, p148.

479 Jeffrey Weeks, *Sex, Politics and Society*, p190.

480 Lesley A Hall, *The Life and Times of Stella Browne* (IB Tauris, 2011).

481 Friedrich Engels, *The Origin of the Family*, p96.

482 Lise Vogel, *Marxism and the Oppression of Women*, p144.

483 Kate Adie, *Fighting on the Home Front* (Hodder & Staunton, 2013), p 54.

484 Joyce Marlow (ed), *The Virago Book of Women and the Great War* (Virago, 1998), p171.

485 Angela Holdsworth, *Out of the Dolls House: The Story of Women in the Twentieth Century* (BBC Books, 1989), p71.

486 Philip Grant, "Brent's Women at War and at Peace, 1914-1919" (September 2008), http://brent.gov.uk/ media/387425/Brents%20WW1%20 women%20workers.pdf.

487 Arthur Marwick, *Women at War 1914-1918* (Fontana 1977), p127.

488 Barbara Drake, *Women in Trade Unions*, p108.

489 John Costello, *Love, Sex and War 1939-1945* (Pan Books, 1986), p365.

490 Celia Briar, *Working For Women? Gendered Work And Welfare Policies In Twentieth Century* (Routledge, 2004), p57.

491 http://www.undp.org/content/undp/ en/home/ourwork/povertyreduction/ focus_areas/focus_gender_and_ poverty.html.

492 For information on campaigning go to abortionrights.org.uk. Abortion Rights is Britain's main campaigning organisation on the issue, it was formed by the merger of the National Abortion Campaign and Abortion Law Reform Association in 2003.

493 Catherine Redfern and Kristin Aune, *Reclaiming the F Word*, p133.

494 Anna Coote and Beatrix Campbell, *Sweet Freedom*, p257.

495 Helen Wilkinson, "The Thatcher Legacy: Power feminism and the birth of girl power" in Natasha Walter (ed), On the Move, p39.

496 Graham Boustred quoted in *Business Day*, Johannesburg, 8 July 2009.

497 http://www.theguardian.com/ commentisfree/2011/jul/18/diversity-boardroom-corporate-decisions.

498 30percentclub.org.

499 "Working Women vs Bourgeois Feminism—Eleanor Marx: How Should We Organize?" in Hal Draper, *Women and Class*, p309.

500 "A New Model of Social Class? Findings from the BBC's Great British Class Survey Experiment", *Sociology*, April 2013, http://soc.sagepub.com/ content/early/2013/03/12/0038038513 481128.full.pdf+html.

501 Martha Gimenez, "Marxism, and Class, Gender, and Race", p31.

502 Frigga Haug in Shahrzad Mojab (ed), *Marxism and Feminism* (Zed Books, 2015), p78.

503 Marx and Engels, *Communist Manifesto*, p39.

504 Marx and Engels, *Communist Manifesto*, p38.

505 World Bank Group, *Gender at Work: A Companion to the World Development Report on Jobs*, 2014, p8, available at http://www.worldbank.org/content/ dam/Worldbank/document/Gender/ GenderAtWork_web.pdf.

506 TUC, *Women and Recession: How will this recession affect women at work?*, 2009, available at https://www.tuc. org.uk/sites/default/files/extras/ womenandrecession.pdf.

507 Natasha Walter, *The New Feminism*, p23.

508 Nina Power, *One Dimensional Woman*, p20.

509 Alison Spence, *Labour Market, Social Trends* 41 (Office of National Statistics, 2011).

510 Jenny Chanfreau, Sally Gowland, Zoë Lancaster, Eloise Poole, Sarah Tipping and Mari Toomse, *Maternity and*

Paternity Rights and Women Returners Survey 2009/10, Department for Business Innovation and Skills (BIS), Department for Work and Pensions, available at https://www.gov.uk/government/uploads/system/uploads/attachment_data/file/214367/rrep777.pdf.

511 BIS, *Work and Families Act 2006 Evaluation Report*, March 2010, p15.

512 http://www.fawcettsociety.org.uk/2013/11/equal-pay/.

513 Silvia Federici, *Revolution at Point Zero*, p20.

514 Nancy Fraser, *Fortunes of Feminism*, p28.

515 Nancy Fraser, *Fortunes of Feminism*, p33.

516 Deborah Cameron, *On Language and Sexual Politics* (Routledge, 2006), p124.

517 BIS, *Trade union membership 2013: Statistical Bulletin*, 2014, p11.

518 BIS, *Trade union membership 2013: Statistical Bulletin*, 2014.

519 BIS, *Trade union membership 2013: Statistical Bulletin*, 2014, p14.

520 Hester Eisenstein, *Feminism Seduced*, p216.

521 Philip S Foner (ed), *Helen Keller, Her Socialist Years: Writings and Speeches* (International Publishers, 1967), p32.

522 Karl Marx and Frederick Engels, *The German Ideology*, p64.

523 Hal Draper, *Karl Marx's Theory of Revolution*, p42.

524 Karl Marx and Frederich Engels, *The German Ideology*, p94.

525 E P Thompson quoted in Louise A Tilly and Joan W Scott, *Work, Women and Family*, p55.

526 http://www.dailymail.co.uk/news/article-2964511/Fury-unions-tell-MPs-not-make-gender-abortion-crime-divide-communities.html.

527 John Reed, *Shaking the World* (Bookmarks, 1998), p132; see the original newspaper front page at https://www.marxists.org/history/usa/pubs/ohio-socialist/031-aug-28-1918.pdf.

528 Karl Marx and Frederich Engels, *Communist Manifesto*, https://www.marxists.org/archive/marx/works/1848/communist-manifesto/cho2.htm

529 Lenin, *The State and Revolution* (Foreign Languages Press, 1976), p147.

530 Engels, from his Introduction to Karl Marx's *Class Struggles in France*.

531 Albert Soboul quoted in Paul McGarr, "Marxism and the Great French Revolution", *International Socialism* 43, Summer 1989, p95.

532 Hal Draper, *Karl Marx's Theory of Revolution*, p73.

533 Rosa Luxemburg, "Women's Suffrage and Class Struggle" in Hal Draper, *Women and Class*, p287.

534 Karl Marx and Friedrich Engels, *The German Ideology*, p1845.

535 Barbara Evans Clements, *Bolshevik Women*, p130.

536 Richard Stites, *The Women's Liberation Movement in Russia: Feminism, Nihilism and Bolshevism, 1860-1930* (Princeton University Press, 1978), p287.

537 Barbara Evans Clements, *Bolshevik Women*, p120. This book offers lots of fascinating detail about many of the leading Bolshevik women, or Bolshevichki as she refers to them. But is of no use in giving any political analysis of the revolution and its impact on women's lives. She refers to the Bolshevik women who took on work organising among women workers as "feminist Marxists" (p107) because she says they were committed to bring women into the revolutionary movement, claiming that such activity invited "disapproval" from "more conventional" revolutionaries. This is in plain contradiction to what she writes elsewhere in the same book about "the party's long standing practice of engaging women in all its activities" (p125) and the many regular references leading Bolsheviks, women and men, made to the importance of involving women, and not least the

538 Barbara Evans Clements, *Bolshevik Women*, p120.

539 Leon Trotsky, *The History of the Russian Revolution* (Pluto Press, 1977), p122.

540 V I Lenin, *The Emancipation of Women* (International Publishers, 1984), p60.

541 Tony Cliff, "Alexandra Kollontai: Russian Marxists and Women Workers", *International Socialism* 14, Autumn 1981, p100.

542 Jane McDermid and Anna Hillyar, *Midwives of the Revolution: Female Bolsheviks and Women Workers 1917* (UCL Press, 1999), p80.

543 Leon Trotsky, *The History of the Russian Revolution*, p128.

544 Barbara Evans Clements, *Bolshevik Women*, p174.

545 Jane McDermid and Anna Hillyar, *Midwives of the Revolution*, p178.

546 Chanie Rosenberg, *Women and Perestroika: Present, Past and Future for Women in Russia* (Bookmarks, 1989), p82.

547 John Reed, *Ten Days that Shook the World* (Penguin, 1977), p40.

548 Tony Cliff, "Alexandra Kollontai", p77.

549 Cathy Porter, *Alexandra Kollontai: A Biography* (Merlin Press, 2013), p304.

550 Richard Stites, *The Women's Liberation Movement in Russia*, p332.

551 Rosa Luxemburg, *Rosa Luxemburg Speaks* (Pathfinder, 1970), p395.

552 Chanie Rosenberg, *Women and Perestroika*, p86.

553 V I Lenin, *The Emancipation of Women*, p63.

554 V I Lenin, *The Emancipation of Women*, p63.

555 Leon Trotsky, *Women and the Family*, p75.

556 Ronald Fraser, *Blood of Spain: An Oral History of the Spanish Civil War* (Pimlico, 1994), p286.

557 I reported for *Socialist Worker* from Cairo during the first 18 days of the revolution in 2011 that brought down Hosni Mubarak. See socialistworker.co.uk/art/23303/Egypt+in+revolt+-+Judith+Orrs+Cairo+diary

558 Sameh Naguib, *The Egyptian Revolution: A Political Analysis and Eyewitness Account* (Bookmarks, 2011), p19.

559 socialistworker.co.uk/art/33838/Fighting+harassment+in+Cairos+Tahrir+Square.

560 Joel Beinin in Rabab El-Mahdi and Philip Marfleet (eds), *Egypt: The Moment of Change* (Zed Books, 2009), p81.

561 Anne Alexander and Mostafa Bassiouny, *Bread Freedom and Social Justice: Workers and the Egyptian Revolution* (Zed Books, 2014), p70.

562 Anne Alexander, "Women were braver than 100 men", *Socialist Review*, January 2008, http://socialistreview.org.uk/321/women-were-braver-hundred-men.

563 Karl Marx, *Class Struggles in France, 1848-1850*, https://www.marxists.org/archive/marx/works/1850/class-struggles-france/.

564 Chris Harman, *The Lost Revolution: Germany 1918 to 1923* (Bookmarks, 1997), p85.

565 See Steven Rose, *Lifelines*.

566 Eleanor Burke Leacock, *Myths of Male Dominance*, p110.

567 For more information of defending and extending access to abortion go to abortionrights.org.uk.

568 Clara Zetkin, *Selected Writings*, p14.

BIBLIOGRAPHY

Adie, Kate, *Fighting on the Home Front: The Legacy of Women in World War One* (Hodder & Staunton, 2013).

Alexander, Anne, and Bassiouny, Mostafa, *Bread Freedom and Social Justice: Workers and the Egyptian Revolution* (Zed Books, 2014).

Allen, Sandra, Sanders, Lee and Wallis, Jan (editors), *Conditions of Illusion: Papers from the Women's Movement* (Feminist Books, 1975).

Aschenbrand, Periel, *The Only Bush I Trust is My Own* (Corgi, 2006).

Assiter, Alison, *Pornography, Feminism and the Individual* (Pluto Press, 1989).

Balfour, Reuben and Allen, Jessica, *A Review of the Literature on Sex Workers and Social Exclusion* (UCL Institute of Health Equity for Inclusion Health, Department of Health, 2014).

Banyard, Kat, *The Equality Illusion: The Truth about Women and Men Today* (Faber and Faber, 2011).

Barrett, Michele, *Women's Oppression Today: The Marxist/Feminist Encounter* (Verso, 2014).

Baumgardner, Jennifer and Richards, Amy, *Manifesta: Young Women, Feminism and the Future* (Farrar Straus Giroux, 2010).

Baumgardner, Jennifer, *F'em!: Goo Goo, Gaga, and Some Thoughts on Balls* (Seal Press, 2011).

Black, Clementina (editor), *Married Women's Work: Being the Report of an Enquiry Undertaken by the Women's Industrial Council* (Virago, 1983).

Boston, Sarah, *Women Workers and the Trade Unions* (Davis-Poynter, 1980).

Brown, Heather A, *Marx on Gender and the Family: A Critical Study* (Haymarket Books, 2013).

Callinicos, Alex, *The Revolutionary Ideas of Karl Marx* (Bookmarks, 2004).

Cameron, Deborah, *On Language and Sexual Politics* (Routledge, 2006).

Cameron, Deborah, *The Myth of Mars and Venus: Do Men and Women Really Speak Different Languages?* (Oxford University Press, 2007).

Carter, David, *Stonewall: The Riots that Sparked a Gay Revolution* (St Martin's Griffin, 2005).

Charles, Nickie, *Gender in Modern Britain* (Oxford, 2002).

Childe, V Gordon, *Man Makes Himself* (Watts, 1941).

Clements, Barbara Evans, *Bolshevik Women* (Cambridge University Press, 1997).

Cliff, Tony, *Class Struggle and Women's Liberation: 1640 to the Present Day* (Bookmarks, 1984).

Cohen, Aaron, *Amazing Grace* (Continuum, 2011).

Coote, Anna and Campbell, *Beatrix Sweet Freedom* (Blackwell, 1987).

Costello, John, *Love, Sex & War: Changing Values 1939-1945* (Pan Books, 1986).

Criado-Perez, Caroline, *Do It Like A Woman...and Change the World* (Portobello Books, 2015).

Dangerfield, George, *The Strange Death of Liberal England* (Stanford University Press, 1998).

Davies, Ross, *Women and Work* (Arrow Books, 1975).

Dawkins, Richard, *The Selfish Gene* (Granada, 1978).

Delamont, Sara, *Sex Roles and the School* (Methuen, 1980).

Delphy, Christine and Gay, Roxane, *Separate and Dominate: Feminism and Racism after the War on Terror* (Verso, 2015).

Dinnis, Rob and Stringer, Chris, *Britain: One Million Years of the Human Story* (Natural History Museum, 2014).

Douglas, Susan, J, *Enlightened Sexism: The Seductive Message That Feminism's*

Work Is Done (Times Books, 2010).

Drake, Barbara, *Women in Trade Unions* (Virago, 1984).

Draper, Hal, *Karl Marx's Theory of Revolution*, vol 2, *The Politics of Social Classes* (Monthly Review Press, 1978).

Draper, Hal, *Women and Class: Towards a Socialist Feminism* (Center for Socialist History, 2013).

Durham, Gigi, *The Lolita Effect: The Media Sexualization of Young Girls and What We Can Do About It* (Overlook, 2008).

Dyhouse, Carol, *Girl Trouble: Panic and Progress in the History of Young Women* (Zed Books, 2013).

Eagleton, Terry, *Marx* (Phoenix, 1997).

Echols, Alice, *Daring to be Bad: Radical Feminism in America, 1967-75* (Minnesota University Press, 1989).

Ehrenreich, Barbara, *For Her Own Good: Two Centuries of the Experts' Advice to Women* (Anchor Books, 2005).

Ehrenreich, Barbara and Hochschild, Arlie Russell, *Global Woman: Nannies, Maids and Sex Workers in the New Economy* (Metropolitan Books, 2002).

Eig, Jonathan, *The Birth of the Pill: How Four Pioneers Reinvented Sex and Launched a Revolution* (Macmillan, 2014).

Eisenstein, Hester, *Feminism Seduced: How Global Elites Use Women's Labor and Ideas to Exploit the World* (Paradigm, 2010).

Eliot, Lise, *Pink Brain, Blue Brain: How Small Differences Grow Into Troublesome Gaps—And What We Can Do about It* (Oneworld, 2009).

El-Mahdi, Rabab and Marfleet, Philip (editors), *Egypt: The Moment of Change* (Zed Books, 2009).

Elver, Hilal, *The Headscarf Controversy: Secularism and Freedom of Religion* (Oxford University Press, 2012).

Empson, Martin, *Land and Labour: Marxism, Ecology and Human History* (Bookmarks, 2014).

Engels, Friedrich, *The Origin of the Family, Private Property and the State.*

Evans, Sara, *Personal Politics: The Roots of Women's Liberation in the Civil Rights Movement & the New Left* (Vintage, 1980).

Faludi, Susan, *Backlash: The Undeclared War Against Women* (Chatto & Windus 1992).

Faludi, Susan, *Stiffed: The Betrayal of Modern Man* (Vintage, 2000).

Farrell, Warren, *Myth of Male Power: Why Men Are the Disposable Sex* (Finch Publishing, 2001).

Federici, Silvia, *Revolution at Point Zero: Housework, Reproduction, and Feminist Struggle* (PM Press, 2012).

Fekete, Liz, "Enlightened fundamentalism? Immigration, feminism and the Right" in *Race & Class* 48:2 (2006).

Field, Nicola, *Over the Rainbow: Money, Class and Homophobia* (Pluto Press, 1995).

Fine, Cordelia, *Delusions of Gender: The Real Science Behind Sex Differences* (Icon Books, 2011).

Firestone, Shulamith, *The Dialectic of Sex: The Case for Feminist Revolution* (The Women's Press, 1979).

Flannery, Kent and Marcus, Joyce, *The Creation of Inequality: How Our Prehistoric Ancestors Set the Stage for Monarchy, Slavery, and Empire* (Harvard University Press, 2012).

Foot, Paul, *The Vote: How it Was Won, and How it Was Undermined* (Bookmarks, 2012).

Franks, Suzanne, *Having None of it: Women, Men and the Future of Work* (Granta Books, 1999).

Fraser, Nancy, *The Fortunes of Feminism: From State-Managed Capitalism to Neoliberal Crisis* (Verso, 2013).

Fraser, Ronald, *Blood Of Spain: An Oral History of the Spanish Civil War* (Pimlico, 1994).

Friedan, Betty, *It Changed My Life: Writings on the Women's Movement* (Victor Gollancz, 1976).

Friedan, Betty, *The Feminine Mystique* (Penguin Modern Classics, 2010).

Gamble, Sarah (editor), *The Routledge Companion to Feminism and Postfeminism* (Routledge, 2001).

German, Lindsey, *Material Girls: Women, Men and Work* (Bookmarks, 2007).

German, Lindsey, *Sex, Class and Socialism* (Bookmarks, 1998).

Gimenez, Martha and Vogel, Lise (editors), "Marxist-Feminist Thought Today" in *Science and Society*, vol 69, no 1, (January 2005).

Gould, Stephen Jay, *The Mismeasure of Man* (Penguin, 1992).

Hall, Lesley A, *Outspoken Women: An Anthology of Women's Writing on Sex, 1870-1969* (Routledge, 2005).

Hall, Lesley A, *The Life and Times of Stella Browne: Feminist and Free Spirit* (IB Tauris, 2011).

Harford, Barbara and Hopkins, Sarah, *Greenham Common: Women at the Wire* (The Women's Press, 1984).

Harman, Chris, *A People's History of the World* (Bookmarks, 1999).

Harman, Chris, *The Lost Revolution: Germany 1918 to 1923* (Bookmarks, 1997).

Hartmann, Heidi, *The Unhappy Marriage of Marxism and Feminism*, edited by Lydia Sargent (Pluto Press, 1986).

Hennessy, Rosemary, *Profit and Pleasure: Sexual Identities in Late Capitalism* (Routledge, 2000).

Holdsworth, Angela, *Out of the Dolls House: The Story of Women in the Twentieth Century* (BBC Books, 1991).

Hole, Judith and Levine, Ellen, *Rebirth of Feminism* (Quadrangle, 1971).

hooks, bell, *Outlaw Culture* (Routledge, 2006).

Humphries, Steve and Gordon, Pamela, *A Man's World: From Boyhood to Manhood 1900-1960* (BBC, 1996).

Humphries, Steve and Gordon, Pamela, *Forbidden Britain: Our Secret Past 1900-1960* (BBC Books, 1994).

Humphries, Steve, *A Secret World of Sex: Forbidden Fruit, the British Experience 1900-1950* (Sidgwick & Jackson, 1988).

Hunt, Judith and Adams, Shelley, *Women, Work and Trade Union Organisation* (Workers Educational Association, London, 1980).

Hymowitz, Kay S, *Manning Up: How the Rise of Women Has Turned Men into Boys* (Basic Books, 2011).

Jakubowski, Franz, *Ideology and Superstructure in Historical Materialism* (Pluto Press, 1990).

Jeffreys, Sheila, *Beauty and Misogyny: Harmful Cultural Practices in the West* (Routledge, 2005).

Jolly, Susie, Cornwall, Andrea and Hawkins, Kate (editors), *Women, Sexuality and the Political Power of Pleasure* (Zed Books, 2013).

Kanter, Hannah, Sarah Lefanu, and Shaila Shah (editors), *Sweeping Statement: Writings From the Women's Liberation Movement 1981-1983* (The Women's Press, 1984).

Kaplan, Judy and Shapiro, Linn (editors), *Red Diapers: Growing up in the Communist Left* (University of Illinois, 1998).

Keller Helen, Foner, Philip S (editor), *Helen Keller, Her Socialist Years: Writings and Speeches* (International Publishers, 1967).

Kimmel, Michael and Ferber, Abby L (editors), *Privilege: A Reader* (Westview Press, 2010).

King, Laura, *Family Men: Fatherhood and Masculinity in Britain, 1914-1960* (Oxford University Press, 2015).

Klein, Naomi, *No Logo* (Flamingo, 2000).

Koedt, Anne, Levine, Ellen, Rapone, Anita (editors), *Radical Feminism* (Quadrangle, 1973).

Kollontai, Alexandra, *Selected Writing of Alexandra Kollontai* (Allison and Busby, 1977).

Labriola, Antonio, *Essays on the Materialistic Conception of History* (Cosimo, 2005).

Landry, Donna and MacLean, Gerald,

Materialist Feminisms (Blackwell, 1993).

Laurie Penny, *Meat Market: Female Flesh Under Capitalism* (Zero Books, 2011).

Leacock, Eleanor Burke, *Myths of Male Dominance* (Monthly Review, 1981).

Lenin, V I, *The Emancipation of Women* (International Publishers, 1984).

Lenin, V I, *The State and Revolution* (Foreign Languages Press, Peking 1976).

Leslie B Tanner (editor), *Voices from Women's Liberation* (Signet, 1971).

Levy, Ariel, *Female Chauvinist Pigs: Women and the Rise of Raunch Culture* (Free Press, 2005).

Lewis, Jane, *Women in England, 1870-1950: Sexual Divisions and Social Change* (Wheatsheaf, 1984).

Lewontin, Richard C, *It Ain't Necessarily So: The Dream of the Human Genome and Other Illusions* (Granta Books, 2000).

Liddington, Jill and Norris, Jill, *One Hand Tied Behind Us: The Rise of the Women's Suffrage Movement* (Rivers Oram Press, 2000).

Liebau, Carol Platt, *Prude: How the Sex-Obsessed Culture Damages Girls (and America, Too!)* (Center Street, 2007).

Long, Julia, *Anti-Porn: The Resurgence of Anti-Pornography Feminism* (Zed Books, 2012).

Lowe, Marian, "Sociobiology and Sex Differences", *Signs*, vol 4, no 1, "Women, Science, and Society", (Autumn, 1978).

Luxemburg, Rosa, *Rosa Luxemburg Speaks* (Pathfinder, 1970).

Mackay, Finn, *Radical Feminism: Feminist Activism in Movement* (Palgrave Macmillan, 2015) .

Marlow, Joyce (editor), *The Virago Book of Women and the Great War* (Virago, 1998).

Martin, Courtney E, *Perfect Girls, Starving Daughters: The Frightening New Normality of Hating Your Body* (Piatkus, 2007).

Marwick, Arthur, *Women at War 1914-1918* (Fontana, 1977).

Marx, Karl and Engels, Friedrich, *Communist Manifesto* (Progress, 1977).

Marx, Karl, and Engels, Friedrich, *The German Ideology*, 1845 (Lawrence and Wishart, 1994).

Marx, Karl, *Capital* vol 1 (Penguin, 1979).

McDermid, Jane and Hillyar, Anna, *Midwives of the Revolution: Female Bolsheviks and Women Workers in 1917* (UCL Press, 1999).

Meszaros, Istvan, *Marx's Theory of Alienation* (Merlin Press, 1986).

Mitchell, Juliet, *Woman's Estate* (Penguin, 1974).

Mojab, Shahrzad (editor), *Marxism and Feminism* (Zed Books, 2015).

Molyneux, John, *The Point is to Change It: An Introduction to Marxist Philosophy* (Bookmarks, 2012).

Moran, Caitlin, *How to be a Woman* (Ebury Press, 2012).

Morgan, Lewis Henry, "Ancient Society" (1877), http://www.marxists.org/ reference/archive/morgan-lewis/ ancient-society/.

Naguib, Sameh, *The Egyptian Revolution: A Political Analysis and Eyewitness Account* (Bookmarks, 2011).

Nelson, Jennifer, *Women of Color and the Reproductive Rights Movement* (NYU Press, 2003).

Nimtz, August H, *Marx and Engels: Their Contribution to the Democratic Breakthrough* (State University of New York Press, 2000).

Noir, Anne and Bill, *Why Men Don't Iron: The New Reality of Gender Differences* (Harper Collins, 1999).

Pankhurst, Sylvia, *The Suffragette Movement* (Virago, 1978).

Paoletti, Jo Barraclough, *Pink and Blue: Telling the Boys from the Girls in America* (Indiana University Press, 2012).

Patterson, Thomas C, *Karl Marx, Anthropologist* (Berg Publishers 2003).

Patterson, Thomas C, *Marx's Ghost: Conversations with Archaeologists* (Berg Publishers, 2005).

Pinchbeck, Ivy, *Women Workers and the Industrial Revolution 1750-1850* (Frank Cass, 1977).

Porter, Cathy, *Alexandra Kollontai: A Biography* (Merlin Press, 2013).

Power, Nina, *One Dimensional Woman* (Zero Books, 2009).

Ramelson, Marian, *The Petticoat Rebellion: A Century of Struggle for Women's Rights* (Lawrence and Wishart, 1967).

Raw, Louise, *Striking a Light: The Bryant and May Matchwomen and their Place in History* (Continuum, 2011).

Redfern, Catherine and Aune, Kristin, *Reclaiming the F Word: The New Feminist Movement* (Zed Books, 2010).

Reed, Evelyn, *Woman's Evolution: From Matriarchal Clan to Patriarchal Family* (Pathfinder Press, 1975).

Reed, John, *Shaking the World: John Reed's Revolutionary Journalism* (Bookmarks, 1998).

Reed, John, *Ten Days that Shook the World* (Penguin, 1977).

Rees, John (ed), *The Revolutionary Ideas of Frederick Engels: International Socialism* 65, special issue (Winter 1994),

Reiter, Rayna R, *Toward an Anthropology of Women* (Monthly Review Press, 1975).

Reynolds, Simon and Press, Joy, *The Sex Revolts: Gender, Rebellion, and Rock 'n' Roll* (Serpent's Tail, 1995).

Richardson, Brian (editor), *Say it Loud! Marxism and the Fight against Racism* (Bookmarks, 2013).

Roberts, Elizabeth, *A Woman's Place: An Oral History of Working Class Women 1890-1940* (Blackwell 1984).

Roberts, Elizabeth, *Women and Families: An Oral History, 1940-1970* (Blackwell, 1995).

Rose, Hilary and Steven, *Alas, Poor Darwin: Arguments Against Evolutionary Psychology* (Jonathan Cape, 2000).

Rose, Lionel, *Massacre of the Innocents: Infanticide in Great Britain 1800-1939*, (Routledge and Kegan, Paul, 1986).

Rose, Steven, *Lifelines: Biology Beyond Determinism* (Allen Lane, 1997).

Rose, Steven, Lewontin, R C, and Kamin, Leon J, *Not in Our Genes: Biology, Ideology and Human Nature* (Penguin, 1990).

Rosen, Michael and Widgery, David (editors), *The Chatto Book of Dissent* (Chatto & Windus, 1991) .

Rosenberg, Chanie, *Women and Perestroika: Present, Past and Future for Women in Russia* (Bookmarks, 1989).

Rosin, Hanna, *The End of Men and the Rise of Women* (Viking, 2012).

Rowbotham, Sheila, *Century of Women: The History of Women in Britain and the United States in the Twentieth Century* (Penguin, 1999).

Rowbotham, Sheila, *Dreamers of a New Day: Women Who Invented the Twentieth Century* (Verso, 2010).

Rowbotham, Sheila, *Hidden from History* (Pluto Press, 1983).

Rowbotham, Sheila, Segal, Lynne and Wainright, Hilary, *Beyond the Fragments: Feminism and the Making of Socialism* (Merlin Press, 2013).

Rowbotham, Sheila, *Women, Resistance and Revolution* (Penguin, 1972).

Sargent, Lydia (editor), *The Unhappy Marriage of Marxism and Feminism* (Pluto Press, 1986).

Sayers, Janet, Evans, Mary and Redclift, Nanneke, *Engels Revisited: New Feminist Essays* (Tavistock Publications, 1987).

Schneir, Miriam (editor), *The Vintage Book of Feminism* (Vintage, 1995).

Segal, Lynne and McIntosh, Mary (editors), *Sex Exposed: Sexuality and the Pornography Debate* (Virago Press, 1992).

Segal, Lynne, *Slow Motion: Changing Masculinities, Changing Men* (Virago, 1990).

Segal, Lynne, *Straight Sex: The Politics of Pleasure* (Virago, 1994).

Shorter, Edward, *A History of Women's Bodies* (Penguin, 1984).

Simons, Mike, *Striking Back: Photographs*

of the Great Miners' Strike 1984-1985
(Bookmarks, 2004).

Smith, Joan, The Public Woman
(Westbourne Press, 2013).

Stites, Richard, The Women's Liberation
Movement in Russia: Feminism,
Nihilism, and Bolshevism, 1860-1930
(Princeton University Press, 1978).

Stringer, Chris, The Origins of Our Species
(Penguin, 2012).

Taylor, Barbara, Eve & The New Jerusalem:
Socialism and Feminism in the
Nineteenth Century (Virago, 1983).

Terkel, Studs, Hard Times: An Oral History
of the Great Depression (The New
Press, 1986).

Tilly, Louise A and Scott, Joan W, Work,
Women and Family (Methuen, 1987).

Todd, Janet, Mary Wollstonecraft: A
Revolutionary Life (Weidenfeld &
Nicolson, 2000).

Trotsky, Leon, The History of the Russian
Revolution (Pluto Press, 1977).

Trotsky, Leon, Women and the Family
(Pathfinder, 2009).

Valenti, Jessica, Full Frontal Feminism:
A Young Woman's Guide to Why
Feminism Matters (Seal Press, 2007).

Valenti, Jessica, He's a Stud, She's a Slut
and 49 Other Double Standards Every
Woman Should Know (Seal Press,
2008).

Vogel, Lise, Marxism and the Oppression
of Women: Towards a Unitary Theory
(Brill, 2013).

Vogel, Lise, Woman Questions: Essays for a
Materialist Feminism (Routledge, 1995).

Walter, Natasha (editor), On the Move:
Feminism for the Next Generation
(Virago Press, 1999).

Walter, Natasha, Living Dolls: The Return
of Sexism (Virago 2010).

Walter, Natasha, The New Feminism
(Little, Brown 1998).

Wandour, Michelene, Body Politic:
Women's Liberation in Britain 1969-
1972 (Stage 1, 1972).

Weeks, Jeffrey, Sex, Politics and Society:
The Regulation of Sexuality Since 1800
(Longman, 1981).

Weigand, Kate, Red Feminism: American
Communism and the Making of
Women's Liberation (John Hopkins
University Press, 2001).

White, Kevin, Sexual Liberation or Sexual
License? The American Revolt Against
Victorianism (Ivan R Dee, 2000).

Winslow, Barbara, Sylvia Pankhurst:
Sexual Politics and Political Activism
(UCL Press, 1996).

Wolf, Alison, The XX Factor: How Working
Women are Creating a New Society
(Profile Books, 2013).

Wolf, Naomi, Vagina: A New Biography
(Virago, 2012).

Woodward, Kath and Woodward, Sophie,
Why Feminism Matters: Feminism Lost
and Found (Palgrave Macmillan, 2009).

Younge, Gary, Who Are We—And Should
It Matter in the 21st Century? (Viking,
2010).

Zetkin, Clara, Clara Zetkin: Selected
Writings, edited by Philip S Foner
(International Publishers, 1984).

INDEX